ANY WAY YOU SLICE IT

ANY WAY YOU SLICE IT

The Past, Present, and Future of Rationing

Stan Cox

THE NEW PRESS

NEW YORK
LONDON

Requests for permission to reproduce selections from this book should be mailed to:
Permissions Department, The New Press, 38 Greene Street, New York, NY 10013.

Published in the United States by The New Press, New York, 2013
Distributed by Perseus Distribution

ISBN 978-1-59558-809-8 (hc)
ISBN 978-1-59558-884-5 (e-book)
CIP data is available

The New Press publishes books that promote and enrich public discussion and
understanding of the issues vital to our democracy and to a more equitable world.
These books are made possible by the enthusiasm of our readers; the support of a
committed group of donors, large and small; the collaboration of our many partners
in the independent media and the not-for-profit sector; booksellers, who often hand-sell
New Press books; librarians; and above all by our authors.

www.thenewpress.com

Composition by dix!
This book was set in Minion

Printed in the United States of America

10   9   8   7   6   5   4   3   2   1

For Wes Jackson

CONTENTS

ACKNOWLEDGMENTS

I greatly appreciate the help of Monal Abdel-Baki, Abdel Aziz Ezzel Arab, Altef, Ashraf, Mary Ann Baily, Gladson Dungdung, Garry Egger, Nadine El-Hakim, Marian Fadel, Joshua Farley, Tina Fawcett, Carl Finamore, Leonard Fleck, Alan Honick, Bulu Imam, M.S. Kamath, Dadaji Khobragade, Kishore, Fred Magdoff, Mahesh, Negah, David Orr, Priya, Hugh Rockoff, Mark Roodhouse, Gene Sandberg, Satish, Sharmila, K.P. Sinha, Taheya, Brian Tokar, Vijaya, and Martin Weitzman. I am especially and deeply grateful to Paul Cox, Sheila Cox, Gouda Abdel-Khalek, Jud Brodie, David Evans, Jaideep Hardikar, Karima Korayem, Mohammed, Maged Nosshi, and Usama Rekabi. My special thanks, as always, go to Sarah Fan, whose tireless efforts have made this a much better book than it might have been. I want to thank my parents, Tom and Brenda Cox, and my mother-in-law, Santosh Gulati, for their unflagging support as I was writing this book, and Sheila Cox and Greg Cox for their help in editing the manuscript. And no words can express the gratitude I feel toward Priti Gulati Cox—translator, backup memory, photographer, and the love of my life.

Cars crowd into a gasoline station during the 1979 energy crisis.

INTRODUCTION

On the afternoon of September 11, 2001, I left work at a little after 5 P.M. Driving home, I was surprised to see long lines of cars stretching into the street at every gas station I passed. At some stations, police were having to direct traffic. What was going on? This was Salina, Kansas; the embattled East Coast was thirteen hundred miles away. The national news was on the car radio, and there was nothing about a threat to petroleum supplies. What did people know that I didn't know? I even took a glance at my own car's gas gauge but then decided I had better just go home.

I soon learned that the gas rush was not just a Kansas phenomenon. A station owner in Milwaukee told a reporter, "It's probably never been this busy. Ever. It's unbelievable!" Some drivers in Oklahoma City were lining up to pay $5 a gallon—almost four times the prevailing rate at the time—to fill their tanks. At stations around Des Moines, where lines of as many as eighty-five cars were forming, rumors circulated of $8 gas in Boston. Drivers in Iowa and Minnesota were seen loading pickup-truck beds with 55-gallon drums and trash cans and pumping gas into them.[1]

A Kentucky psychologist later explained the irrational fuel rush as a knee-jerk reaction: "Those people had been at work all day, not able to do anything, thinking about previous incidents that had caused gas shortages." Another psychologist speculated, "They wanted to have a sense of control, not feel stranded or trapped in any way"[2] By the next day, Americans seeking a way to render aid were lining up for hours at blood-donation centers. But for many of us not directly affected by the attacks on New York and Washington, the seemingly instinctive first reaction had been to get in line to stock up on fuel. Images of past scarcity and conflict had welled up in our collective memory, and those recollections had brought little reassurance that America would be able to deal fairly with whatever scarcity might come next. Drivers middle-aged and older undoubtedly recalled the 1970s, when gas pumps ran dry and stations became battlegrounds. Back then, station owners could have shortened the lines by doubling or tripling their prices, but the government wouldn't allow that. Instead, there were weekend closings, gallon limits, minimum-purchase requirements, and alternate-day access based on license-plate numbers. As the White House and Congress were considering per-vehicle gas quotas as a last resort, the oil suddenly resumed flowing, the lines vanished, and America once again picked up its growth in consumption not just of gasoline but of all resources. Through the 1980s and 1990s, it was a top priority of political leaders to keep the economy fueled up by reassuring us that whatever calamity might come our way—war, terrorism, hurricane, earthquake, flood, or disease epidemic—our capacity to consume would not be interrupted by shortages. The reaction of motorists on 9/11 indicated that we didn't quite buy those reassurances.

In the days following the attacks, New York mayor Rudolph Giuliani provided his own suggestion to those not directly involved in emergency operations. Praising residents of his city as "the best shoppers in the world," he called on them to start spending money on food, entertainment, and consumer goods again. Tony Blair, the British prime minister, echoed that advice: "People in this country ask what should they do at a time like this. The answer is that they should go about their daily lives: to work, to live, to travel, and to shop." In a speech two weeks after the attack, President George W. Bush encouraged Americans to "get on the airlines, get about the business of America." As the years passed and the list of official foreign enemies grew, that message persisted. In a news conference in late 2006, Bush assured Americans that his administration and the Pentagon had gained control in both the war in Iraq and a dispute with Iran. Therefore, he said, "I encourage you all to go shopping more."[3] Responding to the clamor for patriotic consumerism, the syndicated columnist Marsha Mercer lamented, "The president hasn't asked ordinary Americans to sacrifice at all. . . . 'I want to do something to help,' a nurse told me the other day. 'I don't want to shop.'"[4] But today, more than a decade after 9/11, more than three decades since the era of oil embargoes and gas lines, and, it appears, well into an era of ecological crisis, no movement for shared responsibility and sacrifice has emerged.

The spiral of production and consumption that built today's world cannot spin upward forever. It may begin winding down because some combination of fuels, ores, building materials, soils, water, or food becomes depleted. It could wind down because the atmosphere-, land-, and water-based ecosystems that provide both tangible necessities and myriad unseen benefits become degraded. Or maybe we ourselves will attempt to restrain the growth spiral by preemptively limiting resource consumption and curbing climatic and ecological disruption. In the process, societies will face a vexing two-part puzzle: How can we reduce the burden we place on the Earth's ecological and mineral resources while at the same time ensuring that everyone can consume enough resources to maintain a good quality of life? To do both will require thoroughgoing changes in the way economies function.

People don't like even thinking about entire economies practicing restraint. In 2007, the *New York Times* columnist Thomas L. Friedman wrote, "One thing that always struck me about the term 'green' was the degree to which, for so many years, it was defined by its opponents— by the people who wanted to disparage it. And they defined it as 'liberal,' 'tree-hugging,' 'sissy,' 'girlie-man,' 'unpatriotic,' 'vaguely French.' " [5] Friedman declared it his intention to give "green" a more macho definition, to make it, in his words, "geostrategic, geoeconomic, capitalistic and patriotic." His macho approach hasn't caught on, nor have we found a green vision that is tough-minded and practical and can't be hijacked by big business. Meanwhile, green behavior continues to trigger equal and opposite reactions in those who hold different beliefs. In the years leading up to the automobile industry's 2008–9 crash, an especially intense area of eco-conflict concerned choice of personal transportation. There arose a war of words (and sometimes spray paint and tire irons, on both sides) between Hummer owners and their critics (the latter often branded as "tofu-eating Prius drivers," and many did in fact own hybrid cars). That conflict grew, according to marketing researcher Marius Luedicke and colleagues, into a "nationalistic morality play." While critics accused Hummer owners of "exhibiting a reckless degree of selfishness and an unconscionable level of social ir-responsibility," Hummer owners accused their critics of being in league with an incongruous assortment of opponents whom they regarded as "hostile to their rugged individual ideals," including "communists, PETA members, terrorists, and liberals."[6]

Current enthusiasm for "conspicuous conservation" (or "going green to be seen") among consumers who can afford it has been har-nessed by marketers to increase sales of green products.[7] However, green consumers risk being regarded by others as self-righteous pains in the neck. There's no need to lose sleep over the unfair caricatures of greenness propagated by anti-greens, but what about the much larger segment of the population who may be less than inspired by attitudes like that of the ecomarketing executive who boasted to a *New Yorker* reporter, "I do daily yoga with my wife. We live in an energy-efficient house with solar-panel appliances. We use organic linens and towels"?[8] Those are all fine practices, but you don't have to be a Hummer-driving oil executive to bristle at that style of example setting. The ecofriendly *Slate* columnist Emily Bazelon had an especially strong reaction: "Don't you want to punch this guy? I do."[9] Research shows that some-times people really do become irritated with those who act responsibly, even when it's done completely out of personal motivation, with no boasting or intentional example setting. Rightly or wrongly, we tend to interpret the good deeds of others as implicit criticism of our own actions (or inaction) and that creates ill will.[10]

Public displays of green abstinence can be just as frustrating as the flaunting of green consumption. In an online chat about the column in which she had criticized the yoga- and-towel-consuming executive (and in which she was self-critical as well; the piece ran under the sub-title "Is My Hybrid Turning My Kids into Eco-Snobs?"), Bazelon heard from a commenter in Kensington, Maryland, who, in an effort to show how to avoid ecosnobbery, painted a grim picture indeed:

> Environmentalism is hard, it is not fun. It requires pretty much being uncool and old-fashioned. But it is worth it. The fleet of bikes my family uses to get around was pulled from the garbage. So were some of our furniture, building materials, television,

several vacuum cleaners and assorted computer equipment. We actually sew our clothes to patch holes and extend their useful life indefinitely. We compost. I use the dishwater on the lawn. . . . There is nothing to be snobby about in being green. It is about being humble, not showing off consumer excess, using less and living simpler, more selfless lives. Your kids, like mine, actually will hate it.

Bazelon responded, "But here's my question for you: if it's grim and a slog, and we portray it that way, won't most people decide to do nothing at all?" [11]

While it's true that talk of a tough future can induce apathy and inaction, the obvious mismatch between the scale of looming ecological crises and the limited nature of most of the lifestyle-based recommendations for solving them can be just as demobilizing. If a good citizen need only install a "smart" thermostat, empty the dishwater on the lawn, and keep tires properly inflated, then the situation may appear to be under control. Like the "global war on terror"—in which our only assignment as civilians was to "be aware of your surroundings" and go shopping—the global ecological crisis has so far meant no significant sacrifices or even adjustments by the U.S. public. It's not because people in general are "unaware, hypnotized, selfish, and lazy," as some environmental activists have been accused of characterizing us. [12] It's just that we're still looking for a common struggle in which to join—a struggle for fairness, resilience, and resourcefulness, in which everyone is playing by the same rules.

The question of consumption reaches its stickiest point when it comes to the basic necessities of life. When there is a shortage of essential goods, and a portion of the population struggles even to meet minimum requirements, some very tough choices have to be made. In this book, I will examine what happens when society finds it necessary to limit consumption but decides collectively that it is not acceptable simply to have supplies dwindle, allow prices to rise, and let people scramble for what they need. I will ask if it is possible to devise a fair, objective, transparent system for averting both privation and excess. In other words—to use what has been called a "six-letter four-letter word"[13]—this is a book about how rationing happens today and how we might ration more fairly in the future.

THE PRICE WE PAY

The high-occupancy-vehicle (HOV) express lane has long been a feature of urban freeways around the world. In the traditional version of the HOV lane, only vehicles with two or more occupants are allowed entry, thereby providing an incentive to carpool, conserve fuel, and reduce air pollution. In the 1990s, some cities opened HOV lanes to non-carpoolers if they paid a toll, and, in 2004, California cities began admitting solo drivers if they were in hybrid, electric, and other more fuel-efficient vehicles.[14] In 2011, the notoriously traffic-choked city of Atlanta attempted to lure more drivers into its HOV lanes by converting some stretches into "high-occupancy toll" (HOT) lanes. Under the new regime, solo drivers on a busy sixteen-mile-long stretch of Interstate 85 are now eligible to use the express lane if they buy an electronic "PeachPass" through which they are automatically assessed a fee that ranges between one and ninety cents per mile—the heavier the HOT traffic, the higher the toll. But now, two-occupant vehicles also must pay. Only vehicles with three or more occupants—the rarest of rare sights in Atlanta—may enter free of charge. The lanes, once used to promote conservation, have thereby been redirected almost entirely toward congestion relief and revenue generation.

The scheme has brought little congestion relief, however, and the high-tech "Lexus lanes," as they are often called, have been highly controversial. When HOT lanes made their Atlanta debut in October 2011, drivers veered away from them by the tens of thousands. Very few were willing to buy a pass even if it allowed them to sail past nonpaying traffic. With two-occupant cars now forced to squeeze over into the regular traffic, congestion worsened and commutes stretched even longer. HOT traffic then did begin to pick up, growing steadily over the next few months, and the cost of using the lane rose accordingly, surpassing $4.75 for the full sixteen miles in early 2012. Ninety-four percent of drivers were still using the free lanes, where traffic continued to crawl along as slowly as ever, and cars in the HOT lanes moved at an average of only six to nine miles per hour faster. One driver complained, "So, you're paying four dollars to be stuck in traffic still when you could just drive in the regular lanes and you're going to be stuck in traffic anyway." Furthermore, it was estimated that 20 percent of drivers in the toll lane were cheaters who carried with them neither a PeachPass nor two other passengers.[15] Needless to say, no fuel was conserved.

The logic of the HOT lane is straightforward enough. By adjusting fees, authorities can move toward "getting the price right"—in this case, to determine the rates that will induce the desired number of drivers to shell out a few bucks for a faster trip at a given time of day. One driver, a lawyer, told the *Atlanta Journal-Constitution*, "It's awesome. I'm glad [other drivers] hate it. They can stay out of it—that's why it's moving."[16] The HOT system and the HOV system it replaced are both means of rationing scarce driving space, but HOV applies what is called the criterion of reciprocity—in this case, distributing the resource to those who carpool to conserve resources—while HOT rations space according to drivers' willingness to pay the toll, with a dash of reciprocity for those phantom three-occupant cars. But during rush hour under either system, most drivers are subjected to another time-tested rationing device: waiting in line. Although it can be argued that the classic HOV lane is unfair because it favors commuters who can afford hybrid cars or happen to live and work under circumstances that allow them to carpool, it is the HOT lane's pay-or-crawl requirement that has inspired outrage.[17]

Prices are the key to efficiency in market economies. They direct resources toward more profitable uses by industry; then, once industry has turned out commodities, prices ration the commodities among consumers. That is said to provide maximum benefit to society as a whole, because the ways in which people spend their money reflect what they believe will increase their own well-being. But do markets really zero in on the optimum distribution? "The thesis that efficiency maximizes welfare," the economist Mark Sagoff has written, "states a specious tautology, since 'welfare' and 'efficiency' are both defined in terms of 'willingness-to-pay'"; furthermore, willingness to pay can be expressed only by those with the ability to pay. And it has long been well known that when consumers make purchases, they are not simply expressing preferences that spring from somewhere deep within. Back in 1958, for example, the Harvard economist Edward Mason argued that in the then-new era of the giant corporation and "managerialism," consumers often did not even have the chance to express their preferences. Rather, their purchasing patterns were being largely dictated by those from whom they were buying. This didn't fit the theory of classical economics, in which, Mason wrote, " 'tastes' or 'wants' on the demand side and, on the supply side, technological and resource limitations to production were 'given data' " and the test of an economic system "lay in the efficiency with which it accomplished, within these limitations, the satisfaction of human wants." In the twentieth century, things had changed:

> In an economy whose supreme talent is devoted not only to the creation of the new product but to making the customer like it, [consumer] sovereignty turns out to be limited indeed. The consumer may have a biological need for food but not necessarily in cellophane wrapping; he may have a culturally determined desire for transportation, but he can presumably get there without fins on his car. . . . If this is so, what happens to the doctrine of consumer sovereignty and the tests of the efficiency of an economic system that are cast in terms of its capacity to satisfy human wants? The measuring rod turns out to be highly elastic—to be extended or shrunk at the whim of those who manage the system.[18]

In many situations, markets turn out to be highly inefficient, and they fail.[19] In other situations, even when the economy is operating at high efficiency, it can produce results that "may well be thoroughly unequal and nasty," in the words of the noted economist Amartya Sen.[20] When resources go to the high bidders, the economic tide may rise, but only for those who have a boat—and yachts always rise the fastest.[21]

Consider quinoa. Three to four thousand years ago, farmers in South America took a wild plant species with edible seeds called *Chenopodium quinoa* and, through observation and selective breeding over many generations, increased the yield and size of the plants' seeds, thereby giving their continent, and eventually the world, a new grain crop. Today, with its tastiness, high nutritional value, and association with an exotic ancient civilization, quinoa grain has become popular in North America and Europe as an alternative to cereal grains such as wheat and rice.[22] In 2011, the *New York Times* reported from Bolivia that "demand for quinoa is soaring in rich countries, as American and European consumers discover the 'lost crop' of the Incas. The surge has helped raise farmers' incomes here in one of the hemisphere's poorest countries. But there has been a notable trade-off: fewer Bolivians can now afford it, hastening their embrace of cheaper, processed foods and raising fears of malnutrition in a country that has long struggled with it." The problem was that health-conscious consumers in the global North had stimulated exports of quinoa, driving up prices in its region of origin. The *Times* noted that although Bolivia's malnutrition rate as measured nationwide has fallen in recent years, the rate of chronic malnutrition in children has risen, specifically in quinoa-growing areas. Asked about the situation, the president of the Quinoa Corporation of Los Angeles responded with cool rationality: "It's kind of discouraging to see stuff like this happen, but that's part of life and economics."[23]

Countless such situations illustrate the principle that even when markets work as intended and at high efficiency, they allocate resources "toward those who have money and unmet wants, not toward those who have unmet needs," in the words of the ecological economist Joshua Farley. One of Farley's choice examples of prices in action concerns a pharmaceutical compound called eflornithine, which kills the parasite that causes East African sleeping sickness.[24] The company Hoechst Marion Roussel began to manufacture the drug in 1990, but soon after Hoechst was bought by the pharmaceutical giant Aventis in 1995, the new owners noted the inadequate profits generated by eflornithine and began phasing it out. By 1998, little or no supply remained; approximately three hundred thousand people contracted sleeping sickness that year in Africa, with tens of thousands dying. Farley writes:

> Although the only other treatment for second-stage sleeping sickness [a concoction that is, according to one observer, essentially "arsenic dissolved in antifreeze"[25]] is extremely painful to

administer, often ineffective, and often lethal, Aventis could not profit from selling [eflornithine] to poor Africans and discontinued production for that purpose. At the same time, however, Bristol Myers Squibb and Gillette were profitably producing eflornithine to remove unwanted facial hair in women. Aventis and Bristol Myers Squibb agreed to again produce eflornithine for the treatment of African sleeping sickness only after the NGO Médecins Sans Frontières threatened to publicize the issue.[26]

Had the market been left to its own devices, he notes, the rationing function of prices would have reserved eflornithine exclusively for cosmetic purposes rather than for saving lives. Another of Farley's cautionary tales is the 2001 electricity crisis in California, which triggered "rolling blackouts" and financially crippled power utilities. When energy trading companies, led by Enron Corporation, created shortages in the state's recently deregulated power industry, they caused wholesale electricity prices to jump by as much as 800 percent, with economic turmoil and suffering the result. The loss to the state was estimated at more than $40 billion. That same year, Brazil had a nationwide electricity shortfall of 10 percent, which was proportionally larger than the shortage in California. But the Brazilian government avoided inflation and blackouts simply by capping prices and limiting all customers, residential and commercial, to 10 percent lower consumption than that of the previous year, with severe penalties for exceeding the limit. No significant suffering resulted. The California crisis is viewed as one of America's worst energy disasters, but, says Farley, "No one even remembers a 'crisis' in Brazil in 2001."[27]

Rationing of water to those who can afford to spend the most has had profound consequences around the world.[28] The more extreme the wealth gap, it seems, the more unfair the allocation. From a survey of tropical tourist destinations in Africa and Asia, the London-based nonprofit Tourism Concern concluded in a 2012 report that "tourism development is negatively impacting the quality, availability and accessibility of freshwater for local people, amounting to an infringement of their water and sanitation rights." In Zanzibar, for example, resort hotels and guesthouses sited in three coastal villages consume 180 to 850 gallons of water per room per day (with the more luxurious hotels consuming the most), while local households have access to only 25 gallons per day for all purposes. Each of the villages depends on a small electric pump for its supply, and the power is often interrupted; meanwhile, the hotels employ more powerful, higher-volume pumps, with the result that water pressure in the villages is further reduced. In southern India, luxury tourist houseboats that ply the scenic backwaters of Kerala are using the waterways not only for transportation (leaking gas and oil in the process) but also as a toilet and garbage receptacle. Most local people depend on the backwaters for all their water needs and for the fish they eat; now pollution is rendering their water undrinkable, and their fish often tastes like kerosene. And in the Gambia, on the west coast of Africa, tourist hotels are supplied with ample water through systems of oversized pipes and can store it in large reserve tanks, while 75 percent of households in the area have no piped water at all.[29]

In these few examples spanning four continents, the distorted distribution of food, drugs, energy, and water is striking. Ill effects of rationing by price are especially troubling when, as in these cases, they affect commodities that in certain quantities are recognized as necessities—and that people often desire to acquire them in much larger quantities. In times of scarcity, whether encountered or created, governments sometimes build a floor under consumption to secure basic needs at the bottom of the economy, and they often find it necessary also to put a ceiling in place as well, to conserve resources that would otherwise be consumed in excess by some. In other words, they practice rationing by means other than price. The mechanisms for nonprice rationing are many and varied. The more familiar include rationing by queuing, as at the gas pump in the 1970s; by time, as with day-of-week lawn sprinkling during droughts; by lottery, as with immigration visas and some clinical trials of scarce drugs; by triage, as in battlefield or emergency medicine; by straight quantity, as governments did with gasoline, tires, and shoes during World War II; or by keeping score with a nonmonetary device such as carbon emissions or the points that were assigned to meats and canned goods in wartime. Whether to ration by price and, if not, the choice among other means of rationing can have profound consequences. Any way you slice it, the manner in which we share the burden of scarcity is something that arises from conscious choices. Resources don't decide for themselves where to go.

As we will see, rationing of household consumption does not work as a primary means of limiting total resource use; rather, it is a measure that becomes necessary when the use of resources "upstream," in production, is limited. Should shortages strike on continental or global scales sometime in the future, or if governments should begin treating fossil fuels *as if* they are scarce, as part of an effort to curb ecological disruption, then rationing by price could create intolerable hardship for many. If it becomes clear that nonprice rationing is necessary, societies can learn from past experience; wartime provides many of the most-discussed examples, but, as we will see, there are many others. Nonprice rationing has so far been employed chiefly as a response to temporary scarcity in specific geographical areas. Might we one day face global, persistent scarcity and along with it the prospect of formal rationing? It is not just a hypothetical question. We are seeing a continuous stream of research-journal articles and news stories, and shelves full of books, anticipating a future racked by ecological breakdown, resource depletion, and scarcity.[30] Be assured that this book isn't one of those; in my view, the healthiest approach to the forecasts of gloom and doom hanging over us is to weigh them seriously but then move on quickly to consider what can be done. What societies have done before and what we could do in the future in four crucial realms of life—energy, water, food, and medical care—will be the subjects of the chapters that follow.

The Great Recession of 2009 brought the long-disdained word "austerity" back into wide usage, but it's now defined as a narrow form of frugality that only governments, not corporations or individuals, must practice. Governments are told that they can no longer live beyond their means. Fair enough; that logic is typically applied only to fiscal means, however, while rarely acknowledging that governments and corporations are also living beyond their ecological means. Protests across North America and Europe since 2009 have rightly condemned government austerity measures that protect the fortunes of the richest 1 percent while ignoring the needs of working people and the unemployed. When the demands of those popular movements have focused on restoring the middle-class dream of ever-expanding affluence, they have ignored the fact that limitless economic growth is neither possible nor desirable. When they have focused more on redistribution of resources, they have been more consistent with the need to construct a fairer economy within ecologically necessary boundaries (even if that need is not explicitly recognized).

Meanwhile, attempts to limit greenhouse emissions through a combination of weak treaties and market mechanisms have continued to stumble over issues of fairness. Those efforts have failed because, as the economist James K. Galbraith argues, "polite" approaches do not go far enough, and explicit planning is required. Whether we see it or not, he adds, "in the modern world, planning happens: it is what corporations exist to do. The only issue, therefore, is whether the planning function is to be left entirely in the hands of private corporations . . . or whether the government and the larger public are entitled to play a role."

Although in today's political world, Galbraith notes, "syphilis, leprosy, and planning more or less rank together" in popularity, we may be living in a very different world before long.[31] If we allow the future to be created by veiled corporate planning, the fairly predictable consequence will be resource conflicts between the haves and have-nots—or rather, among the haves, the hads, and the never-hads. Even if we wrest planning out of corporate hands, it is not so obvious what to do next or what the consequences will be. Nevertheless, we can try to foresee those consequences, with some help from past and current efforts to plan rationally.

For now, none of that is happening. And it is not just a witless devotion to consumption for the sake of consumption that is responsible for our resisting any attempt at restraint. It's quite possible (indeed very common, I would guess) to be simultaneously concerned about the fate of the Earth and worried that the necessary degree of restraint just isn't achievable. We've been painted into a corner by an economy that has a bottomless supply of paint. Overproduction, the chronic ailment of any mature capitalist economy, creates the need for a culture whose consumption is geared accordingly. The converse holds true as well. If consumer rationing (nonprice rationing, that is) were employed in the resource-limited world of the future, its role would not be to curb overproduction and overexploitation of resources directly; rather, it would be as a necessary *response* to externally imposed limits on production and prices of consumer goods. It would be a means of ensuring that everyone has enough in those times of scarcity when the laws of supply and demand fail.

Whenever there's a ceiling on overall availability of goods, no one is happy. And when a consumer unlucky enough to be caught in such a situation is confronted with explicit rationing—a policy that she experiences as the day-to-day face of that scarcity—it's no wonder that rationing becomes a dirty word. That has always been true, but an economy that is as deeply dependent on consumer spending as ours would view explicit rationing as a doubly dirty proposition. In America, freedom of consumption has become essential to realizing many of our more fundamental rights—freedom of movement, freedom of association, ability to communicate, satisfactory employment, good health care, even the ability to choose what to eat and drink—and no policy that compromises those rights by limiting access to resources is going to be at all welcome. If we do make a serious effort to corral the national and world economies within ecologically supportable boundaries, the method we choose for divvying up the resources that humanity *can* afford to consume must be a method we can all live with. In fact—considering the many tragic consequences of rationing by ability to pay in a world with such enormous imbalances of economic power—we might even find that we can devise ways of sharing scarce resources that produce a happier, better-fed, healthier, more comfortable, and more secure world than the one we inhabit today. But such methods cannot be expected to pop up spontaneously. That is why it is important to examine how nonprice rationing works, on paper and in the real world, and to find out if it will be possible to paint our society out of its corner.

1

THE MATERIAL EQUIVALENT OF WAR

No patriotic American can or will ask men to risk their lives to preserve motoring-as-usual.
> —Secretary of the Interior Harold Ickes explaining the U.S. government's gasoline rationing plan, April 23, 1942 [1]

When we enter the moral equivalent of war, Mr. President, don't issue us BB guns.
> —from a U.S. citizen's letter to President Jimmy Carter, as quoted by Carter in his energy policy speech of July 15, 1979 [2]

In a 1906 essay, the philosopher William James discussed the deep human needs that militarism appears to fill, and he chided pacifists and utopians of the time, whose vision, he wrote, "tastes mawkish and dishwatery to people who still keep a sense for life's more bitter flavors," while at the same time offering "no substitute for war's disciplinary function, no *moral equivalent* of war." [3] Seven decades later, President Jimmy Carter echoed James in a speech on the then-unfolding energy crisis, declaring, "Our decision about energy will test the character of the American people and the ability of the President and the Congress to govern this Nation. This difficult effort will be the 'moral equivalent of war,' except that we will be uniting our efforts to build and not to destroy." [4]

Carter was neither the first nor the last leader to use martial language when urging conservation and sacrifice. According to the environmental scholar Maurie Cohen, "Experience suggests that the use of militaristic representations can be an effective device with which to convey seriousness of purpose, to marshal financial resources, to disable opponents, and to mobilize diverse constituencies behind a common banner. Martial language can also communicate a political

UNITED STATES
OF AMERICA
War Ration Book One

WARNING

1 Punishments ranging as high as *Ten Years' Imprisonment or $10,000 Fine, or Both,* may be imposed under United States Statutes for violations thereof arising out of infractions of Rationing Orders and Regulations.

2 This book must not be transferred. It must be held and used only by or on behalf of the person to whom it has been issued, and anyone presenting it thereby represents to the Office of Price Administration, an agency of the United States Government, that it is being so held and so used. For any misuse of this book it may be taken from the holder by the Office of Price Administration.

3 In the event either of the departure from the United States of the person to whom this book is issued, or his or her death, the book must be surrendered in accordance with the Regulations.

4 Any person finding a lost book must deliver it promptly to the nearest Ration Board.

OFFICE OF PRICE ADMINISTRATION

N° 901503 —347
canning sugar – 6/1/43
10 lb.

FOLD BACK ✦ FOLD BACK

Certificate of Registrar

This is to Certify that pursuant to the Rationing Orders and Regulations administered by the OFFICE OF PRICE ADMINISTRATION, an agency of the United States Government,

(Name, Address, and Description of person to whom the book is issued.)

Brodie (Last name) *Judson* (First name) *Maurice* (Middle name)

Aiken (Street No. or P. O. Box No.)

Aiken (City or town) *Aiken* (County) *S. C.* (State)

5 ft. 8 in. 168 lbs. Blue (Color of eyes) Brown (Color of hair) 54 yrs. Sex { Male ☐ Female }

has been issued the attached War Ration Stamps this 3rd day of May, 1942, upon the basis of an application signed by himself ☐, herself ☐, or on his or her behalf by his or her husband ☐, wife ☐, father ☐, mother ☐, exception ☐. (Check one.)

Catherine N. Summerall (Registrar) (Signature)

Local Board No. 2-1 County *Aiken* State *S. C.*

Stamps must not be detached except in the presence of the retailer, his employee, or person authorized by him to make delivery.

WAR RATION STAMP	WAR RATION STAMP	WAR RATION STAMP
24	22	20
23	21	19

A ration book issued by the U.S. government, with stamps, 1943.

message that success may take time and that public sacrifice may be required as part of the struggle."[5]

In the future, we could be devoting a much larger percentage of available energy and economic effort to the acquisition of fuels and other resources, construction of alternative-energy capacity, and protection of ecological life-support systems. That could consume a share of national resources similar to the share consumed by war production in the past. As happened then, the need for a fair way to apportion the resources available to the rest of the economy could arise. Therefore, it could be useful to examine in some detail those times during the past century when the government controlled prices and, at times, rationed goods. Life in America during World War II tends to be romanticized in the public imagination, while almost nothing positive lingers in most memories of the 1970s.[6] But the economic interventions by the government that characterized both periods were rarely either cheered or condemned by the public at large at the time. Rather, most people stoically tolerated limits on consumption in the hope that better times were on the way. Although polls taken during both periods tended to show broad support for rationing, it was viewed as a necessary evil at best. It was imposed only as a last resort. If there is a chance that we will once again grapple with the question of whether to ration, lessons learned when we faced that question in the past—for example, in 1918, 1943, and 1979—may be well worth studying.

THE LEAST BAD LAST RESORT?

As World War I ground on into its third year in the summer of 1917, U.S. exports of wheat and other foods were all that stood between Europe's battle-weary populations and mass hunger. America's annual food exports rose from 7 to 19 million tons during the war. As a result, the farms of the time, which were far less productive than those of today, were hard-pressed to satisfy domestic demand. By August 1917, with the United States four months into its involvement in the war, Congress passed the Lever Act, creating the United States Food Administration and the Federal Fuel Administration and giving them broad control of production and prices. Commodity dealers were required to obtain licenses from Food Administrator Herbert Hoover, and he had the power to revoke licenses, shut down or take over firms, and seize commodities for use by the military.[7] In September, the *Toledo News-Bee* announced that the "entire world may be put on rations soon" with Hoover acting as "food dictator of the world."[8] But as it turned out, Hoover wasn't much of a dictator. According to the historian Helen Zoe Veit, restrictions consisted mostly of jawboning, as "food administrators simultaneously exalted voluntarism while threatening to impose compulsory rations should these weak, 'democratic' means prove insufficient"; however, "many Americans wrote to the Food Administration to say that they believed that compulsion actually inspired cheerful willingness, whereas voluntarism got largely apathetic results."[9] There were in fact a few mandatory restrictions. Hoarding of all kinds of products was prohibited, and violators could be punished with fines or even imprisonment. "Fair-price lists" ran in local newspapers and retailers were expected to adhere to them. But controls on prices of wheat and sugar were not backed up with regulation of demand. That led to scarcities of both commodities, as consumers who could afford to buy excessive quantities often did so.[10]

Meanwhile, the Fuel Administration had to deal with shortages of coal, which at that time was the nation's most important source of energy for heating, transportation, and manufacturing. Heavy heating demand in the frigid winter of 1917–18 converged with higher-than-normal use of the railway system (largely for troop movements) to precipitate what has been called the nation's first energy crisis.[11] The administration resorted to a wide range of stratagems to conserve coal, including factory shutdowns, division of the country into "coal zones" with no trade between zones, and a total cutoff of supplies to country clubs and yacht owners. The administration announced that Americans would be allowed to buy only as much coal as was needed to keep their houses at 68 degrees F. in winter. While acknowledging that "this system will be drastic and will introduce conditions new to the country," one official statement announced, "No one will be deprived of coal actually needed for heating, but no one will be allowed fuel for waste or extravagance."[12] The need to conserve petroleum led to a campaign to stop the pastime of Sunday driving. Even in those very early days of the car culture, Fuel Administrator Harry Garfield remarked that "it was odd to see the streets free of automobiles and to hear the almost forgotten clack of horses' hoofs." The campaign against Sunday driving was carried out enthusiastically, perhaps overly so, by self-appointed volunteer citizens. Garfield complained that the volunteers had become "tyrranous," punishing violators in ways that "would have staggered the imagination of Americans twelve months earlier."[13]

Government officials assumed that their conservation plans would have to be kept in place for several years. Hoover's estimates showed the average American eating about six pounds of bread and four pounds of meat and fat per week, and in September 1918 he recommended a reduction in consumption of less than half a pound a week per person of each type of food. With no way of knowing that the war would be over within two months, Hoover went on to explain,

> Some of our homes, by reason of limited income, cannot now provide more food than they should have to maintain health in the family. They cannot be rightfully asked to make the suggested reduction in consumption. But the great majority of our homes can do more than suggested. We need even greater simplicity of living than last year. . . . This is not rationing—a thing we will never have if our people continue to support us as in the past.[14]

Although food shortages persisted despite the drive for voluntary moderation, rationing remained off the table. Veit explained how the U.S. government's insistence on voluntarism was an effort to draw a contrast between democratic America and autocratic, "overrationed" Germany. Rationing, the argument went, had undermined German morale while the United States was managing to rescue Europe and feed its own population "precisely because it never forced Americans to sacrifice, but instead inspired them to do so willingly." (Hoover's Home Conservation director Ray Wilbur asserted that, before the war, "we were a soft people," and that voluntary sacrifice had strengthened the nation.)[15]

But in World War I America, price controls acting alone did not prevent shortages, unfair distribution, and deprivation. From that experience, the economic historian Hugh Rockoff concluded that "with prices fixed, the government must substitute some form of rationing or other means of reducing demand" because "appeals to voluntary cooperation, even when backed by patriotism, are of limited value in solving this problem."[16] The reluctance to use rationing was tied to views on democracy. According to Veit, the most powerful men in Washington, including Hoover and President Woodrow Wilson, viewed democracy as "synonymous with *individual freedom*," while another view of democracy that was widely held at the time required "*equality of burden*." Under the second definition, "rationing was inherently more democratic as it prevented one group (the patriotic) from bearing the double-burden of compensating for another (the shirkers)."

In practice, Hoover's Food Administration valued free-market economics more highly than either personal freedom or fairness.[17] Official language was always of voluntary sacrifice, but there's more than one way to rope in a "volunteer." Ad hoc committees in schools, workplaces, churches, and communities kept track of who did and didn't sign Hoover's food-conservation pledge or display government posters in their kitchen windows. In urging women to sign and comply with the Hoover pledge, door-to-door canvassers laid on the hard sell, often with the implication of an "or else" if the pledge was refused. Statements from government officials to the effect of "we know who you are" and explicit branding of nonsigners as "traitors" were highly effective recruiting techniques. But millions of poor and often hungry Americans had no excess consumption to give up. A Missouri woman told Hoover canvassers that yes, she would accept a pledge card so that she could "wipe her butt with it," because she "wasn't going to feed rich people."[18] As Veit put it, "the choice to live more ascetically was a luxury, and the notion of righteous food conservation struck those who couldn't afford it as a cruel joke."[19]

With pressure building, the U.S. government probably would have resorted to rationing had World War I continued through 1919. The major European combatants, whose ordeal had been longer and tougher, did have civilian rationing, and the practice reappeared across Europe with the return of war in 1939.

THE "SIEGE MOTIVE"

Rationing has long been associated with war. The word *ration* migrated from French into English sometime in the seventeenth century. It referred to the daily quantity of food allotted to men in the army or on board ship (or, in a different context, to portions of feed given to livestock). The French *ration*, in turn, goes back to the Latin *ratiō*, meaning "reason" or "calculation." The American linguist Kemp Malone, writing during World War II, explained that *ration* as both verb and noun had at that time "remained in living use chiefly in the mouths of soldiers and sailors; the members of the armed services get rations normally and regularly, while civilians are subjected to rationing (and add the word to their vocabulary) in abnormal and irregular times only (such times as the present)."[20] Well into the twentieth century, some lexicographers gave precedence to the pronunciation of *ration* with a long *a*, as in *ratio* and *nation*, but by far the more common pronunciation was to rhyme *ration* with *fashion*. The latter pronunciation was clearly preferred in the military. In his 1942 glossary *Army Talk*, Elbridge Colby has this entry for the word:

> Officially defined as "subsistence for one man for one day," this word is so widely understood that it would not have been included here were it not necessary to caution folk that to pronounce it to rhyme with "nation" is the mark of a civilian and a raw recruit. Old soldiers always pronounce it to rhyme with the first two syllables of "national." Another quirk of speech causes it almost always to be used only in the plural, and loosely so as to mean merely "something to eat."[21]

During the twentieth century, economists began to use *ration* to denote any means of apportioning a factor of production or an end product, but one sees the term used in two different ways. The "rationing function of price" refers to the adjustment of demand through changes in price of a scarce factor or product to bring it into line with supply. To convey this meaning, economists often (but by no means always) use a term like rationing "by price" or "by willingness to pay."

But *rationing* is also commonly used to mean the apportionment of scarce goods when the price is *not* allowed to move to a point at which demand and supply align—as happened, for example, when price controls were imposed in America in the 1940s.

When World War II broke out in Europe, the United States once again mounted a campaign to export food and war materials to its allies. Soon after America entered the war, the first items to require rationing were tires and gasoline. Those moves can be explained, in Rockoff's words, by the "siege motive," the result of absolute scarcity imposed by an external cutoff of supply.[22] The rubber and tire industries were indeed under siege, with supplies from the Pacific having been suddenly cut off. The processes for making synthetic rubber were known, but there had not been time to build sufficient manufacturing capacity. The government's first move was to buy time by calling a halt to all tire sales. With military rubber requirements approaching the level of the economy's entire prewar output, Leon Henderson, head of the Office of Price Administration (OPA), urged Americans to reduce their driving voluntarily to save rubber.[23] But, unwilling to rely solely on drivers' cooperation, the government got creative and decided to ration gasoline as an indirect means of reducing tire wear.

The need for gas rationing had already arisen independently in the eastern states. At the outbreak of the war, the United States was supplying most of its own oil needs. With much of the production located in the south-central states, tankers transported petroleum from ports on the Gulf Coast to the population centers of the East Coast. But in the summer of 1941, oil tankers began to be diverted from domestic to transatlantic trade in support of the war effort, and all shipping routes became highly vulnerable to attack by German submarines. With supplies strictly limited, authorities issued ration coupons that all drivers purchasing gasoline were required to submit, and also banned nonessential driving in many areas. Police were asked to stop and question motorists if they suspected a violation and "check on motorists found at race tracks, amusement parks, beaches, and other places where their presence is prima facie evidence of a violation." Drivers also were required to show that they had arranged to carry two or more passengers whenever possible.[24] Energy consumption was further curtailed by restrictions on the manufacture of durable goods, including cars. At one point, passenger-car production was shut down altogether. That, according to Rockoff, was in a sense "the fairest form of rationing. Each consumer got an exactly equal share: nothing." [25]

LIMITED RATIONING HAD LIMITED SUCCESS

It became clear early on that rationing of food and other goods would become necessary as well. The OPA announced that "sad experience has proven the inadequacy of voluntary rationing. . . . Although none would be happier than we if mere statements of intent and hortatory efforts were sufficient to check overbuying of scarce commodities, we are firmly convinced that voluntary programs will not work." [26] With some exceptions, such as coffee and bananas, the trigger for rationing foodstuffs was not the siege motive. The United States was producing ample harvests and continued to do so throughout the war, but the military buildup of 1942 included a commitment to supply each soldier and sailor in the rapidly expanding armed services with as much as four thousand calories per day. Those hefty war rations, along with exports of large tonnages of grain to Britain and other allies, pulled vast quantities of food out of the domestic economy. Without price controls, inflation would have ripped through America's food system and the economy, and the price controls could not have held without rationing.

In the first year of America's involvement in the war, there was only loose coordination among agencies responsible for production controls, price controls, and consumer rationing, and as a result the government was unable to either keep prices down or meet demand for necessities. In late 1941 and early 1942, polls showed strong public demand for broader price controls. Across-the-board controls were imposed in April 1942. But over the next year, prices still rose at a 7.6 percent annual rate, so in early 1943 comprehensive rationing of foods and other goods was announced. In April, Roosevelt issued a strict "Hold-the-Line Order" that allowed no further price increases for most goods and services. Only that sweeping proclamation, backed up as it was by a comprehensive rationing system, was able to keep inflation in check and achieve fair distribution of civilian goods. In late 1943, the OPA was getting very low marks in polls—not because of opposition to rationing or price controls, but because people were complaining that they needed even broader and stricter enforcement.[27] It's important to note that OPA actions were often motivated as much by wariness of political unrest as by a concern for fairness. Amy Bentley, a historian, explains that the experience of the Great Depression was fresh in the minds of government officials, and they felt that, with the war having reimposed nationwide scarcity, ensuring equitable sharing of basic needs was essential if a new wave of upheaval and labor radicalization was to be avoided. In publicity materials, the OPA stressed the positive, buoyed by comments from citizen surveys, such as the view of one woman that "rationing is good democracy."[28]

Consumer rationing by quantity took two general forms: (1) straight rationing (also referred to at various times as "specific" or "unit" rationing), which specified quantities of certain goods (tires, gas, shoes, some durable goods) that could be bought during a specified time period at a designated price; and (2) points rationing, in which officials assigned point values to each individual product (say, green beans or T-bone steak) within each class of commodity (canned vegetables or meats). Each household was allocated a certain number of points that could be spent during the specified period. Price ceilings were eventually placed on 80 percent of foodstuffs, and ceilings were adjusted for cost of living city by city.[29] Determining which goods to ration and what constituted a "fair share" required a major data-collection effort. The OPA drew information from a panel of 2,500 women who kept and submitted household food diaries. The general rules and mechanics of wartime rationing, while cumbersome, were at least straightforward. Ration stamps were handled much like currency, except that they had fixed expiration dates. Businesses were required to collect the proper value in stamps with each purchase so that they could pass them up the line to wholesalers and replenish inventories. Many retailers had ration bank accounts from which they could write ration checks when purchasing inventory; that spared them the inconvenience of handling bulky quantities of stamps and avoided the risk of loss or theft. Although stamps expired at the end of the month for consumers, they were valid for exchange by retailers and wholesalers for some time afterward. Therefore, the OPA urged that households destroy all expired ration stamps, warning that pools of excess stamps could "breed black markets." The link between the physical stamp and the consumer was tightly controlled. Only a member of the family owning a ration book could use the stamps, and stamps had to be torn from the book by the retailer, not the customer. Stamps for butter had to be given to the milkman in person at time of delivery; they were not to be left with a note.[30]

The people of the United Kingdom had a much longer midcentury experience with rationing than Americans did. British rationing plans started with bacon and butter in 1939, expanded during the war to cover almost all essential goods, and persisted in some parts of the economy for almost a decade after the war ended. In the first three years of rationing, overall consumer spending dropped 15 percent and shifted sharply toward less resource-intensive goods. The purchase of clothing dropped by more than one third, and the use of private automobiles was almost eliminated. Food rationing was prompted in part by the siege motive. In the 1930s, Britain had been heavily dependent on food from other countries, with half of meat consumption and 92 percent of all oils and fats having been imported. By 1944, the tonnage of food imports was cut in half.[31]

When consumption of some products is restricted by rationing, people spend the saved money on nonrationed products, driving up their prices. Therefore, Britain's initial, limited program covering bacon and butter did little to protect the wider economy. Families were plagued by inflation, as well as by shortages and unfair distribution of still-uncontrolled goods; demand swelled for "all-around rationing."[32] Restrictions on sugar and meat began early in 1940, in order to keep prices down, ensure fairness, and reduce dependence on imports. Tea, margarine, and cooking fats were included at midyear. As food scarcity took hold, worsening in the winter of 1940–41, Britons demanded that rationing be extended to a wider range of products to remedy growing inequalities in distribution. They got what they asked for. The quantities allowed per person varied during the course of the rationing period but were never especially generous: typical weekly amounts were four to eight ounces of bacon plus ham, eight to sixteen of sugar, two to four of tea, one to three of cheese, six of butter, four to eight of jam, and one to three of cooking oil. Allowances were made. Pregnant women and children received extra shares of milk and of foods high in vitamins and minerals, while farmworkers and others who did not have access to workplace canteens at lunchtime received extra cheese rations. Quantities were adjusted for vegetarians. In its mechanics, the system differed from America's in that each household was required to register with one—and only one—neighborhood shop, which would supply the entire core group of rationed foods. As the war continued, it became clear that this exclusive consumer-retailer tie was unpopular, so the government introduced a point-rationing plan in December 1941, permitting consumers to use points at any shop they chose.[33]

In both the UK and America, most of the day-to-day management of the rationing systems was, necessarily, handled at the local level. Administration of the system was decentralized. According to Bentley, "The 5,500 local OPA boards scattered across the country, run by over 63,000 paid employees and 275,000 volunteers, possessed a significant amount of autonomy, enabling them to base decisions on local considerations. The real strength of the OPA, then, lay less in the federal office than in its local boards." In large cities from Baltimore to San Francisco, a "block leader plan" was instituted to help families deal with scarcity. The block leader, always a woman, would be responsible for discussing nutritional information and sometimes rationing procedures and scrap drives with all residents of her city block. The Home Front Pledge ("I will pay no more than the top legal prices—I will accept no rationed goods without giving up ration points"), administered to citizens by the millions, was backed by clear-cut rules and was legally enforceable, so it was taken much more seriously than the Hoover Pledge of 1917–18.[34] In Britain's system, the Ministry of Food oversaw up to nineteen Divisional Food Offices, and below them more than 1,500 Food Control Committees, each of which included ten to twelve consumers, five local retailers, and one shop worker, that dealt with the public through local Food Offices.[35]

"FAIR SHARES FOR ALL" ARE ESSENTIAL

Other Allied nations, as well as Germany and the other Axis powers, also imposed strict rationing. In the countries they occupied, the Nazis enforced extremely harsh forms of rationing among local populations in order to provide more plentiful resources to German troops and civilians. A 1946 report by two Netherlands government officials, poignant in its matter-of-factness, shows in meticulous detail through numerous graphs and descriptions how the calorie consumption and health status of that country's population suffered and how many lives were lost under such strict rationing. Average adult consumption dropped as low as 1,400 calories per day during 1944. Meager as it was, that was an average; because of restrictions on food distribution, many people, especially in the western part of the country, received much less food and starved. By that stage of the war, according to the authors, "People were forced more and more to leave the towns in search of food in the production areas. Many of them, however, did not live through these food expeditions." What can be learned from such punitive forms of rationing is simply that they should never be tolerated.[36]

The OPA's job was made easier, notes Bentley, by the fact that "most Americans understood that their wartime difficulties were minor compared with the hardships in war-torn countries."[37] Soon after the initiation of food rationing, the Office of War Information estimated that, conservatively, "civilians will have about 3 percent more food than in the pre-war years but about 6 percent less than in 1942. There will be little fancy food; but there will be enough if it is fairly shared and conserved. Food waste will be intolerable."[38]

Total availability of coffee, canned vegetables, meat, cheese, and canned milk was often as high as before the war. Those items were rationed not because they were especially scarce but in order to hold down demand that otherwise would have ballooned under the price controls that were in effect. There was, for instance, an explosion of demand for milk in the early 1940s, when prices were fixed, but the dairy industry blocked attempts to initiate rationing. Consumption shot up, and severe shortages developed in pockets all over the country. Everything but rationing was attempted: relaxing health-quality standards, prohibiting the sale of heavy whipping cream, and reducing butterfat requirements. But the problem of excess demand persisted.[39]

Huge quantities of fruits and vegetables were exported in support of the war effort, leaving limited stocks for civilian use. The OPA kicked off 1943 with a plan under which households would be allowed to keep in their own homes no more than five cans of fruits or vegetables per occupant at any one time. A penalty of eight ration points would be assessed for each excess can. There is little evidence that the ban was actually enforced, and neither home-canned goods nor fresh produce was covered by the order.[40] Home canners could get a pound of sugar for each four quarts of fruits they planned to can without surrendering ration coupons; however, sugar restrictions sidelined home brewers and amateur wine makers. Commercial distilling for civilian consumption ceased, but the industry reassured customers that it had a three-year supply of liquor stockpiled and ready to sell, so there was no need to ration.[41]

Bread and potatoes were exempted from rationing, to provide a dietary backstop. With caloric requirements thus satisfied by starchy foods, protein became the chief preoccupation. Red meat had already held center stage in the American diet for decades; consumption at the beginning of World War II was more than 140 pounds per person per year, well above today's average of about 115 pounds. During the war, the government aimed to provide a full pound of red meat per day to each soldier; therefore, according to officials, only 130 pounds per year would remain for each civilian. A voluntary "Share the Meat" program, introduced in 1942, managed to lower average annual consumption by a mere three pounds. When the necessity for stronger curbs became evident, rationing was introduced in 1943, and soon consumption dropped steeply, to 104 pounds per civilian.

Farm families were permitted to consume as much as they wanted of any kind of meat they produced on the farm without surrendering ration coupons, but farm owners who did not cultivate their own land were not. Elsewhere, the feeling of scarcity was pervasive. For those who craved more meat, there was little consolation to be found in a chicken leg. At that time, poultry was not highly regarded as a substitute for red meat, so average consumption was only a little over twenty pounds per year—less than one-third of today's level.[42] The OPA tightened price ceilings on poultry but did not ration it.[43]

Soon after meat rationing was instituted, Gaynor Maddox advised newspaper readers in Florida that a forced deviation from the standard meat-heavy diet of those days "won't starve you." Nevertheless, he continued, "The two pounds per week allowed under point rationing will not supply enough protein for nutritional needs. So what's the answer? . . . The brutal truth is that you can go hungry today if you don't master ration arithmetic." Maddox's recommendations for a healthful diet reflect how dramatically the typical American worker's level of physical activity and nutritional norms have changed: "If a man eats one egg, a quart of milk, half a cup of dried beans or soybeans, a cheese sandwich, a serving of fish or shellfish, a dish of wholegrain cereal and four slices of bread, two of them whole wheat, a day, he will get enough protein, even without any meat." When nothing but meat would do, Maddox helpfully pointed out, "You can have 16 pounds of meat a week if you like pig's ears" because of their very low point value. That said, he admitted that "you can lead your husband to a kidney stew but you cannot make him eat it."[44]

By April 1, 1943, even vegetable-protein sources such as dried beans, peas, and lentils had been added to the list of rationed items. To make a half pound of hamburger go further, the American Red Cross Nutrition Service suggested the use of "extenders," including dried bread and bread crumbs, breakfast cereals, and "new commercial types" of filler. Cooks became accustomed to substituting jelly and preserves for butter; preparing sardine loaf, vegetable loaf, cheese, lard, and luncheon meat; and substituting "combination dishes such as stews, chop suey, chili, and the like for the old standby dishes such as choice roasts and steaks and chops." Americans sought out protein- and calorie-heavy food wherever they could, partly because, in those days, thinness evoked memories of hard times. The OPA, for example, "served notice on Americans . . . that they will do well, if they want to preserve that well-fed appearance, to stop dreaming of steaks and focus their appetites and point purchasing power on hamburger, stew, and such delicacies as pig's ears, pork kidneys, and beef brains."[45]

AS CITIZENS, PEOPLE ACCEPTED RATIONING WILLINGLY; AS CONSUMERS . . . NOT SO MUCH

On Sunday, February 7, 1943, Mayor Fiorello H. La Guardia announced to New Yorkers on his regular radio address that, within a few hours, a new nationwide rationing program would commence, and that the commodity involved would not be a food item. He said he was not yet permitted to identify the commodity but slyly hinted, "In the meantime, do not do any unnecessary walking." His inside information proved accurate: that afternoon, James F. Byrnes, who had stepped down as associate justice of the U.S. Supreme Court to become the director of the newly created Office of Economic Stabilization, announced that, starting the next morning, footwear would be subject to rationing, with each American entitled to three pairs of shoes per year. Initially, stamp number 17 in "War Book 1" was designated for shoe purchase. This was the first major extension of rationing beyond transportation and food, and it affected a product about which people tended to have strong feelings. Apparently anticipating that his decree would trigger a nationwide anxiety attack, Byrnes emphasized that all possible strategies had been considered, and that his office had considered and rejected the only feasible alternative: "to compel manufacturers to produce shoes that would be so unattractive that people would not buy them unless absolutely necessary."[46]

We'll never know what the public reaction would have been to the ugly-shoes option, but the reaction to rationing was instantaneous and frantic. Most shoe and department stores were closed on Sundays in that era, but in the few hours that remained before shoe rationing began, there was a rush on footwear at the handful of open stores. During the following week, after the order went into effect, the stampede continued, partly because some shoppers had misunderstood the rationing order to mean that shoes were already in short supply. In one Miami store, "clerks were fitting oxfords on feet accustomed to three-inch heels" and "women were actually having trouble navigating in the flat, heavy shoes." But, added the store's manager, "they'll get used to it." One store was hit with a rush on brightly colored shoes when the store manager speculated "that his present stock of reds, yellows, greens, and blues probably would be replaced by somber colors." At a Palm Beach store, a woman asked what the price of a pair of shoes would be without a ration stamp. A local reporter overheard the answer: "Without blinking an eye, the manager told her, 'We can let you have a pair for about $85,000, madam.' "[47]

The War Production Board (WPB) announced tight regulation of hosiery for both sexes and all ages, specifying manufacturing methods, limiting colors and patterns, and estimating that the order would save almost 15 million pounds of cotton, rayon, and wool yarns per year. WPB quality specifications required larger quantities of material per article but, significantly, they were also expected to provide for greater durability and longer wear. The apparel industry succeeded in blocking rationing plans from being implemented for any articles other than footwear, and that made it very difficult to control demand for clothing.[48] But efforts to reduce resource consumption at the manufacturing stage were ambitious. For most clothing, the WPB established "square-inch limitations on the amount of material which may be used for all trimmings, collars, pockets, etc.," while clothing was designed "to keep existing wardrobes in fashion" so that consumers would wear them longer. In discussing a WPB order regulating women's clothing, the government publication *Victory Bulletin* observed, "The Basic Silhouette—termed the 'body basic' by the order—must conform to specified measurements of length, sweep, hip, hem, etc., listed in the order." Such micromanagement even extended to swimwear, when a skimpier two-piece bathing suit was promoted for requiring less fabric.[49]

Appliance manufacturing for civilian use was tightly restricted. From April 1942 to April 1943, no mechanical refrigerators were produced; that saved a quarter million tons of critical metals and other materials for use in war production. Starting in April 1943, sale of refrigerators, whether electric-run, gas-run, or a nonmechanical icebox type, was resumed; however, in order to be allowed to make a purchase, a household member had to attest on a federal form that "I have no other domestic mechanical refrigerator, nor do I have any other refrigerator equipment that I can use." Stoves for heating and cooking were similarly rationed, requiring a declaration that the purchaser owned no functional stove. The OPA ruled that the 150,000 stovetop pressure cookers to be produced in 1943 would be allocated by County Farm Rationing Committees and that "community pools," each comprising several families who agreed to the joint use of a pressure cooker, would receive preference. The WPB exerted its influence on production of radio tubes, light fixtures, lightbulbs, and even can openers.[50] Bed and mattress production was maintained at three-fourths its normal level. Reports noted, "Sacrificing metal-consuming inner springs, mattress manufacturers have reverted to the construction of an earlier period," using materials such as cotton felt, hair, flax, and twine. The industry produced "women's slips made from old summer dresses; buttons from tough pear-tree twigs; life-jacket padding from cattails; and household utensils from synthetic resins."[51]

In Britain, a series of "Limitations of Supplies" orders governed sales of textiles and household goods. Availability of cotton fabric fell 20 percent and rayon 40 percent. The manufacture of items such as pencils, pots and pans, and furniture was subject to licensing and standardization in order to maintain a minimum level of quality at the fixed price. Soap was rationed because its production required fats, which had to be shared with the food and munitions industries. (Infants and chimney sweeps were awarded extra soap rations.)[52] The idea of clothes rationing was no more popular in Britain than it was in the United States. Prime Minister Winston Churchill didn't like the idea at all, but neither he nor anyone else could come up with an alternative means to keep prices down and all Britons clothed. Apparel was given a page in the ration book originally reserved for margarine, which at the time was not being rationed. Annual allowances fluctuated between approximately one-third and two-thirds of average prewar consumption.[53] To make the system work, production of fabric and clothing had to be controlled, and some traditions suffered. Brides learned that unless they had been saving up yards of the proper fabrics over several months, there would be no white wedding. Noted a columnist in Swindon, "At least 16 coupons would be needed for a long dress made of satin, and it would be a very selfish bride who would expect her bridesmaids to surrender valuable coupons for dresses to be used only on one occasion."[54]

In both countries, people had been accustomed to replacing clothes regularly, in response to either fashion changes or simple wear and tear. With rationing in Britain, that was no longer possible, so the government created an alternative class of apparel adapted to wartime realities. Price-controlled, tax-exempt "utility clothing" was made of fabric manufactured to precise specifications meant to ensure quality and long life. It was conceived in part by "top London fashion designers" and was not necessarily cheap. Yet it was generally well received because of its potential to delay one's next clothing purchase. Utility plans eventually encompassed other textiles, shoes, hosiery, pottery, and furniture. Items had to be made to detailed specifications, and the number of styles was tightly limited.[55]

POPULIST APPEAL WAS A POTENT CATALYST

As the United States shifted from a Depression mind-set into world war gear, a large slice of the population remained poor, and the equal-shares aspect of rationing, together with controls on prices and the rapid creation of well-paying wartime jobs, tended to boost the real incomes of working-class Americans. Food rationing took some getting used to. Amy Bentley notes, "The Depression had trained people to think in terms of agricultural surpluses amid poverty—too much food and too little money—and it took time for Americans to believe that the country now had the opposite problem—too much money and too few goods." Nonetheless, thanks partly to the combination of prosperity, price controls, and rationing, average consumption of protein, calories, calcium, and vitamins all increased during the latter part of the war.[56]

Average people also got many opportunities to sit back and enjoy the public humiliation of well-heeled or politically powerful ration violators. In the summer of 1943, the OPA initiated proceedings against eight residents of Detroit's posh Grosse Pointe suburb for buying meat, sugar, and other products without ration coupons. This gang of "socialites," as they were characterized, included a prominent insurance executive, the wife of the president of the *Detroit News*, and the widow of one the founders of the Packard Motor Car Company who tried to buy four pounds of cheese under the table and got caught.[57] In Maryland, the wife of the governor had to surrender her gas ration book after engaging in pleasure driving in a government vehicle.[58] At about the same time, the newspaper publisher Rives Mathews reported that the Maryland state comptroller J. Millard Tawes had violated the pleasure-driving ban by taking a state-owned vehicle to his son's wedding in Georgia. In a column, Mathews demanded that "Washington start cracking down on the big fellows if you expect cooperation from the little fellows." But it was Mathews himself who was arrested, on libel charges. Eventually, however, Tawes confessed and Mathews went free. The OPA suspended the comptroller's personal gasoline ration for a year.[59] In Pittsburgh, the mayor and a school superintendent had both their driver's licenses and their gas rations suspended when they were found in violation. Meanwhile, one of the city's constables was charged with enjoying some Sunday driving, including a 150-mile round-trip to Johnstown, Ohio. It turned out that he had made the trip simply to win a bet with friends that he could get away with it. When his official pretext—that he was searching for a fugitive—didn't hold up, he lost both the bet and his ability to buy fuel.[60]

Rationing stirred egalitarian feelings in Britain as well. In 1943, an American economist reported, "I was frequently told emphatically that the British people are so constituted that they will stand almost any degree of rationing if they are convinced that everyone is being treated equally, but that they decisively resent any arrangement which smacks of discrimination."[61] And rationing worked primarily to the benefit of poor families who had previously known hunger. Public health improved significantly—primarily because, writes Ina Zweiniger-Bargielowska in her history of Britain's long rationing experience, "the Second World War represented a major turning-point in the history of the British diet. The rise in consumption of brown bread, milk, and vegetables coupled with food fortification resulted in a healthier diet, and no social group fell short of basic nutritional requirements." The British Medical Association concluded in 1950 that the population's health through more than a decade of rationing had shown "continuous improvement throughout the period." Mortality rates, including the rate of infant mortality, dropped.[62] Life expectancy in England

and Wales increased by an extraordinary 6.7 years per decade during the wartime 1910s and 1940s, with their "dramatic increases in many forms of public support including public employment, food rationing, and health care," compared with an increase of only 2.2 years per decade in the peaceful 1920s, 1930s, and 1950s.[63]

Wealthy Britons did not suffer much either under food rationing. Upscale restaurants could serve as much food as their customers could eat, and they were not subject to price controls. Such costly luxuries as wild game and shellfish were not rationed, and word of extravagant banquets in upper-class mansions caused considerable grumbling. There were also frequent charges that shopkeepers favored customers who could afford larger food purchases. Perhaps the greatest class tension arose over rationing of clothing. Because they were given the same number of ration stamps, the well-to-do could buy only the same number of articles of clothing as ordinary people, but they could afford the higher-quality, longer-lasting items, while everyone else had to be satisfied with often flimsy, unattractive clothes. Nevertheless, Zweiniger-Bargielowska concluded that, on the whole, "the great disparity in consumption standards between different social groups gave way to the political imperative of fair shares. This policy was introduced in the context of total war, and equality of sacrifice was central to wartime propaganda. After 1945 the policy formed part of the Labour government's wider commitment to greater social equality." Perhaps most strikingly, the nutritional gulf between rich and poor did not reappear after controls were lifted: the improvements had stuck.[64]

COMPLICATIONS WERE UNAVOIDABLE, ADAPTATION ESSENTIAL

The rationing of goods at controlled prices provides a strong incentive for cheating, as the World War II example shows. For administering wartime rationing and price controls, the UK Ministry of Food had an enforcement staff of around a thousand, peaking in 1948 at over thirteen hundred. They pursued cases involving pricing violations; license violations; theft of food in transit; selling outside the ration system; forgery of ration documents; and, most prominently, illicit slaughter of livestock and sale of animal products. Illegal transactions accounted for 3 percent of all motor fuel sales and 10 percent of those involving passenger cars. Enforcement of rationing regulations and price controls by the ministry from 1939 to 1951 resulted in more than 230,000 convictions; the majority of offenders were retail merchants guilty of mostly minor offenses. An estimated 80 percent of the convictions resulted in fines of less than £5, and only 3 to 5 percent led to imprisonment of the offender. There were fewer problems involving quantity-rationed goods (for which consumers were paired up with a single retailer) than there were with rationing via points, which could be used anywhere. Zweiniger-Bargielowska writes that, although most people at one time or another made unauthorized purchases, the most corrosive effect of illicit markets was to subvert the ideal of "fair shares for all," since it was only those better off who could afford to buy more costly contraband goods routinely.[65]

In the United States, enforcement of price controls and rationing regulations made up 16 percent of the OPA's budget. The agency identified more than 333,000 violations in 1944 alone but prosecuted just 64,000 people that year. Forty percent of prosecutions were for food violations, with the largest share for meat and dairy, and 17 percent were for gasoline. Along with flagrant overcharging, selling without ration-stamp exchange, and counterfeiting of stamps and certificates, businesses resorted to work-arounds: "tie-in sales" that required purchase of another product in addition to the rationed one, "upgrading" of low-quality merchandise to sell at the high-quality price, and short-weighting.[66] As in Britain, the off-the-books meat trade got a large share of attention. Illicit meat was sold for approximately double the legal price, and it tended to be the better cuts that ended up in illegal channels. Official numbers of hogs slaughtered under USDA inspection dropped 30 percent from February 1942 to February 1943, with the vanished swine presumably diverted into illegal trade. Off-the-books deals by middlemen were common, as was "the rustler, who rides the range at night, shooting animals where he finds them, dressing them on the spot, and driving away with the carcasses in the truck."[67] It wasn't only meat that was squandered. *Victory Bulletin* warned, "Potential surgical sutures, adrenalin, insulin, gelatin for military films and bone meal for feeds are disregarded by the men who slaughter livestock illegally"; also lost was glycerin, needed for manufacturing explosives.[68]

Retailers didn't always play strictly by the ration book. A coalition of women's organizations in Brooklyn urged Chester Bowles, director of the OPA, to prohibit shopkeepers from holding back goods for selected customers, demanding that all sales be first come, first served. But some OPA officials pointed out that such a policy would discriminate against working women who had time to shop only late in the day. Restaurants were free to serve any size portions they liked; however, if they decided to continue serving ample portions (for which they were allowed to charge a fittingly high price), they faced the prospect of having to close for several days each week when their meat ration ran out. Private banquets featuring full portions could be held with the permission of local rationing boards. One official justified such use of scarce foods by pointing out that "some banquets are essential and serve a useful purpose." Asked for an example, he cited banquets hosted "by business groups for the purpose of explaining various rationing moves of the government."[69]

Accommodation was made for "persons whose health depends on special diets," with decisions on individual cases made largely at the local level. But diversity in dietary preferences was not widely respected in those days, and the consumption of particular kinds of foods on philosophical grounds was rare. An OPA spokesman announced that "voluntary vegetarians and others who have unusual eating habits governed by a fad or a preference rather than by a health requirement, will not be eligible for special rations." Furthermore, it would "also be impossible for anyone to trade his ration coupons for one type of food he does not like for a type he prefers." On the other hand, "involuntary vegetarians" who presented doctor's certificates stating that they could not eat animal products for reasons of health were allowed to apply for extra coupons for canned vegetables and still let family members use their surplus meat coupons.[70]

The ration stamps issued to a single household were not usually sufficient to purchase a large cut of meat such as a roast, and because stamps had expiration dates they could not be saved up from one ration period to the next in order to do so. Because consumers were required to present their own ration books in person when buying meat, announced the OPA, guests invited to a dinner party would have to buy their own meat and deliver it beforehand to the host cook—an awkward but workable solution if, say, pork chops were on the menu. However, if a single large cut such as a pot roast were to be served, the OPA noted, the host and invitees would have to "go to the butcher shop together, each buying a piece of the roast, and ask the butcher to leave it in one piece."[71]

Rationing so dominated everyday life during the war that even private interests moved to get in on the act. In 1943 the Associated Press reported from Georgia, "Comes now the newest thing in rationing: 'frozen' church seats. For two months starting Feb. 1, worshippers will be admitted to Ellaville Baptist Church by 'V' ration coupons, which will be issued soon for the 300 available seats, says the Rev. Hugh Dozier, pastor. Here is the explanation: The OPA's ban on pleasure driving 'indicates a large increase in church attendance. It is our wish to take care of this revival of interest in the best way we can.' "[72] Late in the war, the National Association of Tobacco Distributors got into the spirit of the times, meeting to consider a recommendation for cigarette rationing. With large quantities of product going to the military, a "smoking crisis" was developing, and association members wanted to ensure "fair distribution of limited supplies" to civilians. The plan never went into effect.[73]

NOTE TO THE TWENTY-FIRST CENTURY: "OFFENSIVE RATIONING" IS NOT EASY

The experience of the 1940s suggests that people are much more receptive to rationing when it is a response to a crisis than when it is a means of heading off crisis. According to Amy Bentley, the U.S. government wanted to avoid "offensive rationing," which she defined as "widespread and conservative control of the nation's food supply over a long period." The approach they took instead, "defensive rationing," meant imposing controls only when they were unavoidable, making quotas as generous as possible, and lifting them at the first opportunity. Yet in August 1942, when only limited numbers of items were being rationed, a poll found 70 percent of respondents feeling they had not been asked to sacrifice enough. Six months later, with controls starting to tighten, 60 percent of respondents to a Gallup poll still felt the government should have acted faster and more decisively in rationing scarce goods. Even with rationing at its height in the 1943–45 period, polls consistently found strong approval, often in the range of two to one.[74] And the government's impulse to lift the foot off the brakes at any opportunity sometimes led to problems. In mid-1944, amid worries that a quick collapse and surrender by Germany could leave the United States with huge food surpluses, the War Food Administration loosened some rationing rules. But, as it turned out, the country had bigger problems than food surpluses to worry about. The Nazis rallied to keep the war in Europe going full blast, and Washington had to clamp down at home, tightly and quickly. Cancellation of all existing ration coupons and tough new limits on consumption were imposed without advance notice, and the order was issued on Christmas Day to avoid spurring a run on stores. Public reaction to the retightening of rationing was much more harshly negative than anything seen before the relaxation.[75]

Support for continued price controls, however, remained strong after the war, hovering between 67 and 77 percent in the six months following Japan's surrender. A wide range of eminent economists endorsed the OPA's view that controls should not be lifted until supply and demand came into balance. Business leaders disagreed. The National Manufacturers' Association funded an aggressive national advertising campaign critical of the OPA. President Harry Truman urged Congress to extend price controls on food and other goods, but a group of lawmakers, led by Senator Robert Taft of Ohio, saw to it that controls were allowed to expire. Still, some rules remained in effect until November 1946. When meat, having been decontrolled, was recontrolled in September of that year, shortages almost immediately ensued. Bowles blamed producers for holding their product off the market. With no external regulation of supply and demand through rationing, it was not surprising that suppression of prices led to scarcity. The 1946 price controls didn't even manage to rein in inflation. According to Rockoff, wartime price controls performed much better

than the postwar controls because "during the high tide of price controls, they were backed up by a vigorous enforcement effort and three
important supplementary measures—wage controls, the seizure of
noncomplying industries, and rationing both of resources and of final
products."[76]

When price controls failed to curb inflation in 1946, they lost public support. But when Truman called for restraint in food consumption in order to permit increased exports for prevention of famine in
war-ravaged countries, approval among American women was strong.
Three postwar polls found that majorities above 70 percent would
tolerate continued food rationing in order to help keep Europe fed.
(Tellingly, only one-third would have made sacrifices to help stave off
hunger in Japan.)[77] Secretary of Labor Lewis Schwellenbach suggested
as late as September 1947 that rationing might be brought back if the
president's "campaign for voluntary conservation" failed to "meet the
need of starving people abroad." He did not phrase his projection as a
threat. Rather, he expressed confidence that Americans would "overwhelmingly support" renewed rationing, partly because it would, he
said, help bring down rising prices.[78]

But the postwar years passed with few if any sacrifices being required of Americans. In forming a Famine Emergency Committee
to deal with the situation in Europe, Truman appointed as its head
none other than Herbert Hoover. With the former food administrator and ex-president back in charge of food policy, and a large share
of the committee's membership representing industry, efforts reverted
largely to World War I–style voluntary, market-based strategies. The
chief rationale was that rationing is not a proper means of regulating supply; rather, control should be exercised only at the production
phase. Yet without domestic rationing, farmers had little incentive to
sell to the government for exports to Europe. They enjoyed a large and
growing domestic market, and, with meat prices decontrolled, they
could also turn a profit by selling grain to cattle raisers. Officials insisted that rationing, which had been so effective during the war, wasn't
really a good means of ensuring food security after all. Turning wartime propaganda on its head, some government publications even began portraying those in favor of rationing as being unpatriotic and

selfish. All of this, writes Bentley, indicated "a distinct agenda aimed at serving the interests of private agricultural producers." The women of the OPA's Consumer Advisory Committee were among those who blasted Truman for not taking tougher action. Their letter to the president read in part, "Voluntary rationing is patently inadequate to meet the present food crisis. It did not work after the last war. It cannot work now when demand is almost unlimited in the domestic food markets. The housewife wants a guarantee that when she takes pains to change her buying habits and the diet habits of her family to curtail her use of scarce foods, all other housewives are doing likewise."[79] The single example of World War II does not necessarily prove that price controls cannot stop runaway inflation unless rationing is imposed. But in U.S. history, there is no case of price controls being effective in the absence of rationing.[80]

When Britain's economy moved from wartime into peacetime, rationing continued almost organically. There, a wide array of products, from sugar to coal to leather, remained in short supply. And the country had learned that it could not rely, as Minister of Food John Strachey put it, "on a sort of improvised rationing by the shopkeeper, which can never work properly."[81] Despite postwar surveys showing that the British population was better fed than ever, there was widespread dissatisfaction with the national diet, which remained low in excitement and variety. Rationing was tolerated, thanks partly to the political spirit of postwar Britain, where surveys showed broad support for egalitarian policies and public planning.[82] But the extension of rationing to bread in 1946–48, a move intended to ensure the flow of larger volumes of wheat to areas of continental Europe and North Africa that were threatened by famine, was highly controversial. People had come to depend on bread, along with potatoes, as a "buffer food" that helped feed manual workers and others for whom ration allowances did not provide sufficient calories. Rationing of the staff of life was unpopular from the start, even though allowances were adjusted to meet varying nutritional requirements and rations themselves were ample.

AFTER A FEW HOURS OF STANDING IN LINE, RATIONING DOESN'T LOOK SO BAD

By the 1970s, the United States was a much wealthier nation than it had been in the 1940s, but the economy suddenly found itself under pressure from several directions at once. As early as 1971, an alarming acceleration of inflation, triggered largely by the prolonged war in Indochina, threatened to sink the economy. That year, President Richard Nixon took two fateful steps: imposing wage and price controls and announcing that the U.S. dollar would no longer be convertible to gold, thereby abandoning the Bretton Woods regime that had stabilized the world economy since World War II. Then, following their 1973 war with Israel, Arab nations belonging to the Organization of Petroleum Exporting Countries (OPEC) imposed an oil embargo on Western countries.

In early 1971 polling, 62 percent of Americans favored federal price controls as the only effective response at the time to inflation. That was a 13-point rise in six months, a shift in public opinion that convinced the administration that a freeze was in order. Polls taken soon after controls were imposed showed that support was even higher, rising to between 68 and 75 percent. Even the business community expressed enthusiasm, provided that wages were controlled as well. (The program Nixon eventually put in place was tougher than expected on both profits and managerial and executive salaries, however, and business leaders turned against it.)[83] Then in mid-1973, despite rising energy costs and the pressure they were exerting on food prices, Nixon lifted price controls on food. Within days, grocery chains were thronged by shoppers who feared an inflationary surge. In response, Safeway and Associated Food Stores, then among the nation's largest food retailers, announced rationing of bacon, chicken, and eggs.[84] Lester Brown, an economist, predicted that nationwide food rationing would soon be necessary. Renewing price controls would not suffice, he advised, because it would put producers out of business and leave empty shelves in the stores that remained open. Instead, Brown urged, America should "limit the intake of certain types of food, as some other countries are doing, in order to export agricultural commodities." He viewed food exports as necessary to balance rapidly growing petroleum imports.[85]

Three months later, the rising inflow of foreign oil was abruptly cut off by the Arab oil embargo. On November 15, Nixon asked all gasoline stations to close voluntarily each weekend, from Saturday evening to Sunday morning.[86] As during World War II, a national allocation plan was put in place to ensure that each geographic region had access to adequate fuel supplies. In establishing allocation plans, the Federal Energy Office assigned low priority to the travel industry and, in an echo of World War II, explicitly discouraged pleasure driving.[87] That same month, Nixon announced cuts in deliveries of heating oil—reductions of 15 percent for homes, 25 percent for commercial establishments, and 10 percent for manufacturers—under a "mandatory allocation program." The homes of Americans who heated with oil were to be kept six to ten degrees cooler that winter. Locally appointed boards paired fuel dealers with customers and saw to it that the limits were observed. Supplies of aviation fuel were cut by 15 percent. The national speed limit was lowered to 55 miles per hour. With Christmas approaching, ornamental lighting was prohibited. Finally, Nixon took the dramatic step of ordering that almost 5 billion gasoline ration coupons be printed and stored at the Pueblo Army Depot in Colorado, in preparation for the day when gas rationing would become necessary.[88]

Energy limits shaped the politics of the 1970s, when, according to the historian Jefferson Cowie, "running out of energy was both a reality and a metaphor, and the problem of limits shaped the entire discussion." The problem was passed down from administration to administration: "By the time [Gerald] Ford filled in after Nixon's resignation, the litany of a restricted future had become less abstract and more particular until Carter was forced to concede that 'dealing with limits' was the 'subliminal theme' of his presidency."[89]

At times during the 1970s, there seemed to be limits on everything—everything, that is, but the length of the lines at gas stations. Here is how *Time* magazine depicted the national struggle for fuel during the 1973–74 embargo:

The full-tank syndrome is bringing out the worst in both buyers and sellers of that volatile fluid. When a motorist in Pittsburgh topped off his tank with only $1.10 worth and then tried to pay for it with a credit card, the pump attendant spat in his face. A driver in Bethel, Conn., and another in Neptune, N.J., last week escaped serious injury when their cars were demolished by passenger trains as they sat stubbornly in lines that stretched across railroad tracks. "These people are like animals foraging for food," says Don Jacobson, who runs an Amoco station in Miami. "If you can't sell them gas, they'll threaten to beat you up, wreck your station, run over you with a car." Laments Bob Graves, a Lexington, Mass., Texaco dealer: "They've broken my pump handles and smashed the glass on the pumps, and tried to start fights when we close. We're all so busy at the pumps that somebody walked in and stole my adding machine and the leukemia-fund can."[90]

The end of the Arab embargo brought relief from gasoline shortages, but the nation's overall energy picture remained grim. As the nation prepared to celebrate the bicentennial of its independence, President Gerald Ford laid out a plan to reduce American dependence on imported oil by imposing tariffs and taxes on petroleum products. His plan was met with almost universal condemnation. A majority of Americans polled said they would prefer gasoline rationing to the tax scheme. *Time* agreed, arguing that rationing would have three crucial qualities going for it—directness, fairness, and familiarity—and adding that "support for rationing is probably strongest among lower-income citizens who worry most about the pocketbook impact of Ford's plan."[91]

In the bitterly cold February of 1977, with the nation facing shortages of heating fuels, the newly inaugurated President Jimmy Carter put on a cardigan sweater and went on national television to ask Americans to turn down their thermostats. To set an example, he ordered that federal offices be heated to only 65 degrees for the rest of the winter. In an April 1977 follow-up speech, he mentioned developments in new energy technologies but gave priority to conservation of resources. The federal government, he said, should challenge Americans to make sacrifices, and its policies must be fair, predictable, and unambiguous. But, he warned, "we can be sure that all the special-interest groups in the country will attack the part of this plan that affects them directly. They will say that sacrifice is fine as long as other people do it, but that their sacrifice is unreasonable or unfair or harmful to the country. If they succeed with this approach, then the burden on the ordinary citizen, who is not organized into an interest group, would be crushing."[92] He was right. Critics in both the private and public sectors rejected Carter's characterization of the energy crisis as the "moral equivalent of war" and viewed any discussion of limits, conservation, or sacrifice as a threat to the economy. Opponents then mocked his call to arms by abbreviating it to "MEOW," while Congress simply ignored Carter's warnings and avoided taking any effective action on energy.[93]

Almost two years passed before another political storm hit the Persian Gulf region and deepened America's anxiety over resource scarcity. This time, it was the overthrow of the shah of Iran by Ayatollah Khomeini and his followers that disrupted international oil markets. Although Iran alone didn't account for a huge share of the world supply, other oil producers managed to take up only part of the slack, and gas prices rose; American motorists were once again seized by panic. As a California newspaper editorial put it, "The government and the oil companies have learned that the public temperament can be as volatile as high-octane fuel if there is any threat to the motorist's presumed right to buy gasoline on demand."[94]

Ground zero for the gas shortages of 1979 was California. The state imposed rationing on May 6, allowing gas purchases only on alternate days: cars with odd license-plate numbers could be filled on odd days of the month and even numbers on even days. Several other states followed suit, but that move alone didn't relieve the stress on gas stations. Many station attendants refused to fill tanks that were already half full or more. That first Monday morning, many drivers who woke up early to allow time to buy gas on the way to work instead found empty, locked cars already standing in long lines at the pumps. The cars had been left there the previous evening by drivers who then walked or hitchhiked back to the station in the morning. Two Beverly Hills attorneys tied their new rides—a pair of Arabian horses—to parking meters outside their office as they prepared to petition the city to suspend an ordinance against horse riding in the streets. The National Guard was called out to deliver gas to southern Florida stations. A commercial driver hauling a tankful to a Miami station found a line of twenty-five cars following him as if, he later said, he'd been "the Pied Piper." In some cities, drivers were seen setting up tables alongside their cars in gas lines so the family could have breakfast together while waiting to fill the tank. The suffering was said to be lighter for the rich person, who had the option of paying someone to take his car to the station and wait in line.[95]

Phone companies reported that, because gas shortages had curtailed travel, there was a record volume of Mother's Day calls. On major highways and in big cities, a lack of fuel brought unusual peace and quiet. One Monday in June 1979, for example, the streets of Manhattan were strangely quiet, with buses doing good business, car traffic volume low, and the sky "an almost blinding blue." Elsewhere, the peace was broken with enough force that to some it threatened "civilizational breakdown." One of the worst incidents occurred in Levittown, Pennsylvania, where a crowd of fifteen hundred gasoline rioters "torched cars, destroyed gas pumps, and pelted police with rocks and bottles." A police officer responded to a question from a motorist by smashing his windshield, whacking the driver's son with his club, and putting the man's wife in a choke hold. In all, eighty-two people were injured, and almost two hundred were arrested.

Large numbers of long-haul truckers across the nation went on strike that summer, parking their rigs. Some blockaded refineries, and a few fired shots at nonstriking truckers. The National Guard was called out in nine states, as "the psychology of scarcity took hold." A White House staffer told *Newsweek*, "This country is getting ugly."[96]

As during World War II, gasoline scarcity was far worse in some regions than in others. But increasing desperation in the nation's dry spots prompted talk of rationing even in conservative quarters. The columnist George F. Will observed, "There are, as yet, no gas lines nationwide. If there ever are, the nation may reasonably prefer rationing by coupon, with all its untidiness and irrationality, to the wear and tear involved in rationing by inconvenience." A *New York Times*–CBS News poll in early June found 60 percent of respondents preferring rationing to shortages and high prices. Stuart Eizenstat, Carter's domestic policy adviser, looked back to "how energy was carefully preserved" during World War II "as a model for how to conserve energy in the future" in his proposal for the formation of a "National Energy Mobilization Board." He stressed the wartime parallel, suggesting that "we can mobilize the nation around a real crisis with a real enemy—OPEC." In contrast, Robert Bellah, a senior adviser to the president, warned Carter not to put all the blame on OPEC. Carter agreed with Bellah, saying, "Americans don't like it when a foreign country can interfere in our life, but we've been interfering in OPEC countries' and most other countries' lives rather heavily for a long time."[97]

Carter wanted the government to have the ability to ration gas, thereby freeing up supplies that could then go to regions that were suffering shortages. Thanks largely to the oil companies' fierce opposition, Congress refused to pass standby rationing in May, but support for the idea continued to grow. A June 29 memo circulated among a group of Carter's advisers summed up the case for rationing:

> Gas lines promote anger, not conservation. . . . People will accept rationing because it implies fairness; "allocations" is a word that suggests special privileges for those who scream the loudest. . . . The inconvenience of gas lines is pointless and infuriating. What further defeats conservation is that in many parts of the country, gas-guzzlers can still get all the fuel they need. Rationing is better than gas lines. If not rationing, some national program to distribute gasoline supplies fairly.[98]

WHAT'LL IT BE: CONSERVATION OR WAR?

On July 15, 1979, Carter gave the most important speech of his presidency. It was more impassioned than his 1977 energy address—more sermon than policy address. He did not resurrect the phrase "moral equivalent of war," but he did appeal to Americans' morality. Once he turned to policy, it became clear that grappling with energy problems would be as much the material as the moral equivalent of war. Although the president called for expansion of domestic liquid fuel supplies—"from coal, from oil shale, from plant products for gasohol, from unconventional gas, from the Sun"—most of his policy recommendations were again focused on conservation. His most specific move was asking Congress once again for authority to order mandatory conservation and set up a standby gasoline rationing system.[99]

Of the five thousand or so telegrams and phone calls received by the White House in response to that speech, an astonishing 85 percent were positive. Carter's approval jumped 11 points overnight. The next day, he spoke in Detroit and Kansas City, both times to standing ovations. But Carter was still being vague about what, specifically, Americans were supposed to do. Meanwhile, renewed political wrangling on other issues and a drop in gas prices drained away the nation's sense of urgency over energy. The deeper problems had not gone away, but without the threat of societal breakdown that had so alarmed the public and stirred Carter to bold oratory, the incentive to take action vanished.[100] Carter had declared in his speech, "Beginning this moment, this Nation will never use more foreign oil than we did in 1977—never." By the time of his 1980 State of the Union address, however, the impossibility of fulfilling that promise had become starkly obvious. In response to the Soviet invasion of Afghanistan, the president proclaimed what came to be known as the Carter Doctrine: that the United States would use military force to protect its interests in the Persian Gulf and surrounding regions. Chief among those interests was access to petroleum.

In August 1980, with only five months left in what would turn out to be his single term as president, Jimmy Carter finally saw his standby fuel rationing plan become law. It had been provided for in the Emergency Energy Conservation Act and was automatically authorized when Congress failed to disapprove it.[101]

The Department of Energy decided to ration gasoline vehicle by vehicle rather than household by household. The quota going to a vehicle of a given type—say, a passenger car or a light truck—would be based on the average annual consumption of all vehicles of that type; pickup trucks and compact cars, for example, would receive different allowances. That provision might also have encouraged people to "trade up" to larger makes and models. Furthermore, assigning ration entitlements to cars and trucks rather than to drivers favored households with multiple vehicles. Business vehicles received the same allotments as personal ones, but firms could apply for additional coupons, depending on their historical fuel use.[102] Analysts asserted, "Implementing this standby plan would be the biggest distribution problem government has ever addressed—even bigger than Social Security."[103] One of the legislators who had struggled long and hard to develop the plan added, "Gasoline rationing is very, very good to contemplate if you have not studied it and do not think about how to implement it. . . . It is nevertheless necessary under some circumstances."[104]

Rationing would be triggered by a 20 percent shortfall in the national gasoline supply. If that occurred, it was estimated that ration allowances would be set at about 33 percent below normal consumption. (The extra 13 percent was to be set aside for federal and state gas reserves, as well as priority allotments for agriculture, public health, and emergency services.) Drivers would be allowed to sell unused ration coupons on a "white market" to those whose requirements exceeded their quota. Gas was selling at about $1.10 per gallon at the time, and it was estimated that ration coupons would sell at about $1.60, so the cost of each gallon of gas purchased beyond a vehicle's ration quota would have been a punishing $2.70 per gallon—more than $7 in today's dollars.[105] The plan, of course, never went into effect. World petroleum supplies stabilized at the beginning of the 1980s, and with much of the U.S. and global economies still stagnant, a massive oil surplus accumulated. In June 1984, the Department of Energy shredded the 4.8 billion gas ration coupons that had been stockpiled by the Nixon administration a decade earlier and buried them. The great energy crisis of the twentieth century was officially over.[106]

During the oil-glutted 1980s, many looked back on the energy crisis as having been a big brouhaha over nothing. But now, with three more decades of rising consumption under our belts, we can ask whether, had they been followed, the conservation plans of the 1970s might have bought us some time for pursuing a transition to independence from fossil fuels. Despite a 28 percent improvement in vehicle fuel economy, America's total annual gasoline consumption has increased 47 percent since 1980, with the consumption rate per person 10 percent higher today than in 1980. Had there been a 20 percent gasoline shortfall at the start of the 1980s, triggering Congress's gas-rationing plan, and had we managed to hold per-capita consumption at the rationed level for the next thirty years (taking into account the rate of population increase that we actually experienced), we would have saved 800 billion gallons—equal to about six years of output from U.S. domestic gasoline refiners.[107] That's a lot in itself, but such long-term restraint would have caused a chain reaction of dramatic changes throughout the economy, changes so profound that America would probably be a very different place today had rationing been instituted and had it continued. That didn't happen. Instead, the U.S. economy focused again on developing new energy-dependent goods and services.

One legacy of the 1970s did persist: the Carter Doctrine. The government and military dedicated themselves to ensuring a continuous and rising flow of fossil energy and other minerals to feed the economy. The three major wars since 1990 were fought in regions viewed as critical to maintaining American access to oil and natural gas. The first and second Iraq wars and the Afghanistan war are distinctive in another way. Unlike earlier conflicts, they were carefully planned to ensure that American civilians, apart from those with friends or family members involved in the fighting, would not be asked to make significant material sacrifices. Perhaps the clearest expression of the current goals of our foreign policy came in an address to the 1992 Earth Summit in Rio de Janeiro by President George H.W. Bush, a year after the first Persian Gulf war. There he announced to the world that "the American way of life is not negotiable," signaling that the country had changed profoundly since the day almost exactly fifty years earlier when Harold Ickes had declared that patriotic citizens would never risk the lives of their soldiers to preserve "motoring as usual." [108]

2

IS THERE A RATION CARD IN YOUR FUTURE?

We need a system that guarantees each human being a certain basic level of necessities. Not that everyone has to live at the same level, but there is no way to satisfy everyone's basic needs and still have a substantial portion of society living at a non-sustainable level.

—Fred Magdoff, 2012 [1]

I was watching that movie Mad Max, *you know that movie where gas is so precious that people are killing each other for a few gallons. It was set in the future—I believe it was August.*

—Jay Leno, May 2008 [2]

In the first chapter of his 2008 book *The Bridge at the Edge of the World*, James Gustav Speth, an environmental scholar at Yale University, includes a lengthy table that categorizes "global environmental threats." Climate change is, of course, prominent, along with marine degradation, desertification, deforestation, freshwater system decline, biodiversity loss, persistent toxic chemicals, ozone depletion, and excess nitrogen release. All of those global crises, as well as myriad local ones, are consequences of uncontrolled growth in the global economy, argues Speth. He adds,

> There are many good reasons for concern that future growth could continue its environmentally destructive ways. First, economic activity and its enormous forward momentum can be accurately characterized as "out of control" environmentally, and this is true even in the advanced industrial economies that have modern environmental programs in place. Basically, the economic system does not work when it comes to protecting

Men hauling coal on bicycles along the highway between the cities of Hazaribagh and Ranchi in the Indian state of Jharkhand, 2012.

environmental resources, and the political system does not work when it comes to correcting the economic system.[3]

CAN A SIZE 18 FOOTPRINT SQUEEZE INTO A SIZE 4 SHOE?

The ecological limits that science has been warning us about for decades are coming into view, and it's now possible to see how little room remains for growth. According to calculations by Vaclav Smil of the University of Manitoba, the human economy has already reduced the total weight of plant biomass on Earth's surface by 45 percent. About 25 percent of each year's plant growth worldwide, and a similar proportion of all freshwater flowing on Earth's surface, is already being taken for human use. If you could put all of our livestock and other domestic animals on one giant scale, they would weigh twenty-five times as much as Earth's entire dwindling population of wild mammals.[4] In 2009, a group of twenty-nine scientists from seven countries published a paper in which they defined nine "planetary boundaries" that define a "safe operating space" for humanity. If we cross those boundaries and don't pull back, they concluded, the result will be catastrophic ecological breakdown. Given the uncertainties involved in any such projections, they proposed to set the limits not at the edge of the precipice but at some point this side of it, prudently leaving a modest "zone of uncertainty" as a buffer. The boundaries were defined by limits on atmospheric carbon dioxide concentration; air pollutants other than carbon dioxide; stratospheric ozone damage; industrial production of nitrogen fertilizer; breakdown of aragonite, a calcium compound that's an indicator of the health of coral and microscopic sea organisms; human use of freshwater; land area used for cultivation of crops; species extinction; and chemical pollution. The group noted that we have already transgressed three of the limits: carbon dioxide concentration, species extinction, and nitrogen output. Furthermore, they concluded, "humanity is approaching, at a rapid pace, the boundaries for freshwater use and land-system change," while we're dangerously degrading the land that is already sown to crops. The ocean acidification boundary is at risk as well.[5] If economic growth lies at the heart of the global ecological crisis, then it seems clear that a reversal of growth would be a crucial part of the solution. But how much smaller must humanity's rate of resource consumption and waste production be if we are to halt and reverse the damage?

The Global Footprint Network (GFN) of Oakland, California, attempts to answer that question each year when it reports on the "ecological footprints" of the world's nations, weighing the resource consumption and waste production of each against its biological capacity to absorb that footprint. Summing up all nations worldwide, GFN finds that humanity's global ecological footprint already far exceeds Earth's biocapacity, creating an untenable situation. In fact, calculates GFN, the global footprint must be reduced by about 45 percent if it is to be brought into line with global biocapacity. If that reduction were accomplished so that every person on Earth ended up with an equal, sustainable share of Earth's capacity, the average person's footprint in China would remain about where it is now, while the average resident of India could actually more than double her impact on the planet. Meanwhile, the average American's footprint would have to shrink by 80 percent, and those in Europe by 60 percent.[6]

Most estimates of the size of the reduction needed in human ecological impact focus on greenhouse-gas emissions, because the numbers necessary for making such calculations are readily available. One-third of Earth's human population creates 90 percent of greenhouse-gas emissions. International climate negotiations have repeatedly broken down over the question of how to share the burden of emissions reductions among rich and poor countries. In the 1990s, the Global Commons Institute (GCI) introduced the "contraction and convergence" model, under which global emissions would contract dramatically while per-capita emissions of rich and poor countries would converge at the global average. In practice, this would mean deep reductions in the global North and modest increases in much of the South. GCI's current figures project that, in order to achieve the required degree of contraction and convergence, the North's emissions should be 80 percent below today's level by sometime between 2020 and 2050.[7] These and other estimates seem to converge on a 60 to 80 percent reduction for the highest-consuming countries. They imply not only reductions of that size in fossil-fuel consumption but similar reductions in the stresses we are placing on all other resources and the ecosystems that provide them.

Could restraints on human activity be adopted involuntarily, enforced by rapid depletion of fossil fuels? Some have suggested that production (more properly, extraction) of affordable fuels will go into steep decline soon enough to prevent catastrophic global warming, even if we fail to curb carbon emissions intentionally.[8] But thanks to new pumping and mining technologies, the quantities of oil and natural gas projected to be within our reach continue to increase. It is seeming less and less wise to count on depletion alone to save the atmosphere; there may be no choice but preemptive restraint. Either way, argue resource pessimists, we can expect to see nonprice rationing become necessary.[9]

Because the supply and price of oil have such swift, obvious impacts on the rest of the economy, the longevity of Earth's petroleum resources has long been a matter of deep concern. A report prepared for the U.S. Department of Energy in 2007 found twenty-one diverse analysts all predicting that global production of conventional oil either had already passed its peak year or would peak by 2020; more than half of them foresaw a peak before 2012.[10] The "peak" isn't an Everest-style summit but rather a bumpy plateau that stretches out over years. The International Energy Agency (IEA) concludes that extraction of conventional oil peaked in 2006, but that with increases in mining of oil from unconventional deposits like the tar sands of Canada, the plateau will bump along for decades.[11] By 2011, discoveries of new oilfields and new drilling methods were convincing many oil analysts that, given continued technological progress and the right market incentives, production could rise by as much as 20 percent over the next twenty years.[12] If vast new reserves do come within reach, we'll continue to enjoy cheap transportation, but at an unaffordable environmental cost. Exploiting Canada's entire endowment of tar sands, for example, would have devastating consequences for air, water, plants, wildlife, and humans, and would strip seven hundred forty thousand acres of forest land.[13]

As the twenty-first century began, natural gas appeared to be heading for a world peak within as little as twenty years, but new extraction technologies have brought large new reserves within reach. The U.S. Energy Information Agency (EIA) now sees domestic gas extraction remaining near its current annual level through 2035. The EIA projects an ample flow of natural gas well into the future; indeed, the biggest problem in recent years, as seen from the industry's point of view, was a gas glut caused by slumping demand during the 2008–9 global recession. But not to worry, says EIA: global demand for gas will leap more than 40 percent in the next twenty-five years, thanks largely to growth in China.[14] Demand for gas may rise even faster than that. It seems that everyone these days is looking to natural gas to bail the world out of all kinds of crises: big environmental groups urge that it be substituted for coal to reduce carbon emissions; the transportation industry wants to substitute it for increasingly costly oil by burning it directly, converting it to liquid fuel, or by feeding power plants that in turn will feed the batteries in electric cars; enormous quantities will be consumed in the process of extracting oil from tar-sand deposits; and high-yield agriculture requires increasing quantities of nitrogen fertilizer manufactured with natural gas. That increasing demand is bad news for the environment, especially near gas fields. The climate impact of gas that is mined through hydraulic fracturing of deep shale deposits (the controversial technology that is permitting access to vast new reserves across the globe) produces more greenhouse-gas emissions than traditional drilling, largely because of increased leakage of methane, the chief component of natural gas.[15] Fracturing has sparked fierce opposition from communities bordering gas fields and from cities, including New York City, whose water supplies depend on aquifers that underlie gas fields. Where the method has been used in locations across the country, water supplies have been polluted by toxic chemicals used in the process, by salts brought back to the surface, and by explosive methane itself. Similarly to nuclear power, natural gas could be subjected to production and consumption limits by a motivated public even while ample fuel remains in the ground.[16]

While "peak oil" has been a perennial subject of discussion, less has been said about coal. Civilization has operated for a long time on the assumption that the world's vast coal reserves can keep us supplied with energy long into the future. For example, simply by taking the total quantity of coal estimated to be in the ground planetwide and dividing it by our current rate of consumption—a method widely discredited by most analysts—the World Coal Institute has managed to promise the world enough coal to keep us going for another 190 years.[17] Other, more sophisticated analyses of the future of global coal supplies have come up with a diverse range of projections. Most foresee a decline in extraction sometime this century.[18] There remains the possibility that large new reserves of coal will be discovered, however—a development that would be even worse news for Earth's atmosphere than new petroleum discoveries.

Just as important as the absolute quantities of energy resources remaining in the ground are the energetic and ecological costs of extracting and using those fuels. The physical foundations of industrial civilization were made possible not just by the burning of extraordinary quantities of fossil fuels but also by the large surplus of energy that is available after you've subtracted the energy expended to extract coal, oil, and gas from geological deposits; turn them into usable fuels; and deliver the energy from those fuels. That energy surplus has narrowed over time and will continue to shrink as we exploit unconventional fuels—a process that requires much more energy and is more ecologically destructive than extraction of traditional fuels. And we will derive a smaller energy surplus from non–fossil fuel alternatives such as solar- and wind-generated electricity and biofuels than we did from coal and petroleum deposits of the past; solar and wind generators provide energy only intermittently and will often require complex storage systems, reducing the surplus further.[19]

The perils of resource scarcity go well beyond fuels. A recent report on the state of the world's soil and water resources by the UN's Food and Agriculture Organization (FAO) can make for disturbing reading. It estimates that 25 percent of the world's food-producing soils are highly degraded or are rapidly being degraded. Add to that other soils that it finds to be degrading "moderately," and the area under threat amounts to one-third of Earth's endowment of cropland. As fuel prices rise, food will become less and less affordable for more and more people. The food production, distribution, and marketing systems of the industrial North achieve very high crop yields but nonetheless often consume more energy than is contained in the food produced. Where soils have become depleted around the world, farmers have still managed to produce harvests by pouring on fossil fuel–derived fertilizers, if they can afford them. Most nitrogen fertilizer—in many crops and regions the key to high yields—is manufactured with the heavy use of natural gas or sometimes coal. Another key element, phosphorus, is a nonrenewable resource that could reach a state of severe shortage in coming decades. In the near term, the process of hauling enough rock phosphate, lime, livestock manure, or even human waste to restore phosphorus-deficient farm soils will be burdened by increasing transportation costs. Then there are tractors, 4.2 million of them on farms and ranches in the United States alone.[20] Field operations on almost all farms in America, including organic farms, are heavily dependent on diesel fuel or gasoline. Finally, the farm economy supports a much larger off-farm food economy, one that is heavily dependent on fossil energy. Now we are asking the industrial mode of agriculture, with its own low energy efficiency, to supply not only food and on-farm power but also billions of gallons of ethanol and biodiesel for the much larger and more energy-hungry transportation sector.

Because expansion of irrigation has been the biggest factor in increasing food production over the past half century, the FAO predicts that improving water application will be a key to boosting crop yields between now and 2050. But the World Bank, working with a multinational group of corporations, has estimated that global demand for freshwater for all uses will exceed supply by a staggering 40 percent in 2030. And even if sufficient water for irrigation can be found, too heavy a reliance on irrigation can deplete local water resources and disrupt the soil's chemical balance. Furthermore, flooding of reservoirs has already driven tens of millions of people out of perfectly good forest and off cropland around the world. The FAO reports, "Municipal and industrial water demands will be growing much faster than those of agriculture and can be expected to crowd out allocations to agriculture. Meanwhile, the levels of soil management and precision application of water will need to rise to meet agricultural productivity increases. This will involve intra-sectoral competition for scarce land

and water and the ultimate source of naturally available freshwater—groundwater—will be hit hard." The U.S. Defense Intelligence Agency foresees political instability erupting worldwide in response to water shortages.[21]

As fossil fuels and water supplies become more deeply depleted—and with it the possibility that their use may become more restricted—humanity will become more and more dependent on soil, rainfall, and sunshine and the more modest way of life those resources are able to provide. If enough good soils and waters are to be maintained to support that life, the currently wasteful means of using water and growing food must be not just adjusted but transformed.[22] Until that happens, the interactions among energy, water, and food will come to look even more like a game of rock-paper-scissors. Energy shortages or restrictions can keep irrigation pumps, tractors, and fertilizer plants idle or make food unaffordable. Water scarcity can reverse advances in food production that have been achieved with irrigation. Current methods for producing food are huge energy sinks and major contributors to greenhouse-gas warming, while the conversion of food-producing land to substitute for mineral resources in providing fuel, fabric, rubber, and other industrial crops will accelerate soil degradation while contributing to wasteful energy consumption.[23] In the United States (and to a lesser extent in other nations), those problems are compounded by the puzzle of how to restrain consumption of resources for health care—one of the largest and fastest-growing sectors of postindustrial economies. The already difficult problem of scaling back overall production and consumption will become impossible if we protect American medicine's current 18 percent share of the economy from cutbacks and let it continue to grow at a rapid, virtually uncontrolled rate.[24]

DO ECONOMIES HAVE A REVERSE GEAR?

Deep cuts in greenhouse-gas emissions would require that vast deposits of fossil fuels planetwide be roped off, never to be extracted. But that's hard to imagine. Instead, it now seems almost certain that Earth's entire stock of fossil fuels will sooner or later be burned up. The next best course is to make it later rather than sooner by leaving fossil fuels in the ground longer. But can economies resist burning fossil fuels that are easily within reach? Might even renewable energy sources be harnessed to the task of obtaining much more potent and versatile fossil energy? That is already happening in various parts of the world, including the poverty-plagued but coal-rich state of Jharkhand in India. Strip mining there is pushing indigenous people off their land, ruining their water supply, and driving them to desperate means of earning an income. Every day for the past decade, it has been possible to witness a remarkable spectacle along a main highway between the coal-mining district of Hazaribagh and the state capital, Ranchi: men hauling coal on bicycles. Each bike, with its reinforced frame, supports up to four hundred pounds of coal in large sacks. The men, often traveling in long convoys, push the bicycles up steep ridges and sometimes stand on one pedal to coast down. Their cargo has been scavenged from small, shallow, village-dug mines, from government-owned deposits that are no longer economically suitable for large-scale mining, or from roadsides where it has fallen, they say, "off the back of a truck." Hauling coal the forty miles from Hazaribagh to Ranchi takes two days, and the men make the round-trip twice a week. These "cycle-wallahs" travel roads throughout the region, delivering an estimated 2.5 million metric tons of coal and coke annually to towns and cities for cooking, heating, and small industry.[25] No one has yet calculated the energy surplus derived from the ratio of the energy obtained to the energy invested in this mode of acquiring and transporting fossil fuel, but in those terms it would undoubtedly be highly efficient. A densely packed bag of coal or coke contains a huge quantity of energy compared with the food that fuels the men with bikes, and it is valued more highly than the health they sacrifice. That sacrifice is making India wealthier in one way and poorer in many other ways.

Breakneck growth in the world's total private wealth, expressed in figures such as the gross domestic product (GDP), may not only be undesirable—it can be viewed as a direct indicator of how rapidly we are dismantling our ecological support system. In recent years, ecological thinkers have once again been highlighting a paradox first articulated by James Maitland, eighth Earl of Lauderdale, in the early nineteenth century. Lauderdale had observed that increases in private riches are associated with decreases in quantities of public goods such as good soil, clean air and water, and mineral resources. The reason is that scarcity gives resources value in the marketplace where private wealth is generated. The ecological economist Herman Daly sees the paradox as having arisen "simply because formerly abundant things with great use value but no exchange value became scarce, and thereby acquired exchange value and were henceforth counted as riches." [26]

Daly wrote those words in response to a 1997 report published in the journal *Nature* that had concluded that the total market value of Earth's ecosystem services and natural capital stocks was at that time $33 trillion.[27] It would be a mistake, wrote Daly, to calculate public wealth as simply the sum of private riches and to take the $33 trillion figure as an indicator of the bounty of resources at humanity's disposal. The reality is quite the opposite, he argued. We should think of it as

> an indirect index of the extent of past sacrifice of natural capital, and thus of the scarcity of remaining natural capital. . . . The higher the measured scarcity value of the remaining natural capital the farther away we are from some historical base period or "Garden of Eden" or "empty world" in which private riches in the form of natural capital were zero and public wealth in that form was a maximum. The higher the measured value, the more we should resist further conversion of natural into manmade capital. The figure of 33 trillion dollars screams at us to save what natural capital is left.[28]

The conventional prescription for dealing with the need to reduce ecological impact includes adoption of efficient technologies: lower-wattage appliances, smaller toilet tanks, aluminum recycling, etc. When economies grow faster than energy consumption and resource depletion, the resulting rise in efficiency can appear to be an appealing solution. But depletion of resources and emission of wastes have continued to rise despite increased efficiency, partly because efficiency itself is a powerful economic stimulant. Whether one is comparing different countries or following change over time within a country, economic growth and increases in energy consumption tend to move in parallel. Per-capita wealth does increase somewhat faster than per-capita energy consumption, thanks to wealthy societies' greater ability to wring more money from a given quantity of material inputs, but one never sees an economy's growth cause a decrease in total energy use or vice versa.[29] Instead, write the investment economists Jeff Rubin and Benjamin Tal, "Across a wide spectrum of activity throughout the American economy, there seems ample evidence to debunk the notion that energy-saving technology reduces energy consumption. Instead, energy consumption has grown steadily as efficiency improvements have steadily lowered the cost of consuming energy."[30] The parallel increases in efficiency and consumption have been explained as being the results of "rebound" and "backfire": the tendency for efficiency gains to be eroded or even canceled out by the growth-stimulating effects of efficiency itself. That argument is largely rejected by orthodox economists. But the most recent reviews of the evidence, which have been methodical and comprehensive, demonstrate how rebound and backfire effects at the scale of individual firms propagate throughout the economy, reinforce one another across industries, accelerate economic growth, and thereby deeply reduce, or sometimes completely wipe out, the original resource savings achieved through efficiency.[31]

Scaling back any nation's resource use will mean reducing the size of its entire economy, and taking the need to relieve pressure on ecosystems worldwide seriously could put the world economy into the equivalent of a trash compactor. In the energy realm, Rubin argues that, "for total efficiency to actually curb total energy usage, as opposed to energy intensity, consumers must be kept from reaping the benefits of those initiatives in ever-greater energy consumption."[32] Daly has written that a "frugality first" policy is always to be preferred over the "efficiency first" approach recommended by most economists. That, he believes, is because "a policy of 'frugality first' induces efficiency as a secondary consequence; 'efficiency first' does not induce frugality—it makes frugality less necessary."[33] Perhaps he should have written, "It makes frugality *seem* less necessary."

Efficiency has been relied upon to keep economic growth a step or two ahead of fast-growing ecological impoverishment and resource depletion. But were we to set out to *reverse* ecological damage and live on fewer resources, we would be playing under very different rules. Under those new rules, argues Ted Trainer of the University of New South Wales, past efficiency improvements will not be a reliable guide for future action. Examining estimates of past efficiency gains, Trainer finds them mushy at best. The technological innovations that have boosted efficiency are themselves heavily dependent on substantial energy inputs. In other words, it is easy to develop new, efficient technologies while riding a wave of ample, convenient energy. But now, improvement of efficiency has already slowed or stopped in many economic sectors. And, Trainer adds, the amount of economic growth per unit energy has come to be badly inflated by "dubious output" from finance and other paper industries, while wealthy economies now have many of their physical needs satisfied by energy-intensive production that occurs outside their borders.[34] To Trainer's observations I would add that, in a future resource-stressed society, one in which necessities take highest priority, gains in economic efficiency will become even less relevant—because no matter how efficiently they are produced, food, shelter, transportation, and other basic necessities generally require greater inputs of resources per dollar's worth of output than do many of the optional products and services that have accounted for much of the current growth in wealthy economies. None of that is a reason for anyone to be anti-efficiency. The more wisely the world economy uses resources, the more we can do with what we have. But even with improved efficiency and beefed-up renewable energy production, it has been estimated that the necessary cuts in carbon emissions will cause growth in world per-capita income to slow to near or below zero; at the same time, building the necessary capacity for renewable energy and efficiency could cost more than $120 trillion. That would be only part of the huge share of economic activity and energy consumption that would have to go into building greener infrastructure rather than into goods and services for consumption. We could find ourselves living in something resembling a wartime economy, in which private consumption must be sacrificed in support of a larger common effort to keep civilization going—except that this time there would be (we should hope) no war-induced boom.[35]

COULD CRISIS BRING ON NEW FORMS OF RATIONING?

If scarcity, either absolute or self-imposed, becomes a pervasive fact of life, will rationing no longer be left to the market? Will more of it be done through public deliberation? Ask ecologists and environmentalists that question today, and you frequently hear that quantity rationing is coming and that we should get ready for it. David Orr, a professor of environmental studies and politics at Oberlin College in Ohio and a leading environmental thinker, believes that "one way or another we're going to have rationing. Rationing goes to the heart of the matter." Although "we assume that growth is humanity's destiny and that markets can manage scarcity," Orr believes that "letting markets manage scarcity is simply a way of not grappling with the problem." And because "there is no question *that* rationing will happen," he says the key question is *how*. "Will it be through growth in governance, either top-down or local, or will we let it happen 'naturally,' " through prices? The latter course, Orr believes, would lead to chaos.[36]

Likewise, Fred Magdoff, co-author (with John Bellamy Foster) of *What Every Environmentalist Needs to Know About Capitalism*, among other books, sees rationing as very likely necessary in any future economy that takes the global ecological crisis seriously. He says there is no escaping the problem of distribution: "There is rationing today, but it's never called that. Allocation in our economy is determined almost entirely in one of two ways: goods tend to go to whoever has the most money or wherever someone can make the most profit." As an alternative, he says, rationing by quantity rather than ability to pay "makes sense if you want to allocate fairly. It's something that will have to be faced down the line. I don't see any way to achieve *substantive* equality without some form of rationing." But, Magdoff adds, "there's a problem with using that terminology. There are certain 'naughty' words you don't use. 'Rationing' is not considered as naughty as 'socialism,' but it's still equivalent to a four-letter word."[37]

Ask almost any economist today, however, and you will learn that non-price rationing simply doesn't work and should be avoided. For example, Martin Weitzman, at Harvard University, who developed some of the basic theory of rationing decades ago, takes the view that "generally speaking, most economists, myself included, think that rationing is inferior to raising prices for ordinary goods. It can work for a limited time on patriotic appeal, say during wartime. But without this aspect, people find a way around the rationing." He adds that rationing would also "require a large bureaucracy and encounter a lot of resistance. I am hard-pressed to think of when rationing and price controls would be justified for scarce materials."[38]

Others see rationing as unworkable not only for technical reasons but simply because people in affluent societies today cannot even imagine life under consumption limits. Maurie Cohen has little confidence that residents of any industrialized society would accept comprehensive limits on consumption because, in his view, "following a half century of extraordinary material abundance, public commitments to consumerist lifestyles are now more powerfully resolute."[39] David Orr agrees that prospects for consumption restraints in America today are dim at best: "We have to reckon with the fact that from about 1947 to 2008 we had a collision with affluence, and it changed us as a people. It changed our political expectations, it changed us morally, and we lost a sense of discipline. Try to impose a carbon tax, let alone rationing, today and you'll hear moaning and groaning from all over."[40]

Have we each become so personally addicted to affluence that we can never agree on how to moderate consumption? Or is broad resistance to any sort of restraint inevitable in Western economies, which tend to fall ill whenever consumers slow their buying even slightly? Could a less consumption-driven global economy emerge? We know all too well that economic circumstances can change suddenly and often wrenchingly. Could such sharp turns create conditions under which rationing by quantity is preferred over rationing by price? Economists of the past have sought answers to that last question, and their calculations may be crucial to our future.

"A CRUDE DEVICE"

Effective solution of the manifold problems posed by rationing offers a challenge to the ingenuity and practical wisdom of the economist—and makes him approach the task with humility.

—Richard Gettell, 1943 [41]

Yosemite National Park has about nine hundred campsites that require advance reservation. To reserve a site for a July vacation in Yosemite—America's third most heavily visited national park—visitors have to phone or log on to the National Recreation Reservation Service (NRRS) at 7:00 A.M. Pacific time on the February 15 preceding their trip. Latecomers needn't bother; usually, all campsites are spoken for by 7:30. At $20, the nightly fee isn't especially high, but camping in Yosemite suddenly became much more costly in 2011 when a group of hackers logged on to the NRRS site, sneaked to the head of the line, and grabbed reservations before legitimate campers could hit "Enter." The ill-gotten permits then showed up for sale on other websites at prices of $150 or more. The scalpers had introduced the power of the market into the campsite allocation process, helpfully demonstrating that the real value of a permit is as much as seven times the official price. But no one applauded their efforts. The *Sacramento Bee* editorialized, "The wonders of Yosemite belong to all of us—not just those who can afford to fork over extra cash to a scalper." The problem, of course, and the reason for the reservation system in the first place, is that even though Yosemite belongs to us all, it would be ruined if everyone who wanted to visit showed up and made camp there. [42]

In theory, shortages are always temporary. As the price of a scarce good rises, fewer and fewer people are able and willing to buy it, while at the same time producers are stimulated to increase their output. The price stops rising when demand has been driven low enough to meet the rising supply. If for whatever reason (often because of absolute scarcity, as with Yosemite campsites) the price is not allowed to rise to the heights required to bring demand and supply into alignment, and there is no substitute product that can draw away demand, the good is apportioned in some other way. At that point, nonprice rationing, often referred to simply as "rationing," begins. Governments do it, but they aren't the only ones. For example, companies that have monopoly-like control over the price of a scarce good sometimes forgo the higher profits they could make by raising the price; so-called rationing by waiting or rationing by queuing is the result. First-come, first-served rationing has worked in the case of Yosemite campsites, and it has been intentionally induced at times by makers of luxury automobiles. Economists say that companies use such seemingly irrational strategies when they want to convince consumers that their brand or product is so highly valued that people will line up for it; that, they believe, will generate greater future sales. This strategy is familiar to any parent who has pushed through throngs of holiday shoppers to buy a hot new toy or game that sells out within hours. Even with mundane metals like copper, lead, and zinc that are not subject to "buzz" or consumer buying frenzies, large firms may keep prices low, triggering rationing by queuing, if they believe that it will increase their profits later on.[43] With basic necessities as much as with toys, rationing by queuing tends to create not buzz but belligerence.

Dreadful memories of rationing by queuing—like the lines that formed at gas stations across America and outside bakeries in the Soviet Union in the 1970s—are burned into the memories of those who lived through those times; few regard such methods of allocation as satisfactory when it comes to essential goods. As an alternative, economists have suggested "pay or wait" schemes in which people are free to choose between parallel sources of a good, one of which sells at a high price and the other at a price low enough to make queuing necessary. Consumers could determine the value of their own time and decide whether to spend more money and less time or spend more time and less money.[44] High-occupancy toll lanes on freeways put the "pay or wait" idea into practice.

When rationing by queuing is not desirable, rationing by quantity may be the next step. In 1977, with America's energy crisis escalating, Martin Weitzman, then at the Massachusetts Institute of Technology, published a paper that posed this question: "Is the price system or rationing more effective in getting a commodity to those who need it most?" He started by noting that economists in general don't like rationing by quantity, which they see as "a crude allocation device which cannot effectively take account of individual differences." First observing that "any rationing scheme typically ends up over-delivering goods to some people who don't really want them so much, at the same time that it will be withholding from others with a genuine need for more," Weitzman then summarized the case in favor of rationing:

> The rejoinder is that using rationing, not the price mechanism, is in fact the better way of ensuring that true needs are met. If a market clearing price is used, this guarantees only that it will get driven up until those with more money end up with more of the deficit commodity. How can it honestly be said of such a system that it selects out and fulfills real needs when awards are being made as much on the basis of income as anything else? One fair way to make sure that everyone has an equal chance to satisfy his wants would be to give more or less the same share to each consumer independent of his budget size.

Acknowledging that arguments both for and against rationing of basic needs "are right, or at least each contains a strong element of truth," Weitzman went on to demonstrate mathematically how rationing by price performs better when people's preferences for a commodity vary widely but there is relative equality of income. Rationing by quantity appeared superior in the reverse situation, when there is broad inequality of buying power and demand for the commodity is more uniform (as can be the case with food or fuel, for example).[45]

In a follow-up to Weitzman's analysis, Francisco Rivera-Batiz showed that rationing's advantage increases further if the income distribution is skewed—that is, if the majority of households are "bunched up" below the average income while a small share of the population with very high incomes occupies the long upper "tail" of the distribution. Rivera-Batiz concluded that quantity rationing "would work more effectively (relative to the price system) in allocating a deficit commodity to those who need it most in those countries in which economic power and income are concentrated in the hands of the few."[46] Writing back in the early days of World War II, the Dutch economist

Jacques Polak had come to a similar conclusion: that rationing had become necessary because even a small rise in price can make it impossible for the person of modest income to meet basic needs, while in a society with high inequality there is a wealthy class that can "push up almost to infinity the prices of a few essential commodities." Therefore, he stressed, it is not shortages alone that create the need for rationing with price controls; rather, it is a shortage that occurs in a society with "substantial inequalities of income."[47]

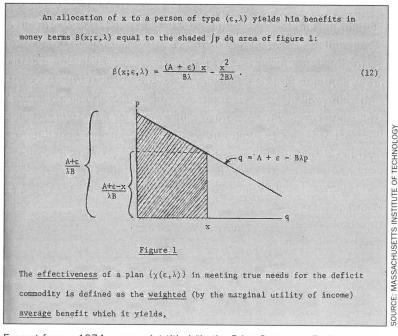

An allocation of x to a person of type (ϵ,λ) yields him benefits in money terms $\beta(x;\epsilon,\lambda)$ equal to the shaded $\int p\ dq$ area of figure 1:

$$\beta(x;\epsilon,\lambda) = \frac{(A + \epsilon)\ x}{B\lambda} - \frac{x^2}{2B\lambda}\ . \tag{12}$$

$$q = A + \epsilon - B\lambda p$$

Figure 1

The effectiveness of a plan $\{\chi(\epsilon,\lambda)\}$ in meeting true needs for the deficit commodity is defined as the weighted (by the marginal utility of income) average benefit which it yields,

SOURCE: MASSACHUSETTS INSTITUTE OF TECHNOLOGY

Excerpt from a 1974 manuscript titled "Is the Price System or Rationing More Effective in Getting a Commodity to Those Who Need It Most?" by Martin Weitzman, then at the Massachusetts Institute of Technology. The paper was published in 1977 by the *Bell Journal of Economics*.

What happens when there is not a current or even imminent shortage but demand must be curbed intentionally for environmental or other reasons? If prices don't rise enough on their own to suppress demand or if they rise to the point at which they inflict unacceptable hardship, governments have the power to put their thumbs on the scales through subsidies, taxes, economic assistance programs, and other interventions. After thousands of years of practice at levying taxes, governments have the revenue-raising part worked out pretty well; however, steering demand indirectly through taxation is not very precise, especially if the goal is to discourage consumption of seemingly abundant resources or reduce ecological footprints. The effects of increasing the cost of goods through taxes can veer even further off target if prices tend to be volatile, as they are in the petroleum and food markets.[48] Then there is the political toxicity factor: to many voters and politicians, the only good tax is a repealed tax.

The burden of consumption taxes weighs most heavily on people in lower-income brackets. It has been suggested that governments can handle that problem by redistributing proceeds from consumption taxes in the form of cash payments to low-income households. But determining the size of those payments is no easier than finding the right tax rate; furthermore, means-tested redistribution programs often come to be seen by more affluent nonrecipients as "handouts" to undeserving people and are therefore more politically vulnerable than universal programs or policies. Weitzman has also observed that problems always seem to arise when attempts are made to put compensation systems into practice. The argument that the subsidies can blunt the impact of the taxes, he says, "is true enough in principle, but not typically very useful for policy prescriptions because the necessary compensation is practically never paid."[49]

In 1952, looking back on America's wartime experience, the economist James Tobin noted that if the nation again faced general scarcity, either income taxes or consumption taxes could be used successfully to bring demand down to match supply. "But probably," he concluded, "neither can be as effective an instrument of equalization of consumption as rationing." Eighteen years later, continuing his examination of the potential of taxes and income subsidies for addressing inequality, Tobin observed that redistributing enough income to the lower portion of the American economic scale through a mechanism like the "negative income tax" being contemplated by the Nixon administration at the time (which would have provided subsidies to low-income households much like today's Earned Income Tax Credit) would require very high—and, by implication, politically impossible—tax rates on higher incomes. He continued, "The layman therefore wonders why we cannot arrange things so that certain crucial commodities are distributed less unequally than is general income. . . . The idea has great social appeal. The social conscience is more offended by severe inequality in nutrition and basic shelter, or in access to medical care or to legal assistance, than by inequality in automobiles, books, clothes, furniture, boats. Can we somehow remove the necessities of life and health from the prizes that serve as incentives for economic activity, and instead let people strive and compete for non-essential luxuries and amenities?"[50]

That question, Tobin acknowledged, has no easy answer. He wrote, "The most difficult issues of political economy are those where goals of efficiency, freedom of choice, and equality conflict. It is hard enough to propose an intellectually defensible compromise among them, even harder to find a politically viable compromise. These are ancient issues."[51] If, in addition to efficiency, freedom, and equality, we add a fourth goal—restraint of total consumption—then conflicts multiply.

THE RATIONING SPECTRUM

The diversity of possible nonprice rationing systems is great, and the range of goods covered can vary from a single item to virtually everything in the economy; not surprisingly, the direct effects and side effects of the various methods of rationing can differ dramatically. With rationing by quantity, people or households use coupons, stamps, electronic credits, or other parallel currencies that entitle them to a given weight or measure of a specific good—no more, no less—over a given time period. Normally, as was the case in World War II–era America and Britain, rationed goods or the credits to obtain them may be shared among members of a household but may not be sold or traded outside the household. The plan may be accompanied by subsidies and/or price controls.

Rationing by quantity is a more direct means of bringing consumption in line with available supplies than rationing by price. Quantities may be constrained indirectly, as with the odd/even date schemes in which access to gas stations was restricted by license-plate number, or outdoor water use is rotated according to street address. Similarly, electric utilities distribute "smart" home thermostats that allow them to turn a household's air-conditioning system off and on remotely in order to rotate supply during peak demand hours. But such practices, which might be called "rationing in time," cannot ensure that savings of the resource will be proportional to the length of time for which supply is denied. For example, consumption doesn't fall by half when alternate-day lawn-watering restrictions are in force, because people can water as much as they like on their assigned days.

Rationing of specific commodities, especially fuels and raw materials, may be most urgently required upstream at the production stage. But the effects of production restraints run downstream, causing shortages and inflation in a wide variety of products and creating a need for price controls, which, in turn, create a need for consumer rationing. When individually controlling a wide range of products isn't feasible, quantity rationing may be applied to groups of goods by assigning individual items in a group different numbers of points, as was done in wartime schemes. Unlike straight rationing, quantity rationing by points cannot guarantee everyone access to every item in the group of rationed items, but it can ensure a fair share of consumption from a "menu" of similar items. Points, like all ration credits, are a currency. Every covered item requires payment in both a cash price and a point price. But points differ from money in that every recipient has the same point "income," which does not have to be earned; points can be spent only on designated commodities; point prices are not necessarily determined by supply and demand in the market; and trading in points is usually not permitted. The range of goods covered by a given point scheme could in theory be as narrow as it was with canned goods during World War II or as broad as desired—if, for example, there were a point scheme covering all forms of energy, with different point values for natural gas, gasoline, electricity, etc.

The values of items in terms of points can be set according to any of several criteria. In the case of wartime meat, items with higher dollar prices also tended to be the ones assigned higher point values (for a time in Britain, dollar and point values were identical), but for other types of products, an item's point value might reflect the quantity of a scarce resource required to produce it—or, as we will see, the greenhouse-gas emissions created during its manufacture, transport, and use. The more closely point values are adjusted to reflect the level of consumer demand that would exist without rationing, the less they interfere with functioning of the market.[52] But of course the objective of rationing is often not only to limit total consumption but also to distribute goods in ways in which the market would *not* distribute them. Although quantity rationing is the most direct way to peg overall demand at a desired level, the average level of demand or consumption that is best for society as a whole may not come close to meeting many individual desires. Among people with differing preferences, there will be winners and losers.[53]

Both theory and experience suggest that once the decision is made to ration, an in-for-a-penny, in-for-a-pound situation soon develops. If only a few items are restricted, people take the extra money that they would otherwise have spent on additional rationed goods and spend it on nonrationed ones, driving up their prices. If price controls are then extended to other goods without rationing them, demand for those goods shoots up even higher, and stocks are further depleted. These goods are then brought into the rationing scheme, thereby extending it to larger and larger numbers of essential goods. But what about nonessential goods, such as swimming pools or rare wines? If the main concern is fair access to necessities, there seems little reason to ration nonessentials. If wealthy people, prohibited from buying as much gasoline or food as they would like, use their increased disposable income to bid up the prices of luxuries, is too little harm done even to worry about? Maybe, but it would depend on the motive for rationing. If the goal is to reduce total resource consumption, the prices of vintage wines or rare books might be left to the market, while the construction of swimming pools would be restricted.[54]

In June 1940, with some goods already being rationed in the United Kingdom, an economist at the Oxford Institute of Statistics named Michal Kalecki published a paper titled "A Scheme of Curtailment of Consumption."[55] As an alternative to a vast, complex system of quantity-rationing schemes for many products, Kalecki proposed simply to ration total spending. Each person would be permitted expenditures only up to a fixed weekly limit in retail shops, with the transactions tracked through coupon exchange. Up to that monetary limit, families could buy any combination of goods and quantities, as long as their total per-person spending stayed under the limit. No such system of "general" or "expenditure" rationing has ever been adopted, but during and after the war, several British and American economists examined the possible consequences of employing it during some future crisis. Once again, they realized, income inequality would complicate things. If the spending ceiling was the same for everyone, as was proposed, then lower-income families could spend their entire paycheck and still have coupons left over. Such families might be tempted to sell their excess coupons to people who had more cash to spend than their coupon allotment would allow. Some economists worried that that would not only stimulate unwanted demand but violate the "fair shares for all" principle.[56]

It was Kalecki who finally proposed a workable solution: that the government offer to buy back any portion of a person's expenditure allowance that the person could not afford to use. For example, if the expenditure ration were £30 but a family had only £10 worth of cash to spend, they could, under Kalecki's proposal, sell one-third of their allowance back to the government and be paid £10 in cash. That could be added to the £10 they had on hand, and they could spend it all while staying within the limit imposed by their £20 worth of remaining ration coupons. The government buyback system would be intended to prevent the exploitation of the worse off by the better off and ensure a firm limit on total consumption, creating a "fairly comprehensive, democratic, and elastic system of distributing commodities in short supply," and it would provide an automatic benefit to low-income families without an artificial division of the population into "poor" and "nonpoor" categories. Well-to-do families would tend to accumulate savings under expenditure rationing, and Kalecki urged that those savings be captured by the government through an increase in upper-bracket income tax rates. That would not only curb inflation, it could also help pay for the coupon buyback scheme.[57] Kalecki's idea of allowing people to return ration credits for a refund rather than sell them to others has since been suggested as a feature of future carbon-rationing schemes.[58]

Quantity rationing of specific goods and general rationing of expenditures lie at the two ends of a spectrum along which the many varieties of point-style rationing lie. At the extremes, point rationing of all goods, with point values tied to market demand, would be essentially the same as expenditure rationing, whereas a scheme that covered a narrow array of goods and assigned point values in line with available supplies or a criterion such as ecological impact would resemble quantity rationing.

In a report written for the U.S. National Security Resources Board in 1952, the economist Gustav Papanek looked back at the wartime discussion of expenditure rationing and saw plenty of deficiencies when he compared the concept with that of straight rationing of individual goods. He noted that if the same spending ceiling were applied to everyone, it could mean a dramatic change in lifestyle for the wealthy, who would probably push back hard against such restrictions. As one of many examples, he cited people with larger houses, who would plead that they had much higher winter heating bills and that allowances would have to be made. Nevertheless, a uniform spending ceiling would be necessary, wrote Papanek, because allowing those with larger incomes to spend more money "not only would make inequality of sacrifice in wartime evident, but would also place upon it the stamp of government approval." [59]

As we will see, the specific mechanisms used in rationing vary in other ways as well. In many countries, a large portion of the supply of food, water, cooking fuel, or other essentials is subsidized and rationed by quantity, while the remaining supply is traded on the open market. Such two-tier systems provide a floor to ensure access to the necessary minimum but have no ceiling to contain total consumption. Some also treat different people or households differently by, for example, steering subsidized, rationed goods toward lower income brackets. And in some, there is the option of allowing the barter or sale of unused ration credits among consumers and producers. Such markets were proposed as part of Carter's standby gas rationing plan, and they have been included in more recent proposals for gas rationing and for limiting greenhouse-gas emissions.

OUTLAWS AND SNOOPS

The consequences of rationing can be difficult to predict, but one thing is certain: nobody wants to be told what we can and cannot buy. There will be cheating. There are always people—often many people—who want to buy more of a rationed product than they can obtain legally; otherwise, there would be no need to ration it. They will also be willing to pay more than the ration price. That creates an incentive for someone to meet the extra demand, and the more those consumers are willing to pay under the table, the stronger the incentive for others to sell.

Given the frequency with which rationing laws were flouted in Britain during World War II, Maurie Cohen has predicted that any future attempt to ration carbon emissions would be badly handicapped because "black markets are inevitable outcomes of the regulation of consumption, and the combination of scarcity and high demand will always lead to various forms of innovative commerce." Widespread circumvention of regulations poses a dilemma. On the one hand, Cohen wrote, attempts to enforce total compliance are "ineffectual in the short term and counterproductive in the long term," while on the other, lax enforcement "will lead to the erosion of public support." Cohen concluded that "there is no easy solution to this dilemma other than agile and adept management."[60]

Evasion of wartime price controls and rationing was less extensive in Britain than in the United States. Conventional wisdom long held that the difference could be explained by a greater respect for government authority among British citizens, reinforced by their more immediate sense of shared peril (the "Dunkirk spirit"). But an analysis of wage and price data before, during, and after the war shows that the most important factor was the British government's tighter and more comprehensive control of supply and demand. Enforcement in both countries went through mid-war expansion in response to illicit activity, but key measures taken by the British—complete control of the food supply; standardization of manufacturing and design in clothing, furniture, and other products; concentration of manufacturing in a smaller number of plants; the consumer–retailer tie; and rationing of textiles and clothing—were not adopted in America, where industry opposition to such interference was stronger. The British also invested much more heavily in the system. In 1944, with rationing at its peak in both countries, British agencies were spending four and a half times as much (relative to GDP) as their American counterparts on enforcement of price controls. They were also employing far more enforcement personnel and filing eight times as many cases against ration violators, relative to population.[61] At its peak, the entire U.S. federal apparatus for administering price controls and rationing employed about 150,000 people, which was about 40 percent as many as were employed by the Postal Service at the time. Private industry employed an estimated 160,000 people to deal with the regulations. Relative to employment by the government and the economy as a whole, and considering the vast and complex system being administered, these are not considered especially huge numbers.[62]

The differential impact of rationing and underground markets on economic classes should not be ignored. Theory says that the rich are better off in a pure market economy, while those with the lowest incomes are better off in an economy that incorporates rationing; however, the poor benefit even more under rationing (whether it's by coupons or queuing) that is accompanied by an underground market, because secure access to necessities is accompanied by some flexibility in satisfying family needs. This is thought to be one of the many reasons that there was such widespread dissatisfaction with the conversion from a controlled economy with illegal markets to an open, legal market economy in the former Soviet Union and Eastern Europe in the 1990s.[63]

Ration cards, books, stamps, and coupons are not only clumsy and inconvenient; they invite mischief as well. Some of the biggest headaches for past and current systems have involved the theft, sale, and counterfeiting of ration currency. Some have suggested that in the future it would be easier to head off cheating by using technologies such as smart cards and automatic bank debits that were not available during previous rationing eras. Several countries are currently pursuing electronic transfers for their food-ration systems. Of course, electronic media are far from immune to outlaw trading; consumers, businesses, and governments have long battled a multibillion-dollar criminal market that exploits credit and debit cards, ATMs, and online vulner-abilities. Were rationing mechanisms added to that list of targets, en-forcers would be drawn into similar kinds of cat-and-mouse games with hackers and thieves. Cohen argues that while smart cards and similar technologies can reduce administrative costs and red tape, they cannot eliminate cheating and that it is unrealistic to expect "high-tech rationing" to wipe out evasion and fraud. It will still be necessary, he predicts, "to use customary enforcement tools to limit the corrosive effects of unlawful practices."[64]

Some have argued that the biggest problem with rationing is not so much the existence of underground markets or the expense of en-forcement as it is the criminalization of buying, selling, and other ac-tivities that were formerly considered natural and harmless. Overnight, law-abiding people would find themselves engaged in illegal activity. The increase in enforcement power and the creation of an outlaw cul-ture can be socially unhealthy, it is argued. Rockoff concluded that the suppression of activities made illegal by wartime price and ration regulations led to the growth of a kind of Big Government on steroids: "Suppression of the black market, to put the matter more simply, led gradually toward a significant regimentation of the economy. Ulti-mately, it is the inevitability of this process which makes permanent controls on the World War II model an unacceptable alternative."[65]

No law is ever met with total compliance, but there are many ex-amples of laws and regulations that appear to be accomplishing their goals despite routine violations. Compare limits imposed by rationing to speed limits. Around the world it is common for a large share of motorists to be exceeding posted speed limits at any one time. Like the majority of wartime rationing violators, who dipped only lightly into the underground market, most drivers fudge just a few miles per hour. A relatively small proportion of drivers break the limit by ten miles per hour or more, and a still smaller percentage of speeders are ticketed; nevertheless, speed limits succeed in preventing accidents and fatali-ties. Existence of a speed limit is cited by drivers as an important reason for driving more slowly than they otherwise would, whereas concern about pollution or fuel consumption is not.[66]

Also relevant to a discussion of rationing compliance is the example of tax laws, which are routinely violated in all countries. U.S. federal income tax evasion has been estimated to result in a loss of approximately 19 percent of the total due—almost $500 billion. The 2012 budget of the Internal Revenue Service (IRS) was about $13 billion, less than half of which was for enforcement. The IRS estimates that it can recover $4.5 million in lost revenue for each $1 million spent on enforcement.[67] The federal government could reduce its budget deficits by spending heavily to eliminate much of the fraud and evasion that occurs, but the necessary expansion of government intervention and the ill will that would result are prices too high to pay. Here, too, some toleration of cheating does not scuttle the system.

There is another, possibly just as important political issue to be addressed by any future attempt at rationing: the risk to privacy. The same digital technologies that would make rationing less cumbersome could also allow even deeper intrusion by governments and corporations into our personal lives. Yet we have already routinely allowed businesses to maintain data on our consumption patterns for years. Banks and credit card companies know much more about our finances and spending than do our close friends. Google, Facebook, Amazon, and countless online sellers hold and exchange extensive information on customers. Retail chains offer discounted prices only if we use their "loyalty cards," allowing them to keep records on all of our shopping habits so that they can target us with incentives to buy specific goods. During the 2012 U.S. presidential campaign, the costliest in history, the Associated Press revealed that Republican candidate Mitt Romney's campaign was operating "a secretive data-mining project that sifts through Americans' personal information—including their purchasing history and church attendance—to identify new and likely wealthy donors." Also in 2012, the municipal governments of the San Francisco Bay Area launched a study of a proposed "vehicle miles traveled" tax under which, reported the Associated Press, "drivers could be required to install GPS-like odometers or other devices in their vehicles and pay from less than a penny to as much as a dime for every mile driven." Already, police patrol cars across the United States have been collecting vast quantities of data through automatic license-plate readers. Seven million numbers were collected in just two years in Kansas City,

Missouri, alone. The American Civil Liberties Union has argued that by storing data that locate law-abiding motorists in specific places at specific times, the government is threatening Americans' freedom of movement. And Progressive Insurance, Inc., may have set a new standard for intrusiveness with its "Snapshot" program, under which the company provides customers with a device that, when attached to the car, records and reports information on driving habits. Drivers who perform well are eligible for discounts on their premiums.[68]

Clearly, the Internet would be a much rougher ride—whether the goal is shopping, forming social relationships, or joining in political activism—if there were no give and take of information between humans and online entities. But as matters stand, there is an imbalance of power. Businesses (particularly familiar online behemoths, such as Google) have a strong incentive to keep privacy policies obscure and make it much more convenient for clients to allow intrusions than to bar them. Two independent studies published in 2011 found that (1) 63 percent of Facebook users surveyed had privacy settings that differed from the settings they thought they had, (2) those who are mistaken "almost always" give their information greater exposure than they expect to, (3) people with more online experience tend to spend more money online, and (4) privacy concerns do not appear to curtail online spending.

Reading the *Wall Street Journal*'s extensive coverage of digital snooping in recent years is a hair-raising exercise. Here are only a few of their findings: reporters found that the big online companies were collecting and disseminating not just users' basic data but also information on religious preferences and sexual habits; every year companies were receiving tens of thousands of "national security letters" from the FBI requesting information on users, possibly including financial information; Google had tracked the online movements of Safari browser users by secretly bypassing their privacy settings; and a visitor to the Web's fifty most popular sites would find her computer infiltrated by more than three thousand cookies or other tracking programs.[69] Today, in countless ways, we trade privacy for convenience or cost savings. We do it sometimes voluntarily and at other times unwittingly, but the online data gatherers (and the government) make sure that it is to their benefit.[70]

Any rationing system would probably be resented more intensely than today's digital intrusions, because it would restrict rather than facilitate consumption. The scope of such a system would have to be limited to tabulating purchases, for the sole purpose of ensuring fair and correct shares, with strict expiration dates on data. The system could work well only if viewed as necessary by a large majority of people, and it would have to be clear that everyone is playing by the same rules. There is no reason that the rules for handling ration data could not be conveyed in a brief paragraph of plain language (unlike the byzantine privacy policies of today's corporations—the fine print that's universally ignored by customers).

But in speculating about how rationing could be practiced in a way that protects individual rights, I am obviously asking an even more profound question: who would design and manage the rationing system? Clearly, a system designed to keep a lid on consumption at the national or international scale and not simply deal with local, temporary shortages would require national rules on production and consumption quotas, point values, and other basic elements. That will mean setting limits on total resource use and ecological impact at the production stage before determining, given those limits, the quantities that constitute fair shares for consumers. Once the basic, economy-wide rules have been agreed to, it will be essential that those rules be applied to everyone, with no favoritism toward too-big-to-fail corporations or individuals with wealth, power, or political influence. Day-to-day administration of the system should be carried out locally in the most democratic way possible. It would be helpful to consider in more detail how the highly decentralized U.S. and UK wartime rationing systems handled citizen input and local decision making. Those systems may have been far from ideal, but we can learn from both their successes and their failures.

All of that will work well only in a society with strong democratic institutions. Even then, such sweeping, intrusive decisions are unlikely to be greeted warmly by anyone, let alone a majority of citizens. What will be essential is broad agreement that strong action is needed. As we will see, such conditions have been hard to achieve in the case of medical care in America, while proposals in Britain for carbon rationing have also wrestled with the question of how a society can steel its will and vote into place restrictions on consumption that no one really wants.

3

FAIR SKIES

Carbon really is different. It's a physiological thing. People can eat only so much food, but if we can afford it, we can consume an almost unlimited amount of energy.

—Tina Fawcett, Environmental Change Institute, University of Oxford, 2011 [1]

Ultimately, carbon trading is a means to preempt and delay the structural changes necessary to address climate change. Instead of reexamining the fundamentals of an economic and political system that has led to climate change, carbon trading adjusts the problem of climate change to fit these structures.

—Tamra Gilbertson and Oscar Reyes, *Carbon Trading: How It Works and Why It Fails*, 2009 [2]

Even with evidence of climate disruption having strengthened over the past decade, polls show that the percentage of Americans who choose not to believe in the existence of human-induced greenhouse-gas warming has increased dramatically.[3] Much of that change can be credited to a vigorous climate-denial industry that conjures up apocalyptic visions of deprivation, lost liberty, and stunted opportunity that, it claims, would result from any interference with the right of people and corporations to emit greenhouse gases without restraint. Denial-industry spokespeople have developed a kind of shorthand language for talking about the nightmare world they say awaits us, and the key word in that language is "rationing." Here, for example, is the conservative commentator Daniel Greenfield writing in 2011: "For environmentalists alternative energy was never really about independence, it was about austerity and rationing for the good of the earth. . . . [T]hey will use any conceivable argument to ram their agenda through, but

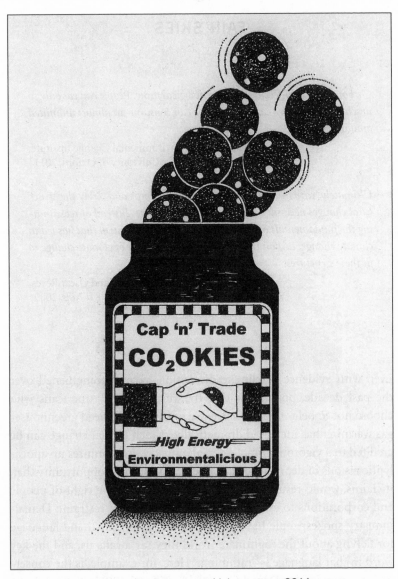

Priti Gulati Cox, *All Trade, No Cap*, pen and ink on paper, 2011.

they are not loyal to anything but their core austerity rationing manifesto. Their goal is expensive sustainable energy. If it isn't sustainable, than it had damn well better be expensive."[4]

According to anti-environmental groups such as the Washington, D.C.–based Heartland Institute, just about any move away from the economic status quo, no matter how small, will trigger rationing—as if rationing by price were not already a fact of life—and catastrophic consequences will ensue. Opponents of recent proposals to install two-way thermostats in all California homes or use the Endangered Species Act to protect polar bears raise the specter of "energy rationing." Companies that have resigned their memberships in the U.S. Chamber of Commerce over its opposition to climate legislation are "energy-rationing profiteers." Green urban design leads to "land rationing." Even First Lady Michelle Obama's anti-obesity campaign was, according to the website EmergingCorruption.com, aimed at "preparing us for food rationing."[5] By implying that rationing would be something strange and new, arising only as a consequence of stronger environmental or health policies, right-wing groups are implicitly urging that sub rosa rationing of necessary goods via individual ability to pay continue as the norm in society, however unfair the results. Commentators like Greenfield would have us believe that activists want climate protection because they are eager to live under rationing for some reason. In reality—and, one would think, self-evidently—heading off climate disaster really is the goal in and of itself. Nobody longs for rationing. Resource allocation by the market may not be satisfactory, but rationing that is imposed by an identifiable authority, naturally enough, tends to provoke a lot more outrage than does the omnipresent rationing that lies hidden behind price tags.

Nevertheless, we may be creating conditions that will make new ways of limiting consumption inevitable. And nobody is certain what rationing in the twenty-first century might look like.

MAKING ROOM IN THE GREENHOUSE

An analysis published in the *Proceedings of the National Academy of Sciences* in 2007 found that almost two-thirds of the increase in atmospheric carbon dioxide concentration since the 1970s can be attributed to growth in economic activity. In particular, the global boom years of 2000–2006 saw the most rapid increase in carbon dioxide concentration since the beginning of the industrial revolution. The relationship works in reverse, too: economic downturns reduce carbon output. The rare occasions when total carbon emissions in the United States have declined were almost always years of economic hardship: 1981–83, 1990–91, 2001, and 2008–12. Over that last five-year period, emissions from energy use fell a startling 13 percent. Likewise, world carbon emissions from fossil fuels, both total and per capita, dropped in the early 1990s with the economic collapse in the former Soviet Union and again in the late 1990s following the Asian financial crisis.[6] Had any of these reductions been accomplished in prosperous times, they would have been regarded as remarkable achievements and as first steps toward much deeper healing of the atmosphere. They resulted from decreased use of fossil energy—something that, if done right, would not only reduce carbon emissions but also prevent all sorts of other ecological havoc. But economic crises and the rising unemployment, growing hunger, and general misery that they engender are not in themselves acceptable means to achieve ecological stability.

Recessions and depressions happen naturally in capitalist economies; there is no need for action to encourage them. But neither deep reductions in total greenhouse-gas emissions nor improvement of living standards for the world's poor majority, and certainly not both, will happen as a matter of course. Both could be achieved, but much of the world would have to give up some material wealth to do it. As a result, two decades of climate negotiations have failed to come up with a way to share the burden of emissions reduction among countries of widely varying size and power. Fair sharing of that burden would mean deep emissions reductions in wealthy countries and modest increases for people in the poorest countries—a means of achieving what has been called "contraction and convergence." But that will not happen if the governments of the global North continue to have their way.

In 2009, a team of U.S. and European researchers sought to find a workable formula for sharing global emissions reductions among individuals rather than countries. Recognizing that there are elite classes in every country, they statistically identified approximately one billion individuals in the world who are responsible for humanity's excess emissions and asked how reductions could be targeted so that Earth's most affluent, highest-consuming households, in whatever country they are located, would bear the burden of reducing emissions. They found that in order to achieve the relatively modest goal of reducing worldwide carbon dioxide emissions 33 percent by 2030 (a smaller cut than climate research says is necessary) would require setting a firm per-person ceiling of five metric tons of carbon dioxide emissions per year. They also included a worldwide floor of one ton of emissions per person per year to ensure that the planet's most impoverished people have sufficient access to food, water, residential energy, health care, education, and employment; while the greenhouse impact of satisfying such basic needs can be softened, it cannot be eliminated. About 3 billion individuals already fit between the one-ton floor and five-ton ceiling. If we were to gather the rest of the world within that range by 2030, about 2.3 billion people would face emissions reductions, and 2.7 billion would see moderate increases.[7]

Worldwide agreement on an individual carbon dioxide ration that varies within the one-ton to five-ton range would achieve contraction but not complete convergence. Although the average North American would still be allowed three times the emissions of the average African, that would be an improvement on the seventeenfold difference that exists today. Those proposed limits may be useful for demonstrating to policy makers that even when we insist that high emitters in the global South be subjected to the same rules as high emitters in the North, deep average cuts will still be required in the North. (It is important to note that those cuts, tough as they are, would address only future emissions, not the North's existing "carbon debt," which has been building up for a couple of centuries.)

The question of burden sharing among countries, however, cannot be dealt with successfully without also solving the problem of how to distribute the burden of emissions reductions *within* countries. With the five-ton ceiling, for example, 95 percent of people in India and Africa can maintain or increase their emissions, while only 5 percent of North Americans will be spared reductions.[8] So in the South, gathering everyone between the ceiling and floor will be largely a matter of rational growth, along with redistribution of economic power and resources from the high emitters to the poor majority. The North, while also needing to redistribute power and resources, would also be required to cut emissions deeply across the board. In a world economy addicted to growth, achieving the necessary cuts in any one country will require a political and economic transformation. Even if that can be achieved, it will be up to individual countries to ensure that the deepest reductions are imposed on businesses and individuals that have the greatest excess emissions available to cut. That need—to distribute cuts where they will do the most good and the least harm—has led to calls for limitations on greenhouse-gas emissions, either by rationing them directly or by rationing fossil-fuel consumption.

RATIONING FUEL

In the view of the social philosopher André Gorz, "the really bad thing about cars is that they are like stately homes or villas on the Riviera: luxury goods invented for the exclusive pleasure of a minority of super-rich people, which were in no way, either in their design or in their nature, meant for popular use." For the full value of either a Riviera villa or an automobile to be realized, he argued, it has to be "beyond the reach of the masses." That fact is acknowledged in the case of the former; no one has ever been heard to insist upon "one villa with a private beach for every French family." The car also was once strictly a luxury. Gorz writes that early-twentieth-century industrialists such as Henry Ford calculated the profits to be made from personal transportation and made this logically impossible promise to the general population: "You too will, in future, enjoy the privilege, like aristocrats and the upper middle classes, of driving around more quickly than everybody else." But mass availability quickly sapped the car of most of its value, because

> they were in a war of all against all. And that general wrangle
> produced general paralysis, since, when everyone is trying to
> move at the privileged speed of the upper middle classes, the

outcome is that nothing moves at all. The velocity of urban traffic falls, in Boston, Paris, Rome, or London, below the speed of the horse-drawn omnibus and the average speed at weekends on the major roads falls below cycling pace. . . . And since cars have killed the cities, more and faster cars are needed to escape along the motorways to even further outlying suburbs. There is a perfect circularity to the argument: give us more cars to flee the ravages caused by cars.[9]

That was written in 1975, before Traffigeddon had descended on most of the world's big cities and before another nasty consequence of generalized car ownership—climate disruption—had become a concern. Today, we know that personal vehicles and other luxuries-turned-necessities not only are bleeding themselves of their own value but could be taking all of us on a trip to ecological doomsday.

To make personal car ownership once again a privilege reserved for the wealthy is clearly neither possible nor desirable. Instead, a revival of fuel rationing has been suggested as a more equitable way of curbing greenhouse-gas emissions while at the same time discouraging the "war of all against all" on the streets and highways. The simple device of odd/even rationing by license-plate number helped reduce the lengths of lines at gas stations during the U.S. energy crisis of the 1970s; however, it would not, on its own, reduce overall consumption very much, nor could it significantly reduce emissions of air pollutants. Several of the world's largest cities have attempted to relieve congestion and improve air quality through rationing usage by license-plate number: if, for example, numbers ending in 1 or 2 must stay off the street on Mondays, 3 and 4 on Tuesdays, etc., with weekends open to all cars, then weekday traffic, in theory, would be reduced by 20 percent. Extending such restrictions to an entire nation and to all times and days of the week has been proposed as a simple strategy to curb greenhouse-gas emissions from transportation. Experience, however, says it wouldn't work. The longest-running such program, initiated by Mexico City in 1989, was almost instantly undermined by several factors. People drove cars more miles on those days when they were allowed to circulate, and there was increased traffic volume on weekends.

Soon after the program was initiated, the more well-off families began acquiring additional cars with contrasting final digits on the tags; often the extra car was a cheap, older used car with poor fuel economy and high pollutant emissions. Traffic volume was reduced by 7.6 percent, not 20, and gas consumption continued to increase.[10] Research on license-plate rationing systems in Mexico City, São Paulo, Bogotá, Beijing, and Tianjin concluded that "there is no evidence that these restrictions have improved the overall air quality." A study conducted for the New York City Department of Transportation found that the proposed adoption of license-plate rationing in that city would run up against the same obstacles that systems in Latin American cities have encountered.[11] The writer David Owen points out another failure of such systems: "Congestion isn't an environmental problem; it's a driving problem. If reducing it merely makes life easier for those who drive, then the improved traffic flow can actually increase the environmental damage done by cars, by raising overall traffic volume, encouraging sprawl and long car commutes."[12]

In 2005, Charles Raux and Grégoire Marlot, French government researchers, outlined a plan for gasoline rationing that bore many similarities to Carter's standby plan of the 1970s. To begin reducing France's average gas consumption, which then stood at about one thousand liters per car per year, Raux and Marlot suggested that in the first year of the plan, free permits be issued that would allow each car nine hundred liters, with the amount to be reduced year by year afterward. The permits could be bought and sold in a central electronic market. To encourage people to make long-term changes in how they got around, they suggested that the government publish each year a rolling ten-year schedule for steadily reducing the per-car allowance. To ease the transition to the permit system, they suggested that in the first few years it could be voluntary but accompanied by a carbon tax on all fuel purchased without a permit. The issuance of permits at no cost to participants would then provide a strong incentive to participate in the system, and the size of the carbon tax would determine the maximum price of permits in the market. Because permits would be issued on a per-vehicle basis, people could get around the limits simply by buying another automobile; however, the authors predicted, the costs of an additional car purchase, taxes, and insurance would provide a strong deterrent. They did acknowledge that the system could be made more fair by issuing permits on a per-capita basis, regardless of car ownership. Then those who do not drive at all could profit from selling their permits.[13]

Along with transportation, home energy consumption accounts for a large share of personal emissions. About three-fourths of electricity generation in the United States is accomplished by burning fossil fuels; similar proportions hold in much of the rest of the world. Rationing via rolling blackouts has been employed to deal with emergency shortages in the global North, but scheduled blackouts, emergency outages, and denial of connections have been used routinely in India, China, South Africa, Venezuela, and a host of other countries that suffer chronic shortfalls in generation capacity.[14] Chiefly a device to hold down peak demand, the rolling blackout has little or no impact on total consumption and emissions, because people and businesses tend to increase their rate of use when the power is on.[15] The way the burden of blackouts is shared among communities determines how fair the compromise is. In India during the summer season, farmers with irrigation pumps are given priority over city dwellers, and poorer areas tend to have much longer blackouts than wealthy ones. The State of California, in an effort to avoid the necessity for rolling blackouts like the ones that struck in 2001, while at the same time curbing greenhouse-gas emissions, has been using "progressive pricing" of electricity, a rationing-by-price mechanism that seeks to ensure a basic supply to everyone while providing a heavy disincentive for overconsumption. Pacific Gas and Electric Company's customers, for example, pay 12 cents per kilowatt hour for all monthly consumption up to the "baseline," which is the average consumption for a household in a customer's climatic region, adjusted by season. Customers who use more electricity pay higher rates for the amount above the baseline. For consumption ranging between 100 percent and 130 percent of the baseline, the rate is just 14 cents, but between 130 and 200 percent, it is 29 cents and rises to 40 cents for consumption exceeding 200 percent of the baseline. An analysis published in 2008 found that the California system provides a modest benefit to lower-income consumers; however, there is no statistical evidence that consumers consciously alter their consumption patterns to stay below any of the thresholds.[16] Progressive pricing of electricity is also used in parts of India, China, and other countries, with similar results. However, neither rolling power cuts nor progressive pricing was sufficient to prevent the total electrical eclipse that struck India on July 30–31, 2012, leaving 684 million people—more than half the population of the world's second-largest nation—without power.[17]

WHO WOULD LIKE A FAIR SHARE OF CARBON?

Perhaps not surprisingly, given its status as world champion in per-capita carbon emissions over the course of the industrial age, its island geography, and its extensive twentieth-century experience with rationing, the United Kingdom has become an incubator for proposals to address greenhouse-gas emissions through national rationing systems. The idea has even been debated on the floor of Parliament. The first personal carbon-rationing plan was proposed in 1991 by Mayer Hillman of the University of Westminster's Policy Studies Institute and has been articulated more recently as a proposal for "personal carbon allowances" (PCA). In 1996, the British environmental writer David Fleming developed a plan for "domestic tradable quotas" (DTQ), later renamed "tradable energy quotas" (TEQ). "Personal carbon trading" (PCT) has also been used as a generic term covering such proposals, all of which aim to reduce per-capita emissions by directly limiting personal consumption of fossil fuels and/or electricity and indirectly limiting upstream energy use. Both PCA and TEQ systems would establish markets in emissions allowances that would run in parallel with the cash markets for energy. Both have been characterized as domestic counterparts to national or international "cap and trade" schemes that have been used in Europe and proposed in the United States.[18]

A PCT scheme can be viewed as a point-rationing system for a group of energy commodities, with buying and selling of points permitted. As originally described, the PCA system would cover only personal consumption, whereas TEQs would tie consumers, retailers, wholesalers, producers, and brokers into a single energy-trading system. As these proposals have evolved, they have been talked about less as rationing schemes than as means of involving individuals, house-holds, and in some cases organizations directly in carbon markets. They are based on the principle of the individual's right to emit an annual quantity of carbon without payment or penalty, as well as the right to buy and sell such rights if they plan to use more or less energy.

The TEQ system can serve to illustrate how personal carbon trading might work, in its generalities if not all specifics. A 2011 report published by the organization Lean Economy Connection (founded by David Fleming), along with twenty members of Parliament, provides many of the details.[19] The plan envisions the UK government's Committee on Climate Change setting an overall annual carbon-emissions budget, one that starts somewhere below the nation's current emissions total and is lowered further every year thereafter. About 40 percent of total UK emissions currently come from direct energy use by individuals and households, primarily for heating, electricity consumption, and driving. Under the TEQ scheme, one year's worth of "carbon units" (each unit represents the release of one kilogram of carbon dioxide) toward such usage is issued. Forty percent of the total national stock of units is shared among individuals, with one equal portion going to each adult, while the other 60 percent of units are sold to primary energy users (utilities, industry, government, etc.) at the same weekly auction where treasury bills are sold.

Individuals must surrender carbon units with each purchase of electricity or fuel, typically when paying the household utility bill or filling up the family car. Payments are debited directly from each person's "carbon account." To facilitate transactions, a card similar to a bank debit card is issued to every adult. According to the proposal, "The TEQ units received by the energy retailer for the sale of fuel or electricity are then surrendered when the retailer buys energy from the wholesaler who, in turn, surrenders them to the primary provider. Finally, the primary provider surrenders units back to the Registrar when it pumps, mines or imports the fuel. This closes the loop." Low energy users who build up a surplus of TEQ units in their accounts can sell them on the national market, and those who require energy above their personal entitlement can buy them.

Households buy and sell TEQ units in the same market where

primary energy dealers trade. Most units in the market are bought through the weekly auction and sold by banks and other large-scale brokers; however, businesses, other organizations, and individuals can buy and sell TEQ units as well. Brokers sell to private businesses, public agencies, and other organizations, all of whom need units when buying energy. A farmer, for example, buys units on the TEQ market in order to buy tractor fuel, while a furniture manufacturer and the corner pub buy and use units to pay their electric bills. Any firm, institution, or individual can sell excess units back into the national market through brokers. Energy sellers like gas stations and utilities can buy units through the market and sell them to customers. In a typical situation, the customer who has run out of units but needs to buy gas or pay the electric bill will have to not only pay for the energy but also buy enough TEQ units (ideally, available for sale directly from the gas station or utility) to cover the transaction. The cash cost of the TEQ units needed to buy, say, a gallon of gas will be higher than the cash cost of the gallon itself. Therefore, a quantity of energy could be bought for, say, £100 if it's within a customer's annual carbon budget, but it will cost more than £200 (possibly much more) when bought in excess of her budget.[20]

The mechanics of PCAs are similar to those of TEQs. The PCA idea has emerged in various forms, including in the 2004 book *How We Can Save the Planet* by Mayer Hillman, Tina Fawcett, and Sudhir Chella Rajan. PCAs would cover both home and transportation emissions but leave upstream emissions to be dealt with through other mechanisms. Like TEQs, PCAs feature an annual carbon budget that declines over time, equal distribution of personal allowances (with the exception that children receive a partial allowance), electronic accounting, and a market in allowances. PCAs cover only individual consumption, however; businesses and other organizations are not included in the plan. Hillman and his co-authors foresee smart cards and automatic bank debits playing key roles. Alongside a sketch of their proposed "Carbon Allowance Card," they explain, "Each person would receive an electronic card containing the year's credits. This smart card would be presented every time energy or travel services are purchased, and the correct number of units would be deducted. The technologies and logistics would be no different from debit card systems." (Today, hand-held wireless devices presumably could be used as well.) Carbon allowances for electricity or gas consumption could be surrendered as part of paying the monthly utility bill, most conveniently through automatic bank debit. When access to energy is thereby limited, the plan's authors anticipate that consumers will seek out more efficient technologies in order to maintain their accustomed lifestyle. They write, "It will be in the interests of manufacturers to supply low-energy goods because this is where the demand will lie."[21] The authors acknowledge that PCAs will not necessarily reduce emissions produced by industry and commerce—they might even increase them if more efficient, more durable consumer goods require more energy and resources to manufacture—so they suggest, "There may need to be a parallel system of rationing with a reducing allocation over time" applied to business and government as well.

No national, mandatory carbon-rationing scheme has ever been put into practice, but there have been some attempts at smaller-scale trials. The eighteen hundred residents of tiny Norfolk Island, which lies about a thousand miles east of Australia, are planning to be the world's first population to engage in personal carbon trading. The island is a largely self-governing external territory of Australia, and the carbon project's chief investigator is Garry Egger, a medical doctor and professor of lifestyle medicine and applied health promotion at Southern Cross University in New South Wales. Egger explains, "We selected Norfolk Island because, as a small, geographically isolated, mostly middle-class population, it will be easy to monitor. But when the carbon trading project was announced in 2010, it was severely attacked by climate-change deniers, who were encouraged by a right-wing radio 'shock jock.' They put out rumors and urged island residents not to go along with the research. I even received some threatening e-mails. In the end, we had to change the program from mandatory to voluntary." Despite all that, surveys have found that 80 percent of island residents are willing to participate.[22]

The PCT program will kick off its first year with an islandwide emissions cap based on average annual consumption of all fossil fuels, and the cap will be lowered each succeeding year. "Carbon credit cards" will be issued each year to keep track of consumption. According to the original plan, islanders who overspend their allowance would have to buy additional credits from those who do not. Now, with the plan scaled back, there will be no requirement to buy additional credits. Those who stay under their limit will be rewarded, and Egger and colleagues will interview those who go over their limit to learn more about what pushed them to exceed it.

Egger's specialty is human obesity and how it relates to economic growth and ecological degradation. He and his colleagues on the carbon project eventually want to add emissions associated with food to the carbon ration. There already exists a health rating for foods,[23] and Egger proposes to combine a health value with a "carbon value" to give each type of food an overall point score that would be printed on the label. (The two scores might not necessarily be correlated. The health value depends on the type of food, where and how it is produced, and whether and how it is processed; the carbon value is also affected by those factors, but not always in the same way.)[24] People would have their carbon quota increased to account for food, and credits would then be deducted for each food purchase. The goal is to give people incentives to eat more healthful and climate-friendly food.

Getting the carbon scheme started, even on a voluntary, experimental basis, has been a struggle. Egger told me, "The people at Oxford [the authors of *How We Can Save the Planet*] make it sound nice and simple, but it's actually a very complicated process." For one thing, the project was sidetracked by a surprise energy crisis in February 2012, just as the research team was gearing up for preliminary data collection. Norfolk Island residents suddenly and unexpectedly found themselves living with involuntary siege-style rationing when a tanker ship bringing a regular delivery of diesel for the island's electricity utility and gasoline for its three filling stations found itself stranded offshore by a period of unusually bad weather. As the tanker sat anchored for ten days without being able to dock (eventually it gave up and headed to its next port), residents were unable to gas up their cars or even their lawn mowers. The island's power plant did manage to keep running, and a small reserve supply of gasoline was designated for filling the tanks of rental cars to be used by tourists, because tourism plays a central role in the local economy. The initial reaction to the fuel cutoff was characterized as "panic," but then many residents found they could get around fine by foot or bike. The island's minister of tourism, industry, and development, Andre Nobbs, pointed out that "Norfolk is five miles by three, filled to the capacity with beautiful scenery," a fine place for a healthful walk, and that the episode should "make us recognize what we can still do on our own without petrol." [25] Garry Egger said his research group had to postpone a baseline survey for determining the island's typical personal energy consumption—an essential step before the initial carbon cap could be set—due to the fuel shortage. This unexpected rationing episode would have distorted the data.[26]

WHY NOT A CARBON TAX?

A widely discussed alternative to carbon rationing is taxation of carbon emissions. Perhaps the most prominent campaigner for a carbon tax has been James Hansen, a scientist at the U.S. National Atmospheric and Space Administration and a climate activist. Hansen has also roundly denounced all forms of carbon trading, telling the U.S. House Ways and Means Committee in 2009, "Except for its stealth approach to taxing the public, and its attraction to special interests, 'cap and trade' seems to have little merit." Hansen calls his alternative a "tax and 100% dividend" plan, arguing that "a tax on coal, oil and gas is simple. It can be collected easily and reliably at the first point of sale, at the mine or oil well, or at the port of entry." He told the committee how his plan would work in the case of motor fuel:

> For example, a carbon price equivalent to $1/gallon of gasoline (about $115 per ton of CO_2), for 2007 rates of fossil fuel use in the United States) generates $670B. If we give one share to each legal resident age 22 and over, one half-share to college age youth (18–21), one half-share to the parents of each child up to two children per family, that yields about 224 million shares in 2007 (this could be off by ~10%; I could not find optimum census data). So the 100% Dividend for a $1/gallon tax rate ($115 per ton of CO_2) is: Single share: $3000/year ($250 per month,

deposited monthly in bank account). Family with 2 children: $9000/year ($750 per month, deposited monthly in bank account). The tax rate and dividend should increase with time. This approach would reduce demand for fossil fuels, driving down the price of fossil fuels on the open market. The next time the price of gasoline reaches $4/gallon most of that $4 should be tax, with 100% of that tax returned to the public as dividend.

Hansen believes that once a stiff tax is in place, the market will take over:

This tax, and the knowledge that it would continue to increase in the future, would spur innovations in energy efficiency and carbon-free energy sources. The dividend would put money in the hands of the public, allowing them to purchase vehicles and other products that reduce their carbon footprint and thus their taxes. The person doing better than average would obtain more from the dividend than paid in the tax. The tax would affect building designs and serve as an effective enforcer of energy-efficient building codes that are now widely ignored. The need to replace inefficient infrastructure would spur the economy. Tax and 100% dividend can drive innovation and economic growth with a snowballing effect. Carbon emissions will plummet far faster than [with] alternative top-down regulations.[27]

Some think Hansen is overselling the carbon tax. Because the biggest individual emitters tend to be more affluent and more willing to spend up to a very high level to maintain their lifestyle, analysts at the Lean Economy Connection argue that "if taxation were high enough to influence the behavior of the better-off, it would price the poor out of the market." Even with redistribution of the tax receipts back to the public, they say there would be no assurance of fair access to energy in times of scarcity. They also contend that a carbon tax won't work if the goal is a stable decline in emissions over the long term: "It is impossible for tax to give a long-term steady signal: if it remains constant, it will be inappropriate at certain periods of the economic cycle; if it fluctuates, it does not provide a steady signal." They conclude that a tax "should concentrate on what it is good at: raising money."[28] Tina Fawcett, co-author of *How We Can Save the Planet*, concedes that "if Hansen's tax were to have the effect he predicts, maybe there wouldn't be a need for personal carbon allowances," but she does not believe it would work. Furthermore, she notes, Britain already has a "hidden carbon tax" through the European carbon trading program, and because "taxation in the UK is not the least bit popular," adding a domestic tax to the existing one would whip up a political storm. Carbon rations deal more explicitly with emissions reduction and require deeper engagement by the public; therefore, Fawcett and her colleagues have "generally proposed them in opposition to taxes, not as a complement." There's always that third, far more palatable alternative, voluntary restraint; however, she has written, such a policy "could not even begin to tackle the scale of the problem because few individuals could be expected to start taking action for the common good, with 'free riders' having so much to gain."[29]

Hansen's proposal does include a spoonful of sugar to help the tax pill go down: the equal-shares dividend. Whatever view people might take of the tax, the dividend would almost certainly enjoy broad popular support, much as the dividend from oil revenues distributed each year by the Alaska Permanent Fund to all residents of that state does. Both types of dividends give everyone an explicit economic stake in atmosphere-damaging activities, though; the share of oil revenues, for example, gives Alaska residents an incentive to support increased drilling. And pumping large sums of cash into the consumer economy through the dividend provides a strong economic stimulus, which in turn generates increased emissions. Australia, for example, adopted a carbon tax-and-dividend plan in 2012, and in the month after the first "carbon compensation" payments went out, consumer spending rose sharply.[30] Some carbon-tax proposals have recommended directing the bulk of the carbon dividend toward lower-income households, in the form of assistance for improvement of insulation or other energy-conservation measures. Means-testing the dividend, however, would probably undermine the popularity of any tax.

In comparing TEQs with other emission-reduction devices,

Richard Starkey and Kevin Anderson of Manchester University acknowledge that, theoretically, the goals of rationing could be reached by having utilities and industries pay to emit, through either a tax or an auction of permits, and then having the government "recycle" the proceeds as a payment to lower-income individuals. But, they wrote, the perception of fairness could be very different under such a scheme:

> Allocating units directly and on an equal per capita basis quite literally makes individuals equal environmental stakeholders by awarding them an equal stake or share of the atmospheric sink. Arguably, the lump-sum recycling of auction or tax revenue does not make it as explicit to individuals that they have these equal shares in the atmosphere. If awarding units directly to the public means that they more clearly perceive they have such equal shares, if the public perceives this equal share to be fair, and if fairness is a condition for public acceptability, then DTQs [now called TEQs] may promote greater public buy-in to the task of substantially reducing emissions. Indeed, is it possible that a sense of common purpose with regard to emissions reduction could be built around DTQs? It is perhaps not inconceivable that the Prime Minister could address the nation along the following lines: "Making deep cuts in our emission is a great challenge, one which must be met for the sake of our children and children's children. As a nation, we've really got to pull together on this and it is only right that the burden of emissions reduction is shared out fairly."[31]

It is easy—mathematically if not politically—to make taxes more progressive. Tax burdens can be shifted among different income or wealth strata directly through legislation. Making carbon-rationing systems more progressive is another matter. In examining carbon rationing, academics have wrestled with one common assumption in particular: the equal-shares provision. Like Hansen's carbon tax, which would redistribute revenues equally to all adult citizens, personal carbon-trading programs as currently conceived would assign equal shares of the national emissions quota. Because higher-income households tend to be higher carbon emitters, the equal-shares provision is designed not only to treat everyone equally but also to lighten the relative burden on low-income families and even to allow them to profit from sales of unused credits. Fair enough, but could there be a better way to slice the pie? Analyses show that significant numbers of low-income families have higher-than-average energy requirements, ones that they cannot afford to lower simply by moving into better houses or closer to their jobs or by buying hybrid or electric cars. The possibility of including household energy requirements when assigning UK carbon rations was examined by the Bristol-based Centre for Sustainable Energy in a 2009 report. Data on income, energy usage, and household characteristics (such as detached houses versus apartments, rural versus urban locations, the presence of children, and heating sources) were used to simulate departures from the equal-shares method of allocating carbon rations. Results showed that taking household energy requirements into account would indeed benefit people with higher energy needs but that low-income households would not be spared hardship to a greater extent than they would be under an equal-shares allocation. In other words, it's hard to beat the equal-shares approach.[32]

Another alternative to the equal-shares approach, termed "luck egalitarianism," would attempt to distinguish a person's carbon emissions resulting from choice (e.g., traveling by air rather than rail) from those resulting from unchosen circumstance (e.g., advanced age, which might preclude walking or bicycling). The purpose is to distribute allowances in a way that allows "normal functioning" while neither rewarding past high emissions nor punishing emissions that result from circumstances beyond people's control. Luck egalitarianism has not yet been incorporated formally into any rationing proposal.[33]

Distribution of the burden depends in part on the choice of goods and services to be put on the list for rationing. Analysts at the Policy Studies Institute (where Mayer Hillman had first raised the idea of personal carbon allowances) compared TEQs with a variety of vehicle and fuel tax plans and predicted how they would affect households in different income brackets. All of the potential tax and quota schemes were progressive, but even in the lowest brackets some individuals were "winners" and others were "losers." Rationing left fewer losers at the low-income end than a tax did if it was applied only to motor fuel and air travel, not utilities, and also included half-credits for children. Under those conditions, almost 90 percent of households in the low-income bracket would come out as economic "winners." But leaving out electricity and home heating would also leave a large share of energy use uncapped.[34]

A carbon-rationing plan that allows the buying and selling of permits controls consumption more directly than a tax but less directly than nontradable rations. Like a tax, it does not put a firm ceiling on individual consumption. By leaving decisions about the final allocation of emissions to a larger carbon market, personal carbon-trading plans would provide consumers some latitude in choosing how to use personal shares of emissions. The British environmental writer George Monbiot calls it a "ration of freedom," contrasting the simplicity of PCAs and TEQs with a nightmare world in which the "carbon police" enforce specific behaviors: "We would need to be punished for failing to turn our televisions off at the wall, or for leaving the lights on when we go to bed. Some technologies would have to be banned outright." But with PCAs or TEQs, "if you can afford it, you can burn your entire ration on a single carbon orgy, then buy what you need for the rest of the year from other people."[35]

It may be hard to predict how consumers in a carbon-trading economy would handle their new invisible asset. Commodities previously rationed by quantity have always been tangible goods that people wanted or needed. Not so with carbon dioxide—it cannot be seen or smelled, and in the market it is valued only by its absence. Most important, almost any tangible good can be valued, theoretically at least, in terms of the carbon dioxide emissions it causes. In that respect, carbon behaves somewhat like money. If everything—not just coal and oil but *everything*—could be assigned a "price" in carbon units and if carbon had a money price, then the distinction between rationing of material quantities and taxation would vanish.

A carbon-rationing approach referred to as "Rate All Products and Services" (RAPS) would move toward that merger. RAPS would parcel out 100 percent of the national carbon budget to individuals on an equal-shares basis; then, for every purchase, the consumer would have to surrender the number of carbon points assigned to the good or service being bought.[36] Monbiot imagines trying to put one small part of such a system in practice: "If, for example, you stopped beside the road to buy a punnet [small basket] of strawberries, you would need to pay, say, £1 for it, plus 0.01588 percent of your carbon entitlement—assuming that someone had worked out that the growing, transport, and packaging of the strawberries had caused 127 grams of carbon to be released." Given the current state of knowledge and technology, such a system is considered unworkable: it would require computing the carbon footprint of strawberries, bicycles, wind turbines, books (by the page?), and everything else that is bought and sold, and the creation and implementation of an unimaginably complex system to keep track of the carbon points. In contrast, a carbon-trading system like the TEQ scheme that encompasses all upstream and downstream emissions would let the market determine point values. Strawberry producers and shippers will have to pay for their carbon allowance, writes Monbiot, so that "by the time you stop to buy the punnet of strawberries, the carbon required to produce it would have already been incorporated into its price, and you need only pay in pounds."[37]

Another proposed feature that would make PCT systems more convenient is the ability of energy retailers like gas stations and convenience stores and electric and gas utilities to buy up credits and sell them directly to their customers. With that provision, the consumer does not even need to keep track of his or her carbon account or carry a carbon card at all. Each month when the consumer's share of credits is deposited into her carbon account, she could immediately sell them all to the national market, with the payment going straight into her checking account. Then, with every energy purchase, she can simply buy the necessary carbon credits from the retailer and hand them right back. In practice, this would involve the retailer's simply tacking on the cost of the credits to the customer's bill. The consumer would not even keep track of whether she had exceeded her monthly carbon allowance unless she compared her carbon card, credit card, and checking account statements. The metamorphosis of "fair shares" carbon rationing into a carbon tax would be complete.[38]

A mechanism distinct from both rationing and taxes but with some characteristics of both is the "common asset trust." In its broadest form, it would manage access to all natural and human-created resources that are considered the common property of all residents of a nation or region. A bill under consideration in the Vermont legislature, for example, would create a Vermont Common Assets Trust to oversee the state's common-property assets, declaring that

> the list of assets that should belong to the people in common because the assets were inherited or created together, and therefore should be preserved in the common interest has expanded now logically to include natural assets such as undisturbed habitats, entire ecosystems, biological diversity, waste absorption capacity, nutrient cycling, flood control, pollination, raw materials, freshwater replenishment systems, soil formation systems, and the global atmosphere; and also to include social assets such as the Internet, our legal and political systems, universities, libraries, accounting procedures, science and technology, transportation infrastructure, the radio spectrum, and city parks. In enacting the regional greenhouse gas initiative . . . which requires the development of a carbon cap and trade program, the state of Vermont already has determined that the ability to discharge carbon into the atmosphere is an ability that belongs to people in common, and that needs to be managed in the common interest.[39]

With such a varied list of items to cover, the trust would have to apply different management mechanisms to different classes of assets. Consider greenhouse-gas emissions. The right to pollute, including the right to emit greenhouse gases, would become the common property of the people of Vermont. An emissions ceiling for the state as a whole would be fixed, and utilities, fuel providers, and other industries would have to purchase emissions rights at auction from the common pool. Designers of the bill have recommended that emissions rights should not be tradable after they have been auctioned off, to prevent speculation. Proceeds from the auctions would belong to Vermonters in common; therefore, conventional wisdom would say that the most politically popular move would be to return all revenues to the people on an equal-shares basis, like the Hansen tax or the Alaska Permanent Fund. But statewide polls have shown that the preferred use of the money, by a three-to-one margin, would be for investment in "preserving natural resources" and "providing social well-being" for the population as a whole. Doing so would have less of a stimulatory effect on economic activity and emissions than would distribution of dividends. The current version of the bill precisely reflects polling preferences by providing that 25 percent of the proceeds be returned to state residents on a per-capita basis, with the rest being spent to enhance the common good.[40]

TO TRADE OR NOT TO TRADE?

Societies that differ in many other ways nevertheless tend to agree that certain things cannot be brought to market. You cannot sell your vote or your family's food stamps or your kidney to someone else. Should emissions rights be on that list as well? Laurence Matthews of Cap and Share UK writes that although PCT schemes have several characteristics that the word "rationing" brings to the public mind, there are differences, including the long-held assumption that "rations ought not to be traded."[41] And there is concern, as recognized by the Vermont Common Asset Trust, that trading will lead to speculation. But the leading proposals for carbon rationing have always assumed tradability, because it emphasizes a " 'conserver gains principle' to complement the 'polluter pays principle.' "[42] Tina Fawcett argues that there is really no way around trading, mostly because households vary so widely in their dependence on emissions-heavy energy—by as much as ninefold in surveys she has done in Britain. If carbon allowances were not tradable, says Fawcett, the personal cap would have to be much, much higher, and a high cap would restrict only the very top emitters. But because PCA proposals include a market, she says, she and her colleagues "have been accused of commodifying carbon. When we were out promoting our book, 'deep green' people would tell us that tradability just provides licenses to pollute for those who can afford to do it." Her response to that is: "If you can think of an alternative emissions-reduction system in the context of a capitalist economy in which the rich don't have the advantage, well, good luck." She claims never to have seen a thoughtful proposal for making a carbon-rationing system work without tradability. To Fawcett, criticism of tradability seems to be "more of a reaction people have" than a serious counterproposal.[43] Monbiot sees the market as also providing a degree of satisfaction to a potentially resource-limited public: "What this means is that the lady in the Rolls-Royce car might still be driving around, but only after she has transferred a great deal of money to people who are poorer or more abstemious than she is. Economic justice is built into the system." And the carbon market would not require a direct, visible income subsidy that stigmatizes recipients and creates political resentment.

Legal selling of carbon credits would indeed tend to redistribute money from high- to low-income households, but critics contend that a carbon market creates a two-tier system: energy conservation becomes mandatory for the less well off but voluntary for the affluent, who can buy their way out of consumption limits. Because the poor would need more money and the rich more carbon credits, those two groups might have the most to gain from a carbon market. Decades ago, James Tobin reckoned that with a legal market in any kind of rations, "the consumers who will be squeezed are those who, whether by income or by taste, were just about satisfied with the ration" without trading.[44] Martin Weitzman acknowledged that although sacrifice is partially compensated with tradable rations, "this does not necessarily mean that pure direct wants for the deficit commodity are better served in the sense that those who 'need' it most actually end up receiving more."[45] In their book, Hillman, Fawcett, and Rajan admit that the wealthy will be able to "get away with" high energy consumption, but they predict that eventually, as the national quota ratchets down year by year, fewer credits will be available on the market, pushing the price high enough that even the rich will be discouraged from buying them and will reduce their energy consumption accordingly.[46] But even if that happens, there would still be a period of years in which the rich could exploit their advantage and permanently extend their lifestyle gap over the majority. A market in rations chips away at the "fair shares for all" aspect of the system. Tobin observed that

> it may be very difficult in practice to prevent inequalities due to transfers of rations among individuals. . . . The individual-istic approach of the theory of consumer choice and of wel-fare economics may well obscure social effects of rationing of much greater importance than the effects which our atomistic theory discloses. For example, the feeling of sharing equally in an emergency situation may be more important for produc-tion and welfare than the individual incentives and choices on which economic analysis has traditionally centered.[47]

Fairness could be served and total emissions reduced more quickly if carbon rations could be "retired" rather than sold. It has been sug-gested that a right to buy and sell rations implies a right to take them out of circulation as well, by returning a portion of one's annual allow-ance permanently to the common pool. Retired TEQ units would be deducted from future national carbon budgets, hastening the shrink-age of total emissions. Starkey and Anderson observe, "Of course any one individual retiring units would make no real difference to overall emissions, but it is perhaps possible that large groups of individuals might retire units as the result of a political campaign."[48] An incentive could be provided as well, by paying people to retire their unneeded ra-tions. That brings back to mind Kalecki's proposal, under which excess ration coupons could be sold to the government but not to individuals or companies. A buyback would reward conservation, ratchet down the national consumption cap over time, keep the price of carbon credits stable, and provide low-income households with greater means to buy energy or other essentials. As Kalecki proposed, the government could offset the expense of buying credits by levying higher taxes on excess income. In that way, the rich would not be able to buy their way out of consumption limits, and they would also have less capacity to overconsume nonrationed goods.

· · ·

There remains the question of market power. Were a carbon-rationing scheme put in place today, even the fairest distribution of energy credits would happen in an economy where distribution of almost all other goods and services, as well as ownership of the firms that produce them, is highly skewed. Brian Tokar of the Institute for Social Ecology in Plainfield, Vermont, points out that most of the economists who have proposed and designed the big upstream carbon-trading schemes "already live in the world of stocks and bonds and derivatives" and know how to design markets that serve big investors. Tokar asked, "Now if you bring the carbon market to street level, where many people's experience with finance doesn't extend beyond their checking accounts or maybe being ripped off every week by check-cashing and payday loan operations, how will they deal with that card or piece of paper you hand them—something unrelated to anything tangible?"[49] The British economist Nick Eyre echoes that worry, writing that if carbon trading is introduced into the everyday economy in which most people live, "a preference for 'cash now, pay later' is very likely, which could plausibly lead to unfair practices by financial intermediaries or even 'doorstep buying' of carbon permits." Furthermore, "the proposed markets have some unusual properties (at least in a modern consumer economy) in so far as they involve individual consumers selling to large corporations rather than vice versa. The implications of this need to be explored far more fully."[50] A parallel here would seem to be agriculture, in which large numbers of grain farmers, each with little power individually, sell to a handful of powerful corporations. The history of agricultural commodity markets is one of booms and busts, with farmers almost always getting the worst of it.

While carbon trading at ground level could be problematic, the trading that might go on up in the financial ether could cause even more mischief. If, as is anticipated, the carbon price tends to be even more volatile than that of, say, wheat, futures markets will spring up in response. Analysts anticipate "markets not just for the immediate trading of [personal carbon rations] (a "spot market") but for the trading of carbon unit options and futures."[51] The American Clean Energy and Security Act, passed by the U.S. House of Representatives in 2009 before failing in the Senate, provided not only for tradable upstream carbon allowances but also for carbon-derivatives markets. The Congressional Budget Office, considering a broad range of possible scenarios under the bill were it passed, estimated that the pool of basic carbon allowances would reach an annual total of $50 billion to $300 billion by 2020—hefty sums in themselves—but that the carbon-derivatives market based on the value of those allowances could have been seven to forty times as large, reaching $2 trillion by 2017.[52]

The ostensible purpose of such devices would be to dampen the volatility of the carbon market, but what are the chances that the tail would end up wagging the dog, as happened in the pre-2008 U.S. mortgage market? Here is how the Minneapolis-based Institute for Agriculture and Trade Policy describes the risks of creating a carbon derivatives market—something that a member of the U.S. Commodity Futures Trading Commission has predicted could be "the most important commodity market ever": "Once a carbon market, and its associated secondary market, is established, it is likely that carbon derivatives will be bundled into index funds. The sharp projected increase in the volume and value of carbon derivative contracts will induce extreme price volatility in commodity markets. To the extent that carbon derivatives are bundled into commodity index funds, it is likely that carbon prices will strongly influence both agricultural futures contract and cash prices."[53]

Advocates of personal carbon trading predict that by holding down demand for energy, the "cap" part of "cap and trade" will keep prices lower. But, predict some economists, it's the "trade" part that could destabilize the system, even if the cash price of electricity or gasoline stays down. Speculation in carbon and carbon-derivatives markets could put the cost of extra carbon rations beyond the reach of many. That wouldn't matter to those who manage to keep their energy consumption below their allowance. But many people live far from work with no transportation other than an old car, or reside in poorly insulated houses, and when they cannot afford to move closer to work or buy energy-efficient technology, they could go broke buying increasingly costly carbon credits. It has been proposed that the government take the money received in the auction of carbon credits and spend it on programs to improve insulation for low-income households or provide affordable means of commuting, but there are no estimates of how much could be accomplished with the funds available.[54]

Rapid inflation of the value of carbon credits could create big political risks for any government and provide a strong incentive to raise, soften, or even abandon the national emissions cap, undermining the system's main goal. Matthew Lockwood of the Institute for Public Policy Research in London wrote in 2010, "The assumption of some PCT proponents that a carbon market allows demand to adjust to meet a firm cap has not been tested (either in the real world or by market modelling) and is therefore open to doubt." He foresees the "virtual certainty of a soft price cap," meaning that high carbon allowance prices and irresistible political pressures will lead to a weakening of the national emissions limit, undermining the system. "Safety valve" mechanisms that would raise the cap on carbon emissions have been common in upstream carbon-trading programs, both existing and planned. "Overdraft" provisions allow polluters to pay a fine when they generate excess emissions. The size of the fine per ton of excess carbon puts a ceiling on the price of carbon, because no one would buy credits if they were more expensive than simply paying the fine. The result is higher total emissions. Another means through which carbon caps are lifted is the "offset" provision that allows polluters to earn additional credits by investing in ostensibly climate-friendly projects, usually in the global South.[55]

Tradability is also intended to make personal carbon rationing seem less like rationing and more palatable to governments and the public. But that appeal has proved weak. In late 2011, Tina Fawcett lamented the fact that "PCAs have moved down the national agenda since the high point three to four years ago," largely because a feasibility study by the UK government concluded that the idea of carbon rationing was ahead of its time. PCA and TEQ advocates have forcefully challenged the assumptions of that report but, says Fawcett, it took the wind out of carbon's political sails, and "with the government having said, 'No thanks,' none of the big environmental NGOs has taken it up. Work has moved for now into the academic and think-tank world. Maybe it was talked about too quickly, before the idea had been fully explored. And it didn't grow out of a broad popular base like, say, recycling." [56]

Mark Roodhouse, a historian at the University of York, has drawn lessons from Britain's wartime experience that he feels help explain the low level of interest. Britons accepted rationing in good spirits because they knew the war would end within a few years and were bolstered by promises that a future of plenty lay ahead. Likewise, writes Roodhouse, people might accept carbon rationing if "the scheme is a temporary measure during the transition from a high-carbon economy to a low-carbon economy and will be removed when the carbon price and/or consumption levels drop below a certain level." [57] But PCT schemes, in view of the very deep reductions necessary to avoid climate disaster, all envision the ceiling on emissions lowering year by year well into the future at a rate that would outpace any conceivable improvements in efficiency or renewable energy. They are, in effect, permanent schemes that would utterly transform our lives and could not be sold to the public as anything else.

The problem, of course, is that, as Fawcett has pointed out, carbon is different from commodities that have been rationed in the past. During World War II, there simply was not enough gasoline to go around, so people were not permitted to buy as much as they could afford to buy. Today, even after everyone's demand for fuel is satisfied, there is some left over. (Even though that will not always be the case, the economy behaves as if it will.) It's far harder to institute rationing in a world of such apparent abundance than it is in a world of obvious scarcity. So will carbon rationing have to wait until supplies of fossil fuels are depleted to a point that falls far short of demand? If so, it may be too late.

For now, says Fawcett, she sees personal carbon allowances as sitting on the shelf where the government put them in 2008, ready to be retrieved in case of emergency. "Maybe," she says, "when other policies haven't worked, people will come back to PCAs."

BIRTH RATIONING?

One wing of the climate movement has argued for almost half a century that unless decisive action is taken to halt or reverse human population growth, all other efforts to prevent runaway climate change or other catastrophes will fail. For example, J. Kenneth Smail wrote in 2003, "Earth's long-term sustainable carrying capacity, at what most would define as an 'adequate' to 'moderately comfortable' standard of living, is probably not much greater than 2–3 billion people." Given that, he argued, "time is short, with a window for implementation that will last no more than the next 50–75 years, and perhaps considerably less. A deliberate program of population stabilization and reduction should have begun some two or more generations ago (say in 1950, when human numbers were 'only' 2.5 billion and demographic momentum more easily arrested) and certainly cannot be delayed much longer." [58]

Prominent in the population-reduction campaign is the London-based Population Matters. Leading figures in the trust have argued that the number of people on Earth should somehow be reduced by 60 percent. One of Population Matters's initiatives includes the selling of "pop offsets," through which anyone can, on paper at least, cancel out the greenhouse impact of, say, a Caribbean vacation by contributing money that will go to fund birth-control programs. This, critics have said, can be interpreted as giving people the opportunity to say, "If I can stop them having babies, we won't have to change our ways." [59]

Advocates for putting birth control first believe the situation is too urgent and time is too short to wait for poor nations with high fertility rates to go through the so-called demographic transition, the fall in birth rates that most affluent nations experience along with rising standards of living. And they see as inadequate the now customary and often highly successful approach to population characterized by the principles of the UN-backed 1994 Cairo Declaration on Population Development: "sustainable development," "reproductive health and family planning," "gender equality and empowerment of women," education, and lower child mortality.

The population lobby's position has been rebutted on the grounds that it is a "distraction" from the urgent need to control fossil-fuel consumption and that, furthermore, in a diverse range of countries, improved quality of life and policies consistent with the Cairo principles have in fact brought deep reductions in birth rates, ones sufficient to end and even reverse global population growth. It has also been pointed out that although people in poorer nations with high birth rates often do very much need stronger women's rights and better access to family planning, they cannot be viewed as sources of the climate problem, since they contribute such a small fraction of total greenhouses gases. Among low-income nations, lower birth rates are associated with greater economic security, a lower degree of globalization, and more equality of wealth and income. Therefore, the argument goes, the more progress that's made by the climate-justice and labor rights movements, the faster the decline in population growth will be.[60]

It has been suggested that people will be friendlier toward policies to curb population growth than they will be toward policies to reduce their greenhouse-gas emissions.[61] Dramatic birth-rate reductions have been made in South Korea, Southeast Asia, Iran, the Indian state of Kerala, and many other places solely through policies consistent with the Cairo principles. Those successes were achieved without mandatory restraints. Significantly, there are no equivalent examples of progress on greenhouse-gas emissions solely through voluntary policies. Although the global emergency described by population activists would appear to be a problem far too formidable to be resolved by voluntary means, few have proposed mandatory curbs—and with good reason. In most countries, public reaction against laws governing reproduction would be almost certainly far more negative than reactions against rationing of, say, gasoline. It would not just be anticontraception politicians, anti-environment libertarians, and pro-procreation religious leaders who would condemn any form of reproductive rationing; the resistance would be almost universal. In light of that, it is worth examining some of the very few examples of nonvoluntary population policies that have been enacted.

In 1975, with poverty on the increase in India despite her national campaign to end it, Prime Minister Indira Gandhi declared a state of emergency, sharply restricting civil rights and giving the central government sweeping powers. In the emergency's second year, she appointed her son Sanjay to oversee poverty-reduction efforts. On the assumption that "India's population growth concerns could not wait for increased development and education to result in a drop in fertility," the Gandhis put in place an official "National Population Policy." Although campaigns began with sex education and rural health projects, the government soon narrowed its focus to "individual fertility behavior rather than structural determinants of population growth." Most prominent were vasectomy campaigns that eventually achieved more than eight million sterilizations. But the targeting of efforts at India's poorer classes and the use of economic incentives gave the so-called vasectomy camps a bad name. Population policy also became connected to some of the emergency's worst abuses of power, as when the central government demolished a poor Muslim neighborhood in Delhi and declared that alternative housing would be provided only on the acceptance of sterilization by adult males. Sterilization also deprived other medical services of much-needed funds and discouraged many families from seeking necessary health, food, or other aid for fear of having male members forced into having vasectomies. Faced with widespread unrest, Gandhi called for elections in 1977. She lost. The election was said to be "the first in the world in which fertility behavior was a deciding factor." [62] Since then, India's family planning efforts have been voluntary only, with one rather odd exception: in some states, no person who has produced more than two children is permitted to run for election to a *panchayat*, or village council. [63]

The most extensive and longest-running involuntary restrictions on reproduction have been those of China's "one-child family policy." Therese Hesketh, Li Lu, and Zhu Wei Xing write in the *New England Journal of Medicine*:

> The policy consists of a set of regulations governing the approved size of Chinese families. These regulations include restrictions on family size, late marriage and childbearing, and the spacing of children (in cases in which second children are permitted). The State Family Planning Bureau sets the overall

targets and policy direction. Family-planning committees at provincial and county levels devise local strategies for implementation. Despite its name, the one-child rule applies to a minority of the population; for urban residents and government employees, the policy is strictly enforced, with few exceptions. The exceptions include families in which the first child has a disability or both parents work in high-risk occupations (such as mining) or are themselves from one-child families (in some areas). In rural areas, where approximately 70 percent of the people live, a second child is generally allowed after five years, but this provision sometimes applies only if the first child is a girl—a clear acknowledgment of the traditional preference for boys. A third child is allowed among some ethnic minorities and in remote, underpopulated areas. The policy is underpinned by a system of rewards and penalties, which are largely meted out at the discretion of local officials and hence vary widely. They include economic incentives for compliance, and substantial fines, confiscation of belongings, and dismissal from work for noncompliance. The policy depends on virtually universal access to contraception and abortion.[64]

When the policy was introduced in 1979, the goal was to keep China's population under 1.2 billion in the year 2000. The country did not overshoot that target by very much and easily stayed below the 2010 target of 1.4 billion. The policy is officially credited with preventing as many as 300 million births.[65] What is discussed less often is that in the decade leading up to the start of the one-child policy, a largely voluntary national program encouraging fewer, later, and more widely spaced births had already achieved a dramatic halving of the fertility rate. But in the late 1970s, according to Tyrene White, a political science professor at Swarthmore College, "a campaign that encouraged a small-family norm and gave interested couples the means to achieve it" evolved into "birth rationing" under the one-child policy.[66] One result of the policy has been a statistically significant increase in the male-to-female ratio at birth. This is believed to be primarily the result of sex-selective abortion, but nonregistration of female births may also play a part. Hesketh, Lu, and Xing pointed to other consequences of the policy: an aging population and the emergence of what has come to be known as "the '4:2:1' phenomenon, meaning that increasing numbers of couples will be solely responsible for the care of one child and four parents." Writing in 2005, they wondered if the time had come to abandon the one-child policy without worrying about a baby boom, because much of China had apparently evolved into a "small-family culture" like those in more economically developed nations. By 2012, there was widespread talk of ditching the policy, and Walmart and other multinational companies were even running advertisements in China featuring two-child families.[67]

Either carbon rationing or "birth rationing" as a way of curbing climate change would face strong resistance. But as much as people might push back against limits on consumption, their reaction against interference in matters of reproduction is, of course, likely to be much more harsh, at least in most countries. Targeting consumption, difficult as it is, would be the more direct approach and have the better chance of success. The economist David Satterwaite echoes a view widely held in the climate-justice community when he writes,

> It is not correct to suggest that it is the increase in population that drives the growth in GHG [greenhouse-gas] emissions, when the lifetime contribution to GHG emissions of a person added to the world's population varies by a factor of more than 1,000 depending on the circumstances into which they are born and their life possibilities and choices. So it is not the growth in the number of people, but rather the growth in the number of consumers and the GHG implications of their consumption patterns that are the issue. In theory (leaving aside the difficulties in measurement), responsibility for GHG emissions should be with individuals and households and based on the GHG implications of their consumption, and not with nations (or cities) based on GHG inventories from the production perspective.

According to Satterwaite's calculations, ensuring a decent standard of living for the world's poor households would require that they generate greater emissions, but that with the right policies the necessary increases "would not be substantial and are unlikely to drive low-income nations into having per capita emissions above the 'fair share' level." But, he continues, "if it is assumed that such needs are met by trickle-down from economic growth, the GHG [greenhouse-gas] emissions implications would be far more serious."[68]

INTERNATIONAL JUSTICE

The sense of urgency that might put domestic carbon rationing back onto the British political agenda and even provide it some visibility in the United States and other countries of the global North could come through the international climate justice movement and its demands that the North pay its "carbon debt."[69] James Hansen points out that as much as the world's long-industrialized countries would like to focus attention on ways to curtail future carbon emissions, we must face the fact that the North is responsible for the vast bulk of excess greenhouse gases that are currently accelerating climate disruption. Add up each nation's carbon emissions from burning fossil fuels between 1751 and 2007, and the top three per-capita emitters are the United Kingdom, the United States, and Germany, in that order. "Their responsibility," calculates Hansen, "exceeds that of China by more than a factor of 10, and that of India by more than a factor of 25."[70]

Because most past and present excess emissions come from the North, countries of the global South contend that deep reductions must begin here. The philosopher Henry Shue adds, "It may ultimately be in the best interests of the poor states to see global warming stopped, but their citizens have far more urgent and serious problems—like lack of food, lack of clean drinking water, and lack of jobs to provide minimum support for themselves and their families." Earth's atmosphere, he argues, cannot be rescued without closing the chasm between the global rich and the global poor:

> If the wealthy states are content to allow radical inequalities to persist and worsen, it is difficult to see why the poor states should divert their attention from their own worst problems in

order to help out with problems that for them are far less immediate and deadly. It is as if I am starving to death, and you
want me to agree to stop searching for food so I can help you
repair a leak in the roof of your house, without your promising
me any food in return. . . . Whatever needs to be done by either
rich or poor countries about global warming, the costs should
initially be borne by the wealthy industrialized states.[71]

Neither activists nor economists have yet hit on a pragmatic solution to linking domestic emissions reductions to international climate
justice. Instead, there has been speculation that personal carbon trading could be connected to international carbon markets. For example,
Starkey and Anderson outlined a process through which the European
Union Emissions Trading Scheme, an upstream carbon cap-and-trade
system in place since 2005, could pull more and smaller businesses,
and then individuals, into its market, eventually becoming an all-
encompassing system. Would that expose personal carbon markets to
the risks and failures that have so far plagued attempts at international
carbon trading?[72] Brian Tokar speaks for many in the climate justice
movement when he says, "Anytime you market something that is in-
tangible and artificially created, you have a recipe for abuse. People
have argued since the first carbon-trading proposals came out in the
late eighties that such a market is *even more* prone to manipulation by
powerful players than is a market in tangible commodities."[73] In particular, carbon offset projects supported to date through international
trading systems have often rewarded activities that would or should
have been carried out anyway; others have simply foundered.

Side effects of many offset projects—land grabs, displacement of
indigenous peoples, political repression, and other problems—have
turned people's lives upside down across the global South. For example, a 22-megawatt electricity-generating plant in Thailand is powered
by burning rice hulls, a process that earns carbon credits because the
hulls are classified as waste; however, since it began operation in the
early 2000s, local farmers are no longer able to afford the hulls they
have always used for mulch, animal bedding, and soil improvement.
Meanwhile, an agreement allowing the UK-based New Forests Com-

pany to earn carbon credits by establishing more than forty thousand acres of forest in Uganda led to the often violent eviction in 2005–9 of more than four thousand people who had been living on and deriving their livelihoods from the land. Around that same time, in the Indian state of Gujarat, a refrigerant factory was earning credits for trapping and destroying a by-product, HCFC-23, which is a potent greenhouse gas; unfortunately, the plant was also releasing fluorine and other pollutants into waters and soils of the area, with serious impacts on crops, livestock, and human health, say local villagers.[74] Lucrative emissions credits for destroying HCFC-23 have had another unintended consequence. The *New York Times* reported in 2012 that for the previous seven years, nineteen refrigerant plants in India, China, and other countries were "churning out more harmful coolant gas [HCFC-22, a potent greenhouse gas used in air-conditioning and refrigeration] so they can be paid to destroy its waste by-product."[75]

Another example of a carbon offset gone bad is provided by Mark Schapiro of the Center for Investigative Reporting. When he checked out a project run by a forest-resource company in the Brazilian state of Minas Gerais, he found an operation producing charcoal from eucalyptus logs that claimed to spare the atmosphere in two ways: by substituting carbon recently fixed by green plants for fossil carbon and by using a process that lowers methane emissions. The project had been fully verified as a legitimate offset for the European Clean Development Mechanism and would be awarded millions of carbon credits. The charcoal was to be used in a factory producing pig iron. But by the time Schapiro arrived at the site in May 2009, "the entire enterprise lay dormant. Stacks of eucalyptus logs ten feet high lay alongside kilns that had not been fired up; and the pig iron factory's rolling machinery had been frozen in place for at least a month." The worldwide recession had idled the faraway automobile and refrigerator factories in which the iron would have been used; the bust in the global economy had thereby reduced emissions without help from the project in Minas Gerais. Meanwhile, thanks to lax oversight, the pig iron company had been able to start selling some of its carbon credits anyway, hoping to collect as much as $100 million.[76]

Policy makers are working to tighten up offset criteria and project verification, but that would not touch the system's more fundamental failing, contend Tamra Gilbertson and Oscar Reyes of the group Carbon Trade Watch. Even if an offset seller's project could be verified as having achieved its goals perfectly, "any gain would by definition be nullified by increased emissions allowed to the buyer, delaying the transition to a post–fossil fuel economy elsewhere." All that would be accomplished would be to "move emissions from one place to another with no net reduction."[77]

Offsets have not been incorporated into personal carbon rationing proposals; there are no provisions, for example, that would award a consumer extra carbon allowances for planting trees or making biodiesel fuel in the garage. But buying personal offsets has become a prominent form of voluntary green action, and, based on the international carbon-trading experience, the need for political compromise could lead to the inclusion of offsets in any carbon-rationing scheme when it is eventually implemented. The offset mechanism, however, would be a Trojan horse that could undo much of what the scheme is designed to accomplish.

For the wealthy nations to acknowledge their carbon debt would mean going beyond tough regulation of carbon trading or the five-ton international carbon dioxide limit, or even contraction and convergence. It would mean not only reducing the North's own fossil fuel use but also providing the economic means for less well-off countries to protect themselves from the impacts of past emissions while they build the technological capacity for low-emissions economic development. Any domestic carbon-rationing scheme in the North should take into account those people around the world who, because of poverty or geography, belong to a group that the legal scholar Maxine Burkett calls "the climate vulnerable." The climate vulnerable actually require an increase in consumption—not only to compensate for their greater exposure to the ravages of climate change but also to account for the fact that they didn't have a century and a half of the access to ample fossil fuels that helped the North reduce its own climate vulnerability while the South's prospects worsened.[78]

Burkett argues that the North owes the South massive reparations both for past climate-disrupting emissions and for helping ensure that future emissions don't aggravate the crisis. The reparations would, in part, take the form of cash transfers; however, she adds, "Adaptation measures, like insurance plans or technology transfers previously floated, are also methods of compensation. In short, the developed world could execute the many adaptation proposals and provide, without delay or distraction, the tens of billions of dollars needed to prepare the developing world." She points out that the UN Framework Convention on Climate Change, ratified by almost two hundred countries (not including the United States), commits nations of the North to the "promotion and facilitation of climate-friendly technology transfers because of the stark differences in their historic contributions to climate change." Furthermore, the climate vulnerable must be able to design their own adaptation strategy. Burkett stresses community-based adaptation, using "initiatives aimed at helping villages most at risk to launch projects with the money going to them rather than trickling down through global and national funds."[79]

The necessity for simultaneously cutting emissions and transferring resources to climate-vulnerable communities around the world will be an enormous challenge. But success in achieving a lower-energy world economy would address a host of other problems—destruction of soils, depletion of biodiversity, poisoning of the world's waters, malnutrition, and others—that fossil energy in pursuit of profit helped create well before global temperatures started rising. The ecological nightmares that the world's affluent are hoping to avoid are already endured daily by billions of people, and in many countries rationing of water, food, and other essential goods has become a matter of survival for a large share of the population. Their day-to-day experience in sharing resources could hold lessons for those of us in the North once we decide to start bringing consumption in line with what Earth can support.

Priya, a resident of Kadam Chawl, a slum in Mumbai, India, with the pots she and her family use to collect water from their community tap, 2012.

4

. . . AND NOT A LOT TO DRINK

Water is a fundamental human right and a public trust to be guarded by all levels of government, therefore, it should not be commodified, privatized, or traded for commercial purposes. . . . Water is best protected by local communities and citizens who must be respected as equal partners with governments in the protection and regulation of water. Peoples of the earth are the only vehicle to promote earth democracy and save water.
—Cochabamba Declaration, 2000[1]

If ever there was a time for a plan of conservation and water justice to deal with the twin water crises of scarcity and inequity, now is that time. The world does not lack the knowledge about how to build a water-secure future; it lacks the political will.

—Maude Barlow, 2007[2]

After sixteen months without rain, the state of Texas started the year 2012 in deep trouble. The previous year had brought the worst drought in the state's history, a scary preview of the intense heat and drought that was to assault most of North America in the coming months. Reservoirs and wells were shrinking fast, especially in south Texas, and water rationing had been imposed in nearly one thousand cities and towns. On January 30, Spicewood Beach, located about forty miles northwest of Austin, became the state's first town that year to run completely out of water; its main well went dry a week after imposition of emergency water rationing. The Lower Colorado River Authority (LRCA), which had been operating the town's water system for the previous ten years, immediately began filling four-thousand-gallon tanker trucks at a fire hydrant ten miles away and hauling water into Spicewood Beach. As the first trucks arrived, one woman chanted, "Just get water! Just get water! We don't care where. Just. Get. Water!" She and her neighbors did get water, but not much. The LRCA planned to bring in three to four truckloads per day, equivalent to about 10 percent of normal consumption for a south Texas community the size of Spicewood Beach.[3]

Watching the trucks slosh into town, several residents expressed more than a little bafflement; for the past year, they had been watching similar trucks fill up at the Spicewood Beach well and haul water *out* of town. It turned out that the LRCA had maintained contracts with two private hauling companies, which together had trucked out at least 1.4 million gallons in 2011 alone to supply residences and industrial sites in other communities; they were asked to stop removing water only when strict water rationing was imposed at the start of 2012. For the water they obtained from the Spicewood Beach well, the companies had paid $6 to $8 per thousand gallons. One of the companies' owners told reporters, "The water is the cheapest part of the equation. We're being subsidized for water. But it should probably be valued like fuel." Now, with the well having run dry, the LRCA was paying a third company $50 per thousand gallons to bring water back into Spicewood Beach.[4]

Trying to put a value on water is always a tricky business. Many of the benefits that it provides, including climatic regulation and health of land and ocean ecosystems, qualify as pure public goods—benefits that are not denied one person when another enjoys them and from whose enjoyment no one can be excluded. Public goods are not marketable, so while water itself can be treated as a commodity, its ecological "services" cannot. Consuming water doesn't destroy it, but it almost always makes water less accessible or useful. And because water is eminently measurable and can be divided into quantities of any size, it can be owned, bought, sold, and taxed. Once upon a time, fresh water free of pollutants was easily within reach of most people, but nowhere was good water obtained and distributed without at least some effort and expense. Now, with growth in human population and economic activity, competition for water is becoming more and more intense in more and more places. The chief competitors are agriculture, industry, commerce, and domestic users. Just as individuals, nations, and the world as a whole have carbon footprints that can be estimated, we also have "water footprints." The footprint of the entire human economy is computed as the volume of water required to produce all goods and services. A whopping 86 percent of the global total is accounted for by production of food, fiber, and other agricultural products, and 9 percent is attributable to industrial production. Although a scant 5 percent of the footprint is residential water use, it is in the domestic supply where shortages are felt most immediately and most intensely by the majority of people. Often, the result is rationing.[5]

BROWN LAWN, DIRTY CAR

In the dry western United States, drought is a way of life, but that has not blocked economic development. Across the region, water conservation traditionally has been defined as making the most profitable use of a scarce resource. The legal doctrine was "prior appropriation," by which a landowner could gain rights to water if he could show that he would put it to "beneficial," that is, economically rational, use. Wasteful use was formally forbidden but has been widely tolerated in practice. In a time of scarcity, the original rights-holder was allowed to fill his needs before those holding "junior" rights, which had been conferred after the initial claim was made, could use what, if anything, was left over.[6] "Beneficial use" implied that the water had to be physically removed from the watercourse, and there were usually "use it or lose it" provisions as well. Groundwater was generally considered the property of whoever owned the land overlying it, however, and did not need to be drawn out to be claimed. In Texas specifically, the "rule of capture" that permitted owners of oil and gas wells to pump as intensively as they liked had long been applied to groundwater resources as well. These simple principles, however, have not spared the West "intense competitions over water, sometimes lasting decades or even centuries."[7]

While the water laws of the West, writes the environmental attorney Daniel Findlay, "may have initially posed no issues in the gluttonous prospecting age in which it arose, the extreme stresses placed on water resources in today's West make for a different story."[8] Such laws, therefore, have been moderated in some states—for example, by giving "optimum use" priority over "first use," by rewarding conservation, and by legally protecting water that is to be "left to flow in its natural course." [9] In recent years, Texas water policy has been modified. Some county groundwater districts are now authorized to set pumping limits (whether they do so is another matter) and rights to pump; users of the Edwards aquifer in central Texas, for example, have been issued tradable permits. [10]

One of the most controversial water restrictions has been Colorado's prohibition on rainwater harvesting. For many years, the state's residents were not permitted to collect water from their own roofs in rain barrels, or otherwise capture it. The reasoning behind the law was that, in an often thirsty state, no one should be able to appropriate for personal use water that would otherwise run downhill into streams, rivers, and reservoirs or seep into aquifers to benefit downstream users and the public good. But for citizens to be liable to prosecution for using the rainwater falling on their own property seemed downright un-American to many, and after years of legal battles the law was finally repealed in 2009. [11]

In the eastern states, "riparian" rights govern the use of surface water, which is treated as a common resource that may be used by anyone whose land abuts a body of water. When water is scarce, rights to it are allotted in proportion to the length of landowners' frontage on the body of water. This doctrine evolved in places and under conditions in which there was generally ample water to fill all needs. But in many localities, even in the East, water supplies are now being pushed to their limits. Although agriculture dominates overall water use in the East as well as the West, an entire region's water supply can be badly stressed by demand from a single large city. An infamous example of rural/urban conflict is the long-running, highly charged dispute among the states of Georgia, Alabama, and Florida over water resources in the Chattahoochee–Flint–Apalachicola River basin. The origins of what J.B. Ruhl, professor of law at Florida State University, has called a "water war, Eastern style," lie in a succession of droughts that have left the region without enough water to fill the huge needs of the greater Atlanta area, as well as the large stretches of irrigated agriculture along the Flint River in south Georgia, while still maintaining sufficient flow rates in Florida's ecologically vulnerable Apalachicola River (which is formed by the confluence of the Chattahoochee and Flint rivers). In 2007, during the most severe drought to hit the region since the dispute began, a fast-wilting Atlanta was forced to draw more than ever on its primary water source, a vast reservoir, known as Lake Lanier, on the Chattahoochee north of the city. But the lake's caretakers, the U.S. Army Corps of Engineers, were obligated to release enough water to keep the Apalachicola flowing adequately as well. As a consequence, Lake Lanier dropped to its lowest levels yet recorded, exposing broad expanses of red Georgia clay around its shoreline.[12]

By October, there was talk of Atlanta's—and many smaller cities'— sources of water being completely tapped out within three months. Cities across the region had already imposed total bans on lawn watering, car washing, and other outdoor uses; Baptist preachers postponed immersion baptisms and joked about going to the Methodist-style "sprinkle" method. But the prospect of a dry Lake Lanier led many to consider more drastic measures, including mandatory rationing with harsh penalties. Jeff Knight, an environmental engineer for the city of Athens, sixty miles east of Atlanta, told the Associated Press, "We're way beyond limiting outdoor water use. We're talking about indoor water use." He added, "There has to be limits to where government intrudes on someone's life, but we have to impose a penalty on some people. The problem is how much and who. That gets political. But it's going to hurt everyone."[13] Indeed, in some parts of the region, fines of $500 or more for illicit lawn watering were being prompted by "snitch patrols." With gardening and yard grooming out of the question, the Southeast's landscaping industry was hit with $1.2 billion in losses.[14] In 2008, Georgia lost a court battle to curb the continuing drawdown of Lake Lanier, but the issue became moot when normal rainfall returned by 2009. And the tristate water war carried on.

Public utilities have a long history of subsidizing urban water consumption, but in more drought-prone areas of North America there is a tendency toward "marginal cost pricing" designed to capture the true cost of water and discourage waste. On the assumption that private water companies can accomplish that goal more efficiently, local officials in about 15 percent of U.S. municipalities have handed over water supplies to the private sector. Yet water shortages have persisted, while there is no shortage of examples in which privatization has failed. Craig Anthony Arnold, a professor of land use in the schools of law and public affairs at the University of Louisville, writes:

> [P]rivatization and commodification of water are unsustainable and fragmenting forces ecologically, temporally, geographically, socially, ethically, politically, and even economically. The examples are legion: Atlanta's water privatization debacle; failed privatization ventures in Laredo, Texas; Felton, California; and East Cleveland, Ohio; the severely stressed Colorado River; the conflict-ridden Upper Klamath Basin in Oregon and northeastern California; the unresolved and unsustainable demands on the Apalachicola–Chattahoochee–Flint River System in the Southeastern U.S.; the once-declining but now-recovering Mono Lake; excessive groundwater pumping in Tucson, Arizona, Tampa, Florida, San Antonio, Texas, and Massachusetts's Ipswich River Basin; and even emerging water crises.[15]

Given such problems, many local governments have de-privatized, once again treating water as a public utility. In times of severe water shortage, water utilities, whether public or private, face no choice but to impose rationing by slapping restrictions on lawn watering and other outdoor uses in order to achieve an immediate reduction. It isn't a simple matter to enforce indoor water conservation (what with customers lingering longer under their low-flow showerheads), whereas lawn watering and car washing are highly visible to neighbors and local authorities. Therefore, by far the most common methods of water rationing in America aim at outdoor use.[16]

Typical of water-rationing orders was one enforced in parts of six counties in northeastern Florida from 2001 to 2006. Residential, commercial, and industrial properties with odd-numbered addresses were permitted to irrigate on Wednesdays and Saturdays, while those with even-numbered addresses were assigned Thursdays and Sundays; no irrigation was allowed on any day between 10:00 A.M. and 4:00 P.M. or when the soil was not dry from lack of rainfall; and consumption was limited to three-fourths of an inch of water over the area irrigated. Resulting water savings were estimated to total approximately 12 percent of the normal amount of combined indoor and outdoor use, and the reductions were sustained over time.[17]

In the summer of 2002 in Colorado, many cities responded to a severe regional drought by restricting outdoor water use. An oft-cited survey of eight municipal water providers, some of which employed voluntary and others mandatory water restrictions, by Douglas Kenney, Roberta Klein, and Martyn Clark, found that

> Four of the eight providers limited lawn watering to once every three days, three cities limited watering to twice a week, while Lafayette restricted lawn watering to once a week. These restrictions often specified the time of day watering was to occur, the maximum length of the watering period, special rules for irrigating trees and perennials, and allowances for hand watering. Other common restrictions included prohibitions against using hoses to wash paved areas, limits on car washing and filling or refilling swimming pools, and restrictions on planting and/or watering new sod. New drought-inspired pricing mechanisms were also implemented in two cities during the study period to discourage and penalize excessive use.[18]

The fact that cities varied greatly in their approaches allowed for comparisons. The results were not surprising. Mandatory restrictions reduced water use, whereas voluntary restrictions were of little value; the greatest savings were achieved where mandatory restrictions were "the most aggressive and stringent"; and whatever action was taken, doing something always appeared to be better than taking no action.

In selecting a rationing plan, cities have to take into account more than just the total quantity of water to be saved; seemingly insignificant scheduling details may also turn out to be important. When Los Angeles was hit with a rash of major water-main blowouts in the summer of 2009—some of which sent geysers several stories into the air and one of which opened a sinkhole that half-swallowed a responding fire truck—officials who tried to identify a cause were initially stumped. Then they realized that the incidence of line breaks had risen immediately following the initiation of a citywide water rationing mandate. Faced with severe drought, the city had, for the first time ever, limited lawn watering to only two days per week. But the schedule did not involve rotating days; everyone was supposed to use water for lawns only on Mondays and Thursdays. Experts suspected (and a report six months later confirmed) that sudden pressure drops in aging pipes, caused when sprinklers came on across the city on Mondays and Thursdays, followed by pressure spikes when the sprinklers were turned off, caused many of the blowouts.[19]

A survey by Sheila Olmstead of Yale and Robert Stavins of Harvard on what is effective and what is not in reducing domestic water consumption showed that "more stringent mandatory policies (when well enforced) tend to have stronger effects than voluntary policies and education programs," and raising the price of water to match the cost of providing it is more cost-effective than nonprice approaches such as installation of low-flow fixtures or imposition of lawn-watering restrictions. Nonprice restrictions tend to be progressive in the sense that high-income households reduce water consumption more than low-income ones do; however, if prices are simply raised in an effort to hold down consumption, the greater share of water saving is done by lower-income households. To compensate, Olmstead and Stavins recommend that a rebate "inversely related to household income, or some other measure" be given. Nevertheless, they note, raising prices is always politically unpopular, while restricting outdoor water use during a drought creates a sense of common adversity and shared burden (and people are more likely to assign the blame to natural causes rather than public officials). Therefore, "water demand management through nonprice techniques is the overwhelmingly dominant paradigm in the United States," the report concludes.[20]

Emma Aisbett and Ralf Steinhauser of Australian National University have urged that water managers not give up on voluntary measures, even though most surveys have found them ineffective. Success, they argue, depends very much on the content of the messages urging restraint. They found that the most effective conservation messages during droughts in Australia were ones alerting consumers to the fact that the water level was dropping in the reservoir that supplied the target area. When information on reservoir level was provided by electronic roadside signs, people responded to alarming drops in the reservoir by reducing their consumption.[21]

TEN POTS IN TWENTY MINUTES

Around the world, 1.8 billion more people have safe drinking water today than had it in 1990. But that achievement, significant as it is, has barely kept up with population growth. The result, according to a recent World Health Organization (WHO)/UNICEF report, is that today, as in the 1970s, almost a billion people lack adequate access to water; more than 60 percent of those people live in sub-Saharan Africa or South Asia.[22]

In the global South, expansion of water availability has made the most headway in large urban areas. Among the beneficiaries have been the residents of Kadam Chawl ("Footsteps Slum"), a row of tiny homes clinging to a narrow terrace on a hillside in the northern part of Mumbai, India's largest city.[23] Even water-rights advocates acknowledge that in trying to provide clean water to almost 14 million people—many of them living in densely crowded, highly impoverished areas—Mumbai's Water Utility Department faces formidable obstacles. In densely populated slums, the city has extended access primarily through community water taps like the one in Kadam Chawl. That tap is connected to a remote branch of a labyrinthine network that funnels water from seventeen reservoirs east of the city through more than four thousand miles of water mains and smaller plumbing.

Kadam Chawl consists of ten one-room concrete homes. A cramped stone path leads up a slope past seven of the homes and then becomes a stairway leading to the other three. Each family has a collection of at least four water pots, known as *hundis*, that hold two and a half gallons or more each. The neighborhood's nightly water-rationing drama begins each evening soon after nine o'clock, when water begins gushing from a single hose one inch in diameter attached to a community tap located near the chawl entrance. By then, families have brought all available empty *hundis* down to an open area surrounding the tap, and someone grabs the hose to start filling them. The tap runs for only twenty minutes each night. With the clock ticking and dozens of *hundis* to be filled and hauled, everyone, including children, pitches in. In a fast-moving, carefully choreographed routine, women and men begin hauling full *hundis* up to their rooms. Most women carry one of the twenty-five-pound pots on their head or hip; most men take two at a time. Smaller pots are filled for younger girls to carry. The path is only about three feet wide and partially obstructed in places by water drums, so that anyone hustling back down to the main tap who meets a neighbor hauling water up the slope is required to duck into a doorway or side space to let the neighbor pass.

The scene is all fast action and little talk. Water inevitably sloshes out of the open-top *hundis*, making for treacherous footing on the irregular, largely unlit stone path. Yet another threat is posed by open drainage holes. The water carriers know without looking exactly where to step, but a nighttime visitor has to be on constant alert for potentially leg-breaking hazards. Families living in the three rooms along the steps at the upper end of the chawl have the longest, steepest climb from the main water source and can manage fewer trips during the short time that the water flows. Satish, a professional driver who lives in one of those three upper rooms with his family, says that neighbors lower on the path make allowances for his family and the others who live at the top, letting them go to the head of the line to fill their *hundis* to make up for lost time.

Sometime before 9:30, the water stops running from the community tap, and families stagger home with the last of their *hundis*. If the Mumbai water department were hitting its declared target of a water supply adequate for a "decent life," a family of four would have ready access to more than one hundred gallons per day. In reality, they get much less. Priya, a slight young woman, has lived in Kadam Chawl with her husband and two children for ten years. She says that, depending on how much water comes in a night, she manages to get four to ten *hundis* full—only one-tenth to one-fourth of the city's goal. But she's grateful for her current water supply, meager as it is. At one time, water would run some days and not others. When it did flow, it would turn on at a random time between midnight and 3 A.M. To protest the impossible schedule, Priya and the other residents staged a sit-in at the municipality's offices—an act of civil disobedience that cost Priya and some of her neighbors a couple of nights in jail but won them their prime-time water slot. The stress created by this method of water rationing does not appear to trigger much serious conflict in Kadam Chawl; nevertheless, say residents, arguments can flare when water supplies dwindle during the hot, dry summer or if the supply is interrupted for other reasons. Some other areas see daily disputes. Sharmila, a resident of a nearby slum, has to rush from her cooking and cleaning job each day to be sure she's home by five o'clock, when her community tap opens, because, she says, "The people there are real *haramis*"—meaning, in the most polite translation, scoundrels. "They fight all the time over who gets the water."

A RIGHT TO WATER AND A TIME TO RATION

WHO suggests that a survival ration of potable water (for drinking, washing, cooking, and other household uses) is about five and a half gallons daily per person but hastens to add that such a quantity cannot sustain a decent quality of life over time—for that, a minimum of about thirteen gallons is considered necessary.[24] As crucial as that thirteen gallons is in sustaining a person's life and health, far more water is required to produce that person's food supply. Vast, often complex mechanisms have been designed to allocate increasingly scarce water supplies among farmers in regions around the world. Most of that water is then delivered to consumers in a "virtual" form that is not counted in the thirteen-gallon requirement for household use: as food, beverages, textiles, and other products. Irrigation is becoming more crucial every year in meeting needed increases in food production. By disrupting rainfall and temperature patterns in the world's major agricultural zones, human-induced climate change is expected to increase irrigation needs globally.[25] In rural areas of the global South where population densities are lower than in cities but where large quantities of water are reserved for irrigation and watering animals, access to drinking water is often the most tenuous. In the state of Punjab, India's agricultural powerhouse, three-fourths of households obtain water from a hand pump, and fewer than half of them manage to get even a scant eleven gallons of publicly supplied water per day per person. Even worse, a majority are finding water supplies diminishing with each passing year. A large share of Punjab's groundwater resources have been declared "overexploited" or in "critical" condition, largely because of overpumping for irrigation.[26] In rural areas and often even in cities, people—which almost always means women—have to haul heavy loads of water over long distances daily. In obtaining a resource, such as water, that's needed in continuous supply, time and distance are at least as important as cost. According to WHO, if people face a round-trip of more than thirty minutes or have to make more than one trip a day to collect water, they "progressively collect less water, and eventually fail to meet their families' minimum daily drinking-water needs."[27]

According to the United Nations, two billion people currently live with "economic water scarcity," defined as a situation in which "human, institutional and financial capital limit access to water, even though water in nature is available locally to meet human needs."[28] When there is not enough usable, affordable water available locally to satisfy everyone's needs and wants, it has to be rationed in some way. Thus, the city of Mumbai's water managers receive a specified portion of the region's total water supply and decide how many minutes or hours per day of water flow will go to each of its neighborhoods; whenever a particular slum gets its twenty minutes' worth of water flow, its own residents then must decide how to ration it among themselves. However small the shares, that water is at least free or provided for only a nominal fee. In less fortunate unauthorized slums with no daily water ration, families must buy water by the liter, paying five to ten times more for water than middle-class or wealthy families do.[29] In the Mumbai metropolitan area, 1.2 million people live under such conditions. The *Times of India* reported that women and children from these slums "have the option of walking three to five kilometers a day or going to the neighborhood shop to purchase" water from bootleggers by the one-liter plastic pouch at extortionate prices. A city official interviewed by the *Times* was unperturbed by the situation: "We cannot supply water to the slums that have come up after 1995. . . . The [municipality's] hands are tied, and people have to rely on informal means and ways to obtain water."[30] In the city's wealthier neighborhoods, which receive up to ten hours of water supply each day, there are few big domestic guzzlers.[31] Thirty percent of Mumbai homes exceed the government's goal of twenty-six gallons per person daily, but only 7 percent get more than thirty-seven gallons. In comparison, per-capita domestic consumption of publicly supplied water in the United States is about one hundred gallons daily.[32] Mumbai's municipal government has made plans to more than double its water supply by 2021. That may bring some relief to people in Kadam Chawl, who get only three to seven gallons of water per person, but it also will require construction of new dams that will submerge tens of thousands more acres and dozens of villages east of the city, driving those villagers off their land. Many will end up in Mumbai, filling their *hundis* each day with water piped from those new reservoirs.[33]

The Millennium Development Goals (MDG) announced by the UN in 2000 declared that by 2015 the share of the world's households with inadequate access to safe water should be cut in half.[34] Meeting that goal, along with the related MDG goal of reducing by half the proportion of people without proper sanitary facilities, can come only at a price that the rich nations have so far shown little willingness to pay. As one legal expert, Barton Thompson Jr., put it, "There has been far more discussion of why water should be a human right than action taken to actually supply the poorer residents of developing nations with an adequate and clean supply of water."[35] Estimates of the global cost of meeting the MDG goals range from $6.7 billion to $75 billion per year. But money invested by wealthy nations and multilateral agencies approaches only $6 billion per year—less than the annual sales of bottled drinking water in the United States alone.[36]

The fact that water is becoming more scarce in so many places is intensifying the debate over how to ration it and whether to treat it as a common resource or a private good. And that debate is being made much more complex by a principle that few political or business leaders would dispute but even fewer, it seems, are prepared to guarantee: the right to water. In the summer of 2010, the UN General Assembly finally got around to recognizing humanity's right to water, a principle that has been described this way:

According to the UN Committee on Economic, Social, and Cultural Rights, an individual's right to water includes "sufficient, safe, acceptable, physically accessible and affordable water for personal and domestic issues." Fulfillment of the right to water requires water that is available, of sufficient quality, and accessible. Water availability is defined as having enough water for personal and domestic issues, including food preparation, sanitation, and washing clothes. Water quality is defined as being free from substances, including microorganisms, chemicals, and other hazards that threaten a person's health. Finally, water accessibility is defined as physical and economic access to water.[37]

The words "physical and economic access" acknowledge that water can be treated as either a public or a private good. But, say Manuel Couret Branco and Pedro Damião Henriques of Évora University in Portugal, the assumption of a right to water puts limits on the role the market can play in providing it:

> The fact that the UN declaration on the right to water states that people should have the means to access water signifies that it is acceptable for water to have a price and therefore to be submitted to economic principles. However, one should not infer that the market should automatically be qualified to promote the human right to water. Indeed, there are reasons to believe that the market alone, and mainstream economics along with it, is not theoretically equipped to meet this challenge without abdicating an important set of constitutive principles.

Markets, say Branco and Henriques, simply have no language "to assert that universal coverage is better than any other structure of water distribution." The fact that some people may not be able to buy water at the price set by supply and demand (the latter being determined exclusively by those who can afford water) "is of almost no concern" to the market. While this is no major problem for, say, the price rationing of Perrier-Jouet champagne, water is a different matter; as Branco and

Henriques put it, "When private goods are taken as rights, as with tap water, exclusion becomes intolerable."[38]

The European Declaration for a New Water Culture, signed in Madrid in 2005 by more than one hundred European experts, proposes dividing water supplies into three categories in order of priority: "water for life," not just for drinking but for sustaining healthy ecosystems; "water for general interest purposes," such as preserving public health, social cohesion, and equity; and "water for economic growth." If the first two categories are encompassed by what we regard as the "right to water," then it is clear, according to the declaration, that they should be protected from markets. The declaration asserts that the last category of water, that used for economic growth, is different and "must be managed under principles of economic rationality in order to optimize economic efficiency." However, if that water is used in ways that could threaten to disrupt future water supplies as well as to degrade or even destroy ecosystems, then there will also be a need for public mechanisms to limit and otherwise control the use of water for economic growth.[39]

WHEN THE METER'S RUNNING

Allocating water supplies has been a high priority for municipal authorities throughout history. Water delivered by aqueduct systems to ancient Roman cities, for instance, often passed through a structure known as a *castellum divisorium*, which split the incoming supply in order to deliver portions to different destinations in the city. Archeologists long assumed that the purpose was to direct water toward various uses simultaneously—for example, dividing the supply among private homes, public monuments, and streetside water fountains. But when Pompeii was excavated from the ashes of Mount Vesuvius, its *castellum* befuddled scholars. They initially thought it was designed to divide the water supply into three streams, but that didn't make sense: the capacity of its three outlets added together was much greater than that of the aqueduct serving them. The explanation became apparent only when it was realized that the *castellum*'s purpose was to rotate the supply, providing most or all of the incoming water to only one-third of the city during any given part of the day.[40]

Today, such rotation of water services is the most common method of rationing in cities with a shortage of water. A survey of twenty-two cities and countries in Asia, Africa, and Latin America found that water services were provided for various portions of the day rather than continuously: from less than four hours in Karachi, Pakistan, to four hours in Delhi and Chennai, India; six hours in Haiti, Honduras, and Kathmandu; three to ten hours in Dar es Salaam, Tanzania; and seventeen hours in Manila. Service in Amman, Jordan—a chronically water-stressed desert environment—was highly irregular, averaging two to nine hours per day.[41]

Rationing water in time rather than quantity is a blunt instrument, providing anything from a deficient to an ample supply to each home or business. The more generous the ration, the lower the incentive to conserve. Higher-income areas often receive more hours per day of service, and more affluent residents also have the economic means to install and fill storage tanks that would allow relief from rationing and subvert the goal of reducing consumption. Few among the poor enjoy such a buffer.[42]

To the west of Jordan, in Palestine's West Bank, there are ample reserves of renewable groundwater, potentially as much as 265 gallons per day per person; however, Israel's heavy extraction of water resources from underneath the West Bank has created an artificial scarcity that makes tight rationing necessary in Palestinian cities and villages. Vast numbers of Israeli wells near the border and separation wall with Palestine pull water from the lower, western portion of the large Western Aquifer that underlies the West Bank. Israel can effectively drain off as much water from the aquifer as desired due to several factors: these wells are numerous and are located at the "downhill" end of the aquifer; the separation wall cuts Palestinian farmers and town dwellers off from dozens of their own wells and cisterns; and Israel has effectively blocked the drilling of new Palestinian wells since capturing and occupying the West Bank in 1967. Israel's drawdown is frequently in excess of what the two nations agreed to in the 1994 Oslo Accords, often by 50 percent or more. What has been called a "reckless" rate of water pumping has hurt the ability of Palestinian wells to withdraw water and threatens to damage the West Bank aquifers permanently.[43]

While 90 percent of the rainfall that recharges the Western Aquifer falls within Palestine's borders, 94 percent of water from the aquifer is consumed by Israel. Eighty percent of water from all aquifers lying under the West Bank ends up in Israel. What Israelis end up using is enough water to supply all domestic demand plus enough to support a sprawling agricultural infrastructure fed by subsidized irrigation, with 22 percent of the harvest (including 33 percent of vegetables and 27 percent of flowers) grown for export. At about 1,400 cubic meters per person consumed annually for all purposes, Israel's per-capita water footprint is equal to that of Australia and Denmark and exceeds that of Japan.[44] But Palestinians living just on the other side of the separation wall have daily access to less than one-fourth the water for domestic use that Israelis have. The average West Bank resident manages to subsist on only thirteen gallons per day, and many get by on only six—near the minimum required simply for bare survival. In both the West Bank and Gaza, public water supplies run not only intermittently but often erratically.[45] Here's a typical scene from the West Bank, reported by the Voice of America:

> It is Wednesday at the home of the Mahmoud family in the village of Rafat, not far from Jerusalem. This is one of the few days of the week that water flows from the taps. Family members rush to take advantage of every precious drop before the afternoon, filling plastic jugs, oil drums, and pails with water for use by the 15 people who live in this home. Intifar Sabre Abu Hassan, one of the women of the family, says she knows the taps will run dry by the afternoon, and then stay dry for several days ahead. She hurries to knead the dough for the bread her family will eat all week. She says that on this day that they have water from the taps, her family bathes, does laundry, washes dishes, cooks, and flushes toilets.[46]

On the other side of Israel, in the Palestinian territory of Gaza, 90 to 95 percent of the tap water is undrinkable, and "trap wells" on the Israeli side of the border, which suck up water from the Coastal Aquifer before it reaches Gaza, are depleting the aquifer to a dangerous degree. Approximately ten thousand residents have no access to water taps anywhere near their homes, and many are coping by drilling unlicensed wells and employing costly small-scale desalinization. For those who do have access to municipal water, it is discontinuous—taps are dry more often than they run.[47]

The economically efficient alternative to the ordeal of rationing water in time is to install meters in every household and business and charge a price for each gallon that is equal to the marginal cost of providing it. Because each additional unit of water costs a little less to deliver than the previous one, a water utility that employs such "marginal-cost pricing" will charge its highest rate for the initial "block" of water consumed each month and successively lower rates for each additional block. Such pricing, also referred to as "decreasing block tariff" (DBT), was widely practiced at one time by cities in the United States and other nations where water supplies were plentiful. Development agencies such as the World Bank have recommended marginal-cost pricing to countries of the global South as well, believing that if water is valued accurately, it will be used most efficiently. And the method is attractive to water systems that are pledged to recover all of their costs through fees, because they are dependent on big water users for a large part of their revenue and don't want to risk encouraging those customers to cut back because of high prices. But with a decreasing block tariff, larger, usually wealthier users are charged less per volume of water consumed than are poor users.[48]

Household water meters, long employed in the global North, are becoming more common in the global South as well, and in all regions the regressive nature of flat-rate or DBT pricing has become a greater concern. If water consumption up to a certain number of gallons per day really is a human right, and if water consumed above that amount can be treated as a private good, then rationing water by price becomes more complicated. In areas with metered connections and a large population of residents living on low incomes, some utilities have begun charging fees on a progressive scale, based either on location (with upscale neighborhoods paying more); on household characteristics; or, most often, on quantity consumed. In South Africa, for example, there is a monthly Free Basic Water (FBW) allowance of about sixteen hundred gallons per month per metered connection, with fees charged for water consumed above that amount. For a family of five, that free water ration is still shy of the global daily per-capita standard of thirteen gallons per head. The South African plan is a form of increasing block tariff (IBT), which is becoming more popular in many localities. With IBT, there are two or more pricing blocks: each month, the initial block of water is supplied either free or at a highly subsidized price, and each successive block becomes more expensive. Ideally, fees in the upper blocks are high enough, and enough customers use that much water, that they generate surplus revenues, which can balance out the subsidy the utility provides on the lower blocks.[49]

An IBT is meant to be progressive with regard to income, because affluent households tend to use more water than poor ones. Sometimes, under an IBT, the intention is not only to have high users subsidize low users but also to discourage overconsumption. Those two goals can easily work at cross-purposes: the more successful the conservation effort, the less money is generated to fund the subsidy that makes such conservation possible. Supporting the subsidy appears to be the higher priority in most cases, and often the rates do not seem to escalate steeply enough to discourage the affluent from overconsuming. For example, in 2003, charges in Jerusalem's three-block system went from US$1.20 to $1.50 and then to $1.90. Given what economists know about spending behavior for water, that reduces consumption in the top block by only about 10 percent.[50] But the higher rates of an IBT sometimes can sting big water users, and when that happens, they can expect little sympathy from the community. When, for instance, the IBT used by the water system in San Antonio, Texas, was attacked by a prominent resident who "passionately represented homeowners with big yards who pay higher rates for keeping a green lawn than those with more modest yards," he got nowhere, even after warning officials that the city's heavy water users included some politically "powerful executives."[51]

Some have suggested that "uniform price with rebate" (UPR) billing be substituted for IBT. Under UPR, the utility would charge a flat per-gallon rate that would cover or exceed the cost of providing the water; then it would provide a rebate to all customers, fully paying for each customer's initial monthly block of water—a block deemed just sufficient to cover all basic needs. That way, water would be 100 percent subsidized for low consumers, while the price of water beyond the initial block could be set high enough to strongly discourage over-consumption.[52] This, of course, would not help families living in the global South who have no individual water connection. The long-term solution is to extend home service to them, but an interim solution might be for the utility to provide every family, water customers or not, with a monthly rebate that would help poor families obtain water from other sources.

SIPHONING PROFITS

Water can be plentiful and still out of reach for many people.[53] Because scarcity begets high prices, many government officials and their friends in business around the world have seen local water scarcity as a potential profit generator. But water utilities serving low-income areas have learned through long, hard experience that it is difficult to guarantee water as a right and still charge enough to cover all the costs of providing it. To expect to extract a profit on top of that may be to expect too much.

Some negotiators working on the UN's right-to-water resolution urged that it refer only to "access to water" (translation: you can have it if you can afford it) instead of declaring an absolute right to water.[54] That effort at diplomatic dilution failed. Having theoretical access to water is one thing; having the source of that water reasonably close to home at an affordable cost is another. Yet city after city and country after country, at the urging of international lending agencies, has moved its water system toward privatization and "full cost recovery." Here was the situation as of 2009, summarized by Craig Anthony Arnold:

> Large multinational water corporations have capital to invest in water systems worldwide in exchange for ownership or control of these systems and the (estimated) substantial profits from these water ventures. These corporations have specialized in

water development, management, and distribution, seeing a globally unmet need that will be increasingly profitable, and they aggressively seek out investment and ownership opportunities in water service systems worldwide. Vivendi (or Veolia Environment) operates in over 100 countries and provides water services to 110 million people; Suez operates in 130 countries and provides water services to 115 million people; and RWE AG provides water services to over 70 million people. The combined revenue potential of these three dominant multinational water corporations is close to $3 trillion.[55]

UNESCO argues in favor of privatization by focusing on efficiency:

Specifically, through efficiency gains, improved management, and better access to finance than public utilities, private companies improve performance (including cost recovery rates) and increase access through extending networks and providing new connections to previously "unserved" customers. This benefits the poor, particularly in urban areas, who are often served by a variety of informal arrangements, such as water vendors, and typically pay much higher prices per unit volume for poorer-quality water than wealthier consumers.[56]

Opponents of privatization typically make the point that it is not only futile but also ethically unacceptable for any private company to attempt to extract profits by selling an essential resource for which most people can afford to pay only very little, because, as Damon Barrett of Harm Reduction International and Vinodh Jaichand of the Irish Center for Human Rights explain,

in relation to the provision of services such as water, which are the bases of fundamental human rights, the legal duty of corporations to generate profits for their shareholders is incompatible with a rights-based approach to the provision of such services. Indeed, the only legal duty of a corporation is to make a profit for its shareholders. The human rights of those in receipt of the vital services provided by corporations, such as the right to water, are not only secondary, but often not even a consideration.[57]

While water customers may at times find that it's difficult to "fight city hall" over poor service, they have even less power when they are forced to deal with a multinational corporation. And there is often plenty to complain about. In Dar es Salaam, Tanzania, City Water, a private water contractor that is a subsidiary of the British multinational BiWater, was caught cutting off service to entire communities in an effort to force payments from some individual households. In Jakarta, Indonesia, Thames Water (the third-largest water company in the world when it signed a contract in 1998 to handle half of the city's supply) forced the closure of private wells, forced poor residents to purchase water, and failed to supply safe water, with the result that people had to boil the water they bought. In the six years following the privatization in 1998 of Jakarta's water supply, only 25 percent of new connections were for public hydrants or "poor" or "very poor" households—the sectors that were assigned to pay the lowest water rates. In Manila, where two multinational corporations shared the water concession from 1997 to 2003, one of them raised customers' water rates by 400 percent and the other by 700, making it impossible for many to use tap water at all. In Nelspruit, South Africa, another BiWater subsidiary raised prices 300 percent over the level that prevailed under the previous public utility, padded the water bills it sent out, and metered individual taps; the meters would start running when the tap was opened, but there would often be a long wait (up to ninety minutes) before any actual water would flow. Meanwhile, the meter would be running the whole time.[58]

Despite the many pitfalls of privatization, companies sometimes do boost the flow of water to poorer neighborhoods. A study comparing four cities in Bolivia—La Paz and El Alto, whose water systems went through several years of private management, and Santa Cruz and Cochabamba, which retained public systems—found that the privatized systems performed better in extending service to previously unserved homes, and that residents of neighborhoods that had had private systems for several years were spending a smaller portion of their income on water.[59] But high connection fees were a sore point, and affordability for the poor deteriorated in La Paz; for El Alto's poorest residents, the cost of water rose three times as fast as their incomes when the supply was privatized. The impressive expansion of metered service in El Alto may simply have been a result of the company's charging for water that residents had previously obtained for free and thus had not been recorded. Removal of traditional, free outdoor standpipes caused some of the strongest opposition, as Degol Hailu, Rafael Osorio, and Raquel Tsukada of the International Policy Centre for Inclusive Growth reported:

> The concession contract required that communal standpipes were eliminated, and dwellings were provided with in-house connections. The underlying reason was helping the government to achieve the political target of providing universal in-house water access, as stated in a national water plan. Standpipes, however, were inexpensive alternatives to in-house connection for some households, especially to those who were unable to afford the high initial connection costs to the utility network. This was a potential source of public discontentment from the low-income households, who would have to search for alternative sources, usually more expensive.[60]

For this and other reasons such as low water pressure and pollution problems, both La Paz and El Alto eventually ditched their contractors and went back to public water provision. (Cochabamba was included in the study as a nonprivatized city, although in 1999 the city government, under pressure from the World Bank, had contracted with a consortium headed by the Bechtel Corporation to operate the city water system. Water prices vaulted by as much as 400 percent, and Cochabamba emerged as the most widely recognized symbol of the worldwide fight against water privatization. Tens of thousands of residents took to the streets and, backed by water activists from across Bolivia and the world, ran Bechtel out of town in 2000.)[61]

In South Africa, the right to water is enshrined in the national constitution and in several laws. Most water services remain publicly owned, but water is nevertheless handled according to a "corporate model" in which, writes Jackie Dugard of the Socio-Economic Rights Institute South Africa in Johannesburg, "water services are run along largely commercial lines, albeit with some obligatory concessions to social equity. . . . Indeed, across South Africa and gaining ground particularly in bigger metropolitan areas, water has become more of an economic product and less of a public health–related service." One feature of this approach was the increasing installation of "prepayment meters" in low-income neighborhoods. While more affluent residents of Johannesburg continue to enjoy water through the public-utility model, paying the bill at the end of the month for whatever quantity they use (after receiving their FBW supply of sixteen hundred gallons), customers in impoverished areas see their water taps go dry as soon as the FBW is exhausted if they haven't fed their prepayment meters. As a result, many people like Ms. Makoatsane of the Phiri section of Soweto township lose access to water for days or weeks at a time. On that, Jackie Dugard wrote:

> Like most Phiri residents, Makoatsane is unemployed and desperately poor. She lives on a 150-square-meter property with nine other people, some in her main house and others in backyard shacks. Because the city's Free Basic Water supply is allocated per stand and only to property-owning account-holders, Makoatsane must share the one allocation with all nine people. With so many people sharing the water, the monthly 6,000 liter—6 kiloliters (6kl)—free allocation never lasts to the end of the month even though household members now flush the toilet only once a day and bathe only every second day. Since the introduction of the prepayment meters, once the FBW allocation is exhausted (usually around the twelfth day of the month), the prepayment water meter automatically disconnects the water supply until further water credit is purchased. In households like Makoatsane's, where there is rarely enough money to purchase additional water to ensure an adequate

supply, the disconnection typically lasts until the next month, when the new monthly FBW allocation is dispensed.[62]

Before prepayment meters were installed, Soweto had a non-metered water supply; residents were charged a flat amount based on their projected monthly consumption. Many could not afford the flat fee and went into water debt, but at least their taps were never disconnected for lack of payment. Prepayment meters were the city's attempt to "rationalize" the system by recovering the costs of supplying that water or, failing that, by simply denying residents water. Prepayment meters are notorious around the world. They have been blamed for increased incidence of dysentery in Birmingham, UK, in the 1990s and a 2000–2002 cholera outbreak in the South African province of KwaZulu Natal in which there were 113,966 illnesses and 259 deaths. (In the previous twenty years there had been just 78 cholera deaths in that part of the province.)[63] But for gut-wrenching immediacy, few stories illustrate the consequences of prepayment meters as well as that of Vusimuzi Paki and his family, as told by Patrick Bond and Jackie Dugard:

> At around two o'clock in the morning on 27 March 2005, Phiri resident Vusimuzi Paki awoke to the shouts of a tenant who was trying to put out a fire in one of the other backyard shacks on Paki's property. Assisted by neighbors, the first crucial minutes were spent trying to extinguish the fire using the pre-paid water meter supply that the Johannesburg Water company had recently installed to control the residents' water supply. However, the water pressure was insufficient to make much impact on the fire and, after a while, the pre-paid meter water supply automatically disconnected due to insufficient water credit. Residents were then forced to scoop up ditch water with buckets in a desperate attempt to put out the fire. More minutes passed. One neighbour tried to telephone the police at Moroka police station but no-one answered the phone. After battling for an hour, residents finally put out the fire, but not before the

shack had burnt to the ground. It was only after Paki's tenant returned home from her night shift that everyone discovered to their horror that her two small children had been sleeping in the shack. They both died in the fire.[64]

WHERE SHARES OF WATER ARE FAIR

Those advocating democratic management of water supplies in both the South and the North often point to the city of Porto Alegre in Brazil, where 99.5 percent of the population receives high-quality municipal water, and 84 percent of residents are served by the sewage system. Both percentages are the highest of any city in the country, while the fees charged are among the lowest.[65] The agency responsible, Departamento Municipal de Agua e Esgoto (DMAE), is a public entity but independent of the city government in its funding and decision making. It fully funds its water and sewage operations through fee collection.

In achieving full water coverage at a low cost, DMAE doesn't employ any marvelous new techniques or secret formulas. The department has a Technical Management Council that functions as a "collective, horizontal leadership," along with a citizens' group called the Deliberative Council, "where different interest groups with some link with water and sanitation can find representation and a more formal influence in decision-making." The result is what has been called a "non-state public sphere." The department's funds are managed through a "participatory budgeting process." The fee for water provision is an IBT, with more than 80 percent of households within the lowest block and consuming less than 176 gallons per day per household. However, people living in poverty or in very small spaces are charged the "social tariff" for water, under which they can receive eighty-eight gallons per day for the price of thirty-five.[66]

Craig Anthony Arnold has proposed a broader "reconceptualization of water" as "public stewardship," based on three principles: that water and water services should be under public ownership and control; that any private property rights should recognize that water is "not merely an economic commodity protected by abstract legal rights, but is also an element of nature with physical, chemical, biological, and ecological characteristics, and an element of society with social, cultural, political, religious, and ethical characteristics"; and that governments should have "fiduciary responsibilities for the ownership, management, conservation, and supply of water as a trustee for the public."[67]

In other words, humanity has no choice but to decide collectively how to protect water and how to guarantee everyone a fair share of it. And dealing with water is just not that complicated. As Maude Barlow argues, it's not a lack of technical knowledge or money that prevents us from undoing the damage. Water justice is something well within our capacity, given sufficient political will. Indeed, if we can't manage to conserve and use water fairly, there is little chance that we will manage to do so with energy, food, or other resources.

Morning delivery of *baladi* bread in downtown Cairo, 2012.

5

OUR MONTHLY BREAD

The people of Egypt import half of the food they eat. Yet the country devotes increasing acreages of cropland to production of organic foods for export to Europe. Almost 60 percent of Egyptian-grown organic food leaves the country on northbound ships or planes. With food exports growing at the rate of 30 percent per year, *Al-Masry Al-Youm* reports that "it is easy to find organic Egyptian herbs and vegetables in Italian and German supermarkets for high prices, while it is difficult to find them in Egypt," where families—42 percent of whom live below the international poverty line—can't afford to bid against Europeans for food produced in their own country and struggle to meet their monthly needs for conventionally produced, no-frills bread, fava beans, and rice.[1] Were those and other staple foods available only at market prices, Egypt would be a very hungry nation today. Instead, basic foods are subsidized and rationed.

Governments around the world, including Egypt's, learned long ago about the dangers of exposing their citizens' daily food needs to the whims of global markets. Recognizing the existence of a right to food—and anticipating the political and social upheaval that can happen if that right is not fulfilled—many countries routinely buy and store staple grains and other foods and then ration consumers' access to those stores at subsidized prices. Like water- and energy-rationing policies, existing public food-distribution systems are designed to provide fair, affordable access to a limited pool of resources. As we will see, no food-ration program so far has been entirely successful; nevertheless, a ration card or food stamp booklet may be all that stands between a family and a week (or even a lifetime) of hunger. And with food rationing, unlike carbon rationing, we can be guided by experience. Public provision of subsidized food rations has been pursued in countries as diverse as Argentina, Bangladesh, Brazil, Chile, China, Colombia, Cuba, Egypt, India, Iran, Iraq, Israel, Mexico, Morocco, Pakistan, the Philippines, the Soviet Union, Sri Lanka, Sudan, Thailand, Venezuela, and Zambia.[2] In those and other nations, we can find examples ranging from excellent to terrible, sometimes within the same country.

The frequent failure of markets acting alone to direct food to where it is most needed can be seen not only in hungry nations but in well-fed ones as well. In the United States, the share of households that suffer from food insecurity has climbed to almost one in six, according to the Department of Agriculture, and hard times had pushed demand at charitable food banks to record levels by 2011.[3] In countries rich and poor, the publicly funded monthly food ration has two faces: first, staving off widespread hunger and the societal disruption that could well arise in its absence; and second, making it possible for the private sector to pay below-subsistence wages. In the latter role, the ration can provide a subsidy to business, allow society to tolerate high unemployment and underemployment, or help undemocratic governments keep a lid on political unrest.[4]

Many food-ration plans take the form of a public distribution system (PDS) that provides specific food items to consumers on a regular, usually monthly, basis. In the typical PDS, consumer food rations are situated at the downstream end of a network that buys up and stockpiles grain at guaranteed prices, imposes price controls and provides subsidies, and rations the stocks it provides to retailers. Today's typical PDS parallels World War II–era food systems in that ration entitlements are adjusted according to the available supply. But most contemporary PDSs differ from wartime floor-and-ceiling rationing in that they provide only for a floor, a minimum supply. The supply of, say, subsidized wheat controlled by the government constitutes only a portion (if sometimes a large portion) of total consumption; there are usually, but not always, other supplies legally available on the open market outside the system as well, for those who can afford them.

The typical PDS is created not for dealing with absolute limits on the food supply (although, as we will see, there are exceptions) but to ward off the prohibitively high food prices that would prevail in their absence. In hungry economies, such as during war, price controls without some form of quantity controls generally don't work. Jean Drèze and Amartya Sen have explained this problem:

> One natural thought in dealing with high prices of provisions is that of imposing direct control on food prices. This has obvious attractions. There are, however, serious difficulties in making good use of this strategy in a largely market-based economy without rationing. For one thing, effective enforcement is very hard. . . . There is the further problem that even if prices are successfully kept low through control, this in itself does not guarantee that the available food will be equitably distributed. If prices are lowered below the level at which total demand is met by supply, the people failing to make a purchase might quite possibly be among those who were among the most vulnerable and deprived in the first place. An additional requirement will then be that of providing a minimal amount of food for all, or at least for the more deprived, through some form of direct rationing.[5]

When governments step in between farmer and consumer to balance things out, there's no free lunch: either the farmer, the government, or the consumer must pay to fill the gap between the higher price a farmer requires to stay solvent and the lower price the low-income food consumer can afford to pay. To help fill that gap and conserve both ends of the food chain, governments keep large buffer stocks of basic grains. India, for example, normally maintains national stocks of between 60 and 70 million metric tons. To do that, the government buys up about one-third of the nation's crop each year—enough to fill a five-thousand-mile-long train of hopper cars stretching from Delhi to Casablanca.[6]

The ascendance of neoliberal economics in the 1980s prompted struggles over curtailment or elimination of many nations' food systems, and those struggles continue. But widespread food insecurity is a risk few governments are willing to run, so few PDSs have been completely eliminated. The usual compromise has been to "target" food assistance to households in greatest need. Attempts to replace PDSs with cash payments have typically failed; for many, apparently, money is not an adequate substitute for an ensured ration of food that can be touched, smelled, and tasted.

This is not the place for a full survey of the world's food-ration systems. But there are a few countries from which much can be learned. India and Egypt have operated PDSs of staggering sizes for decades, ones that continue to evolve, while Iraq and Cuba have run comprehensive rationing systems to deal with absolute scarcity.

IS THE "FAIR-PRICE SHOP" FAIR?

The ability of the poor to have access to public services, and the political support that the provision of these services can command, may depend crucially on the participation of a large part of the population in the benefits of public provisioning. . . . [T]here is so much more to a sound food policy than just fiddling with the food prices.

—Jean Drèze and Amartya Sen[7]

Most of the public food-distribution systems operating today across South Asia and North Africa evolved from rationing systems initially put in place to deal with World War II–era shortages. The diversion of resources to military consumption and the wartime inflationary pressures that prompted rationing in the United States and the United Kingdom also affected many nations and colonies that were not among the principal combatants. War-related food rationing was imposed in India by British colonial authorities in 1939, the same time it began in Britain. But food distribution was badly mishandled in northeastern India, where famine killed millions in the state of Bengal in 1943.[8] PDSs established after independence in India and Pakistan, as well as in many other countries, were designed to avoid the mistakes made in the Bengal famine and the long succession of tragic famines that had preceded it on the subcontinent.[9]

In the years following India's independence, with the prospect of starvation never far from the public mind, the ration system often set a ceiling on food consumption as well as providing a floor. Almost all families had to use their ration cards to buy their staple foods, and there were few sources of such foods other than the so-called fair-price shop where public rations were sold. As late as the mid-1960s, for instance, families planning a marriage or other large celebration would need to apply for a license for feeding a large group of people. Once India dramatically expanded its grain production in the 1970s and 1980s so that there would be enough food to go around, the better-quality grains flowed into the open market instead of the licensed fair-price shop. In the 1970s, state and regional food networks expanded and merged into a national PDS under which every household with a fixed address could obtain a ration card that provided access to specified quantities of food and sometimes other goods. For most of its existence, India's PDS promised food rations to everyone in the country for a fixed low cost. But in 1997, with the liberalization of the Indian economy, the PDS was narrowed to target primarily the low end of the income scale. Two types of ration cards were created, one for "above poverty line" (APL) and one for "below poverty line" (BPL) households. BPL cardholders could buy specified quantities of grains and a few other products at an approximate 50 percent subsidy, while purchases with APL cards were not subsidized. In 2006, there were almost half a million fair-price shops in India, and 222 million families held ration cards. Thirty-two million metric tons of rice and wheat and five million tons of other foods were being distributed annually under the program.[10]

In an attempt to streamline the PDS and improve delivery, the National Food Security Act, presented to Parliament in 2011, further complicated the question of who benefits and who doesn't. The bill as first proposed provided that approximately 46 percent of the rural and 8 percent of the urban population—all below the poverty line—would be assured seven kilograms per month of grain per family member at very low prices: three rupees[11] per kilogram for rice, two rupees for wheat, and just one rupee for sorghum and millet. Another 29 percent of rural and 22 percent of urban dwellers would be eligible for three kilograms of grain per month at half the price the government pays farmers for the grain. That would mean an increase in monthly rations received by many, but not all, low-income Indians. As debate over the bill's specific provisions dragged on through 2012, numerous adjustments were proposed, and the Food Ministry outlined a "Plan B" that would drop the two-tier price and quantity structure, allocating a flat five kilograms per person per month to two-thirds of each state's population. Mandating that exact degree of coverage would have resulted in the exclusion of many millions of low-income people, particularly in poorer states.[12]

Most Indians requiring food support live in rural areas, and under the Food Security Act the PDS would begin to focus its efforts more and more on villages like Dorli, a tiny, poverty-plagued spot near the geographical center of India in the state of Maharashtra. On the eastern fringe of Dorli, next to the community well, stands the fair-price shop, a modest ten-by-ten-foot concrete building with a single, always-shuttered window. Every Tuesday, the owner opens the shop's door and offers public rations of wheat, rice, and sugar. Tuesday is market day, and it's also payday for the landless laborers who make up most of the shop's clientele. Although they are usually paid by the week, ration customers are required to buy their entire month's allotment of each commodity all at once. Many often do not have enough cash on hand to buy the whole month's ration; they may have to subsist on rations for perhaps two weeks and then manage for the next two weeks with less food—whatever they can afford from the market. Locals complain that the Dorli shop owner at one point started urging them to buy *three* months' supply at once, but they had just laughed at the idea.

Many prominent Indian leaders who opposed the Food Security Act would prefer to eliminate the PDS altogether, as a way of furthering market "reforms" that began in the early 1990s. But those who would integrate India's food system more fully into the global marketplace appear to be forgetting that it was increased exposure to the global market that helped create greater need for PDS goods in the first place. Jaideep Hardikar covers a swath of central India for the Kolkata-based *Telegraph* newspaper. His beat takes in, by his estimate, a population of one hundred million people. Much of his work is in a region of Maharashtra known as Vidharba, where Dorli is located. Over the past fifteen years, the agriculture of western Vidharba has been converted from diverse cropping to a near-monoculture of cotton that is shipped out of the region to be spun and woven elsewhere. The most widely publicized outcome of this agricultural shift has been an epidemic of more than a quarter million suicides by farmers, most of whom had made the switch to cotton or other cash crops and, caught between always-rising costs of seeds, fertilizers, and pesticides on the one hand and unstable cotton prices on the other, had sunk into deep debt. The transformation of the landscape has taken a heavy toll on village families' nutrition as well. Hardikar says, "This area once produced a wide variety of grains, vegetables, and dairy. It was prosperous and self-sufficient. People hardly ever needed to buy food. Now they are dependent on the ration shop, where they get only wheat, rice, and sugar. People can afford also to buy some edible seeds of the bean/pea family, onion, maybe eggplant and potatoes in the market, but not much more. And they no longer produce milk and eggs. Now 90 percent of women here are anemic." [13]

In the town of Wardha, in the heart of India's cotton belt, Hardikar introduced me to Vijay Jawandhia, a longtime farmer and leader of a Vidharba farmers' rights organization. Jawandhia recalled, "Back in the early seventies in my village, it was still largely a barter economy. Half of the economy consisted of transactions carried out with food grains, not cash. You'd pay the carpenter, the laundry man, even the barber in sorghum grain. But starting in the eighties, the price of sorghum and other staples was kept low, while cotton was selling for a high price, so eventually everyone switched over. Where we once had 40 percent of the rainfed soil planted in sorghum, it's now less than 1 percent." You can't eat cotton, and Jawandhia says that that fact served business interests well: "The purpose of providing cheap grain rations to keep people fed is to allow industry to keep wages low. It's a subsidy to industry." [14]

Another village, Diwa, lies at the other end of Maharashtra, not far from the metropolis of Mumbai. As of early 2012, customers at Diwa's one fair-price shop could buy up to five kilograms of rice and five of wheat at the subsidized price of nine rupees per kilogram. (The sugar that the shop is supposed to sell as well is never available except during Diwali festival time.) Many villagers with lower incomes cannot afford to buy their whole month's ration, so the shop owner usually has stock left over that he can sell to better-off customers "in the black" for sixteen rupees. Similar dual-price sales in the fair-price shop are common within the city of Mumbai as well. But in and around Mumbai, as in most places, it is rationed kerosene for cooking that is in greatest demand: two liters can be bought on the ration for thirty rupees, whereas the market price is eighty. When kerosene is in stock, word gets around Diwa fast and endless queues form. A longtime customer named Vijaya says that once her mother stood in line at the Diwa shop from noon until four o'clock without reaching the head of the queue; at that point, Vijaya took over her spot and waited another four hours before finally getting the fuel.[15]

Vijaya now lives in Mumbai, working as a housecleaner, but she still travels back to Diwa when she wants to buy rations. Such food-commuting is common in all big cities, where getting a ration card that is accepted at the neighborhood fair-price shop can be difficult. Village families arriving in a city and renting their room or flat must provide an affidavit from their landlord confirming their place of residence in order to get a ration card, and even then they may find it necessary to pay a bribe. In India, "people are always very keen to have a ration card," says Dr. M.S. Kamath, CEO and secretary of the Consumer Guidance Society of India (CGSI), India's first consumer-rights organization, founded in 1966. Among other services, CGSI represents low-income consumers who deal with fair-price shops and the agencies that operate the PDS. Kamath notes, "I have a ration card myself, which I use as identification. The ration card is universally recognized as valid proof of residence," required in interactions with government offices, phone and Internet service providers, and so on. While people who move from one locality to another are supposed to be able to turn in their ration card and immediately receive a new one showing their new address, getting a replacement card sometimes can take months or years, thanks to bureaucratic inertia. Those who do not have a card already must be able to show they have lived in one place for five or more years before they can receive one. CGSI deals with many complaints from people unable to obtain cards, and, says Kamath, "we have to do a lot of work to sort out the genuine applicants from the charlatans."

Kamath, a physician, runs a clinic on a quiet side street in Mumbai's Mahim district but spends a large share of his time on his CGSI duties. Viewed from the consumers' end, he contends, the system has "widened the divide between the haves and have-nots." The divide is more in the quality than the quantity of food. The government buys, at a fixed price, every kilogram of grain that Indian farmers offer to sell to it, but before hauling their harvest to the government market, farmers sell as much of their higher-quality grain as possible on the private market, where they can get a better price. The government gets what's left, and PDS customers who cannot afford to buy most or all of their food from private markets often get stuck with inferior rice and wheat. Likewise, in some areas the vegetable oil is usually low-quality palm oil, which, customers say, they would rather use in ceremonial lamps than in their food. Offering low-quality foods saves the government some money, but it's also a means of informal targeting; it discourages middle-class families, who choose to buy better food on the open market instead. In any case, today in most villages and cities, rations are available only to low-income cardholders.

A fair-price shop may be stocked to serve five thousand cardholders per month, but again, not everyone buys the full ration, because of either lack of cash, inability to make it to the shop when it's open, or other reasons. According to Kamath, because "shop owners do not get a good margin at all, their only way to make a decent profit may be to sell off the extra grain." And they usually sell the very worst quality grain through the legitimate ration system, setting aside their somewhat better stocks for illicit sale. Like many city dwellers with above-subsistence incomes, the nurses and assistants working in Kamath's clinic have ration cards but do not often buy ration goods because "they feel it's below their dignity," Kamath says. They can afford to spend a bit more money to buy low- to mid-grade varieties of rice or flour from the market, as well as a more diverse array of foods.[16]

A decade after the Indian government began targeting rations at the poor, Madhura Swaminathan, a food-policy expert, wrote, "Three key objectives of economic reforms—and these are stated explicitly in many policy documents, including the annual Economic Surveys—have been to reduce food subsidies, to leave distribution to the market and to undermine food policy intervention and subsidies to the 'poorest of the poor.'" It is unfortunate that those goals have been achieved, for millions of needy households have been driven out of the system. One problem is that the exclusive focus of targeting has been on keeping subsidized ration cards out of the hands of purportedly "non-needy" households. That eliminates "errors of inclusion," but in the process it causes far more "errors of exclusion" that deprive the poor of rations. To decide who is eligible to buy from the PDS, state governments must collect data household by household on income, assets, and numbers of family members. That is not easy in a country where employment and housing are often irregular, wages are paid in cash, and few low-income families have bank accounts. Sometimes incomes are estimated indirectly, based on whether families own motor scooters, refrigerators, or other goods. While erroneous exclusion may result from faulty data, it could arise also from a variety of other factors, including a too-low official poverty threshold, poor distribution of information on food programs, or the social stigma that adheres to recipients of targeted food aid. Targeting errors have become so serious that by 2010, one-half to three-fourths of all families living *below* the poverty line in the most badly poverty-stricken states had no subsidized ration card. And India is not alone. In virtually every country that has ended universal food rations in favor of targeting, the rate of errors of exclusion has increased.[17]

Between 1998 and 2005, the first eight years of the PDS targeting era, per-capita calorie consumption decreased for all income groups in India. For upper groups, the decline may have been connected to the lower physical demands of a more sedentary lifestyle; for poorer families, however, stagnant incomes and rising food prices were the more likely culprits. Caloric consumption declined more rapidly for rural families who had recently seen the birth of a child than it did for those who hadn't—indicating that adults were eating less to save food for children—and body weights of young children fell as well. Meanwhile, 36 percent of adult Indian women were underweight—one of the highest rates in the world.[18]

Targeting of the PDS has been especially devastating in the southern state of Kerala, which had long been home to one of the best-managed and most comprehensive PDSs in the country, the product of "a strong people's movement for food." The average rice purchase through the PDS fell sharply from a national high of 4.1 kilograms per person per month in 1999–2000 to only 1.7 kilograms per person in 2004–5, due to errors of exclusion. Ejection of so many customers from the system has cut deeply into the earnings of fair-price shops, and many have had to close down. A wider survey of domestic food-security programs in eight countries concluded that Kerala is not unusual: where a large proportion of the population is poor, targeting generally causes more problems than it solves and can cost more money than it saves. And the problems that targeting is ostensibly designed to address are really nonproblems; even in countries where the well-off receive more than their fair share of subsidized food, the poor end up being much more food-secure than they would have been without the ration system. With that in mind, the predominantly rice-consuming states of Tamil Nadu, Andhra Pradesh, and Chhattisgarh have bucked the targeting trend and maintained near-universal coverage of the PDS, augmenting the central government's grain stocks at state expense while computerizing the system and turning poorly run private fair-price shops into public enterprises. But an especially spiteful provision of the Food Security Act would prevent states from expanding coverage of their PDS to people who have been designated as ineligible under the central government's more tightly targeted criteria.[19]

Many poor families subsist on substandard grains even in the heart of highly productive farm country. The village of Nanded in eastern Maharashtra is a case in point. Dadaji Khobragade, seventy-eight, has been developing new varieties of rice in a plot of ground just outside Nanded for more than three decades. Seeds of his varieties spread quickly from farmer to farmer, and today they are grown on more than a hundred thousand acres across central India's rice belt. Khobragade is a member of India's Dalit community, which occupies the very bottom of the caste hierarchy, and he was landless for most of his life. In 2010, in recognition of his achievements, the government finally gave him title to the plot of one and a half acres where he'd been doing all of his breeding work. The upper floor of his small home is stuffed with hundred-pound bags of new seeds ready to go out to his local network of growers. Khobragade's varieties are known for their cooking quality and taste as much as for their dependable yield, but many of his neighbors aren't able to enjoy them because his rice is never available in the fair-price shops. One warm December afternoon in 2011, standing outside Nanded's local fair-price shop, Khobragade lamented the fact that "the rice they sell from here is the worst-quality rice, the cheapest that the government can buy on the market and ship here. The landless people here have to eat that stuff," he said, waving his hand disdainfully toward the shop, "while all around the village we are producing excellent rice that we ship off to other places." For ration recipients, Khobragade's award-winning rice varieties are never on the menu, even in the village where the varieties were born.[20]

Critics of the PDS complain most about the huge volumes of subsidized rice and wheat stocks that never make it into the hands of consumers. The share of PDS foodgrains that falls out of the system reached a peak of 53 percent in 2005; the government claims that losses have since declined.[21] Some of the losses result from spoilage, but even more grain is illegally diverted into the cash market, where it earns a hefty profit.[22] The Asian Development Bank estimated that in 2005, illegal diversion and inefficient operations together kept more than 70 percent of PDS grains from reaching the poor. Exploitation of the PDS can take even more sinister forms, too. Moneylenders, for example, have been known to hold clients' ration cards until their debt is repaid. The card serves as collateral and provides a form of interest payment. In 2010, Salim Khan, a moneylender in the central Indian town of Jhabua, told the *New York Times* that with clients' cards he can buy grain at fair-price shops for the equivalent of less than two cents per pound and resell it at a 500 percent profit. The earnings can add up. "Sometimes I'll have 50 cards," he told the *Times*. "Sometimes I'll have 100 or 150. It's not just me. Other lenders do this, too." Aside from legal ration cards, there are rumored to be more than 20 million counterfeit "ghost cards" in circulation. And there are complaints that licenses to operate fair-price shops are often used as a form of political patronage.[23]

In the northeastern state of West Bengal, where the PDS has crumbled badly, hungry customers reached the end of their patience in 2007. They looted fair-price shops, ran proprietors out of their homes, set fire to barrels of subsidized kerosene from the shops, and fought back against police riot squads, using "rods, swords and brickbats," according to an *India Together* article. At least one embattled shop owner committed suicide. In one cluster of five villages, residents took a more cool-headed approach, levying a 300,000 rupee "fine" on a fair-price shop owner who'd allegedly been cheating them for twelve years and then subjecting him to a "social boycott" when he refused to pay up.[24]

Bordering West Bengal is the state of Jharkhand, home of the coal-hauling cycle wallahs, and the site of some of India's largest stretches of remaining forest. Created in 2000, along with its neighbor Chhattisgarh, Jharkhand is home to more than 7 million indigenous people known collectively as Adivasis. Since the granting of statehood, vast deposits of coal, iron ore, and other minerals have made Jharkhand's hills and forests a high-priority target for both corporations and the Indian government. The 2005 Forest Rights Act decreed that any Adivasi family living on and cultivating a plot of land in any of the designated areas at the time of the law's passage would have ownership of that land. But, according to Gladson Dungdung of the Jharkhand Human Rights Movement, 125,000 people who have lived for decades in an area called the Saranda Hills in one of those forests have never been given title to their land, for the simple reason that the mining interests want it instead. In 2011, an investigative team led by Dungdung learned that government-backed security forces had looted and destroyed ration shops in two of the forest's villages. In addition, he told me, "the forces destroyed supplies for providing schoolchildren's midday meals, as well as grain stored in people's homes. The district government promised to compensate by distributing grain directly but they have not done so. The purpose of the attacks on the food supply was to compel people to flee the forest. They also destroyed families' ration cards, along with land deeds and ID cards, in an effort to wipe out evidence that the people were living on that spot." The looting helped ensure that the Adivasis' land could legally be taken over by mining companies.[25] Dungdung explained, "The Saranda forest is actually seven hundred small forests with farms in between. If we Adivasis had been left to support ourselves with our forests and farms, there would be no need for ration shops in the first place. Now if the Adivasis have to leave the forest, they'll definitely have to buy all of their food from the shops." Jharkhand has been among the states tagged as having had low PDS performance in the past. Therefore, in early 2011, the state government announced plans to open three hundred new shops to extend coverage in the lowest-income rural areas. But, says Dung-dung, there were no provisions in the plan to restore PDS service in the Saranda Hills villages that had been sacked.[26]

Kaushik Basu, the chief economic adviser to the Indian Ministry of Finance, recommended in a 2010 white paper that transformation of the nation's food system should go well beyond measures like expanding coverage, cracking down on pilferage, and improving the grain procurement and distribution process. He advised the government to convert food subsidies for the poor into a U.S.-style food-stamp program:

> the subsidy should be handed over directly to the poor house-hold instead of giving it to the PDS shop owner with the in-struction that he or she transfer it to the poor. This can be done by handing over food coupons to BPL households, which they can use as money to buy food from any store. The store owner can then take the coupon to any bank and change it back for cash. To allow for differences in preferences, we can allow indi-vidual households to buy any food items within a pre-specified range with these coupons. The subsidy does not have to be a fixed amount for wheat and another for rice but a lump-sum for a list of goods.[27]

Basu and others further recommended that coupons go to "the adult woman of the household," who, it is widely assumed in India, will spend the benefits more wisely than her husband, while becom-ing more "empowered." With the introduction of cash-based benefits, Basu expects the PDS to wither away, and "the state's involvement in the market will be much smaller and will pertain mainly to holding stocks for emergencies and unexpected food shortages." Other offi-cials have recommended that recipients be allowed to use coupons at any designated private grocery store and on any items it sells, not just on staple foods. Montek Singh Ahluwalia, deputy chair of the govern-ment's Planning Commission, believes that although some of the state governments would like the central government to go even further and simply transfer cash subsidies directly into poor families' bank accounts (even though most of the poor currently have no bank account), food coupons would be a safer bet. To prevent coupon counterfeiting, he has suggested the use of a smart-card system like the electronic benefits transfer (EBT) card now used in the United States, which transfers credits from a consumer's subsidy account to the shopkeeper's account. Other experts and commissions have advocated food coupons and smart cards, and the idea has received a warm welcome among free-market politicians. The Food Security Act would allow introduction of coupon- or card-based systems on a state-by-state basis.[28]

The debate over transforming the PDS is actually a debate over three interconnected decisions. The first decision—already made but still controversial—was to target the food subsidy/ration system at low-income groups. The second decision will be whether to replace delivery of physical food with a cash-based benefit. If the latter is chosen, then the third decision will be whether to provide the benefit in the form of food coupons or straight cash that can be spent on either food or non-food products. All three decisions have profound nutritional consequences, but switching to straight cash from food-earmarked benefits would be the most radical change. Economic theory says that in most cases, families will buy the same amount of food whether the benefit is in kind (food or food coupons) or in cash; however, on-the-ground research consistently shows that when families receive a benefit that provides only for food, they consume more food than they do if they receive a cash payment of the same size. In country after country, food aid has been shown to have a bigger impact on nutrition than cash aid, partly because, as the World Food Program's Ugo Gentilini writes, "cash provides people with a choice but it also transfers to them the risk of supply failures." In the United States, the effect is dramatic: an additional dollar's worth of food stamps (now the Supplemental Nutritional Assistance Program, or SNAP) increases nutrient consumption by two to ten times as much as does a dollar in cash.[29] The tendency of people to ignore economic theory and consume more food when benefits are in kind rather than in cash means that if a government wants to invest its money in food security, not just poverty alleviation—which would be in line with the high priority that the World Food Program assigns to "food for nutrition"[30]—it should restrict those benefits so that they provide only for food. Free-market advocates, on the other hand, say food aid should be approached strictly as an income enhancement, because encouraging nutritional improvement is paternalistic and inefficient, restraining recipients from spending as they wish.[31]

Any proposal for conversion to coupons, cards, or cash assumes that changes at the consumer level will work their way upstream to make the whole system less leaky and more efficient. At the headwaters of the Indian system is the Food Corporation of India (FCI), the public agency that purchases and stores tens of millions of tons of grain for the central government and then distributes portions to each state's PDS. The FCI field office for Jharkhand lies at the end of a long dirt driveway near the center of the state capital, Ranchi. In its heavily weathered concrete building are shelves laden with ancient ledger books alongside late-model computer equipment. It is here that the administrator, K.P. Sinha, oversees distribution of the wheat and rice that is funneled from nearby FCI warehouses to fair-price shops throughout the state. In late 2011, as the Food Security Act was becoming bogged down in contentious debate, Sinha said he felt confident that the act, once it became law, would "fix accountability" and tighten up the PDS nationally. But, he said, concerns about grain leakage have been overstated, at least in the case of Jharkand: "Every kilo of grain we acquire goes into the state's system and is distributed. It doesn't matter where the fair-price shops are. If they're in the hills, the sacks of rice may reach there in bullock carts or even on people's heads. But they will get there."

Sinha was not in favor of replacing the PDS with coupons or cash. His opinion is not surprising, because such a conversion would render his office superfluous. Yet he had seemingly objective reasons for opposing a straight cash-transfer system as well: "It's very, very risky. Suppose I receive enough money this month to buy fifty kilos of rice. I might buy just five or ten kilos and spend the rest of the subsidy on other things. And my wife and kids may not get enough to eat." He stressed that it's not necessarily a case of consumer "preference" either. Debt collectors, shady salespeople, and out-and-out cheats will all know which families have that extra cash coming in and, he expects, will set out to relieve them of it.[32]

The PDS remains more or less intact, but widespread enthusiasm for introducing digital technology has entangled the question of food with an equally thorny debate over a national identification card, known provisionally as a Unique Identification Document (UID) or Aadhaar (meaning "foundation" or "support" in Hindi) card. The card would contain standard information, including name, address, date of birth, and a photograph, but would also contain electronic records of iris scans and all ten fingerprints. An eyelash would also be collected from each person for archiving DNA.[33]

The card would be used for all interactions with the government, including the PDS. Officials have promoted it as a means by which all Indians can finally get access to the full benefits of citizenship. Rahul Gandhi, a member of Parliament and a grandson of Indira Gandhi, declared in 2011 that the UID "would give voting rights to migrants who otherwise stood without the basic right of democracy" and "give voice to every person." Critics say the card is yet another manifestation of the "myth of the technology fix" and does nothing to ensure concrete benefits; they worry that it could be used as an instrument of surveillance and repression.[34] When quizzed on this concern by a group of students in Bangalore in January 2011, Nandan Nilekani, chairperson of the central government's Unique Identification Authority, insisted that his agency saw the UID as "imperative for financial and social inclusion" and that "the Aadhaar number was only a point of authentication, and therefore there is no scope for misuse."[35]

With the rush to merge the PDS with proposals for national identification, market liberalization, "financial inclusion," public health and education, and women's empowerment, it's easy to forget the central purpose of any food-ration program: to ensure that no one goes hungry. Reetika Khera of the Indian Institute of Technology observed in a 2011 report, "The prevailing confusion on the performance of the PDS has, in recent months, led to the portrayal of the PDS as uniformly defunct. Such a portrayal, in turn, has been used to make a case for junking it and replacing it with 'cash transfers.' I, however, find that there are divergent trends across states insofar as per capita PDS purchase of wheat and rice and proportion of grain diverted are concerned." For example, in the early 2000s, as illicit diversion of grain shot up to well over 80 percent in some states, it did not rise above 7 percent in Tamil Nadu. Khera urged that those pushing to ditch the PDS instead learn from the experience of the states she identified as "reforming" and "functioning" rather than discarding the whole system. Even advocates of a cash-transfer system admit that it would not be well received in states where the PDS is working efficiently.[36]

But rather than learn from success stories, drafters of the Food Security Act further narrowed the scope of the PDS and raised the ire of many food experts, including an economist many consider to be well worth listening to: Jean Drèze of India's National Advisory Council. Drèze does not believe that any targeted or cash-transfer program can be as effective as a universal food-ration system. Instead, he has argued, India's PDS can deliver affordable food to everyone who needs it with improvement and expansion, and without breaking the national budget. He has condemned all proposals for targeting—a practice that, he argues,

> prevents the emergence of a cohesive public demand for a functional PDS. And vocal demand is very important for the success of the PDS. This is one reason why the PDS works much better in Tamil Nadu than elsewhere: everyone has a stake in it. Chhattisgarh's recent success builds on the same principle—about 80 percent of the rural population is covered. In short, targeting is an ugly business, and it would be particularly dangerous to "freeze" the BPL-APL distinction into law. That will amount to converting a purely statistical benchmark, the "poverty line," into a permanent social division.[37]

While intending to increase the quantity of food distributed per poor household, the government remains intent on giving priority to budget thrift through targeting. It brings to mind a comment by Drèze and his colleague Amartya Sen in their book *Hunger and Public Action*: "In contrast with the largely conservative task of entitlement protection, the exercise of entitlement *promotion* is, in many respects, more radical."[38] It is not crop failures or technical disruptions that have caused India's food-security system to stumble repeatedly; it is because the country's leaders have been conservative enough to keep starvation at bay but not radical enough to promote the right to food for all citizens.

BREAD, DIGNITY, JUSTICE

The two chiefs of police . . . Pharaoh, the accounts scribe Hednakht, the godfathers of this administration, came out to hear their statement. They said to them: "The prospect of hunger and thirst has driven us to this; there is no clothing, there is no fish, there are no vegetables. Send to Pharoah, our good lord, about it, and send the vizier, our superior, that we may be supplied with provisions." The ration of the first month of winter was issued to them on this day.

—Amennakhte, a scribe, on the tomb makers' strike
over food rations at Deir el Medina, Egypt, 1170 B.C.E.[39]

The ultra-right talks about the "free man." But what does it mean to be free if you can't afford food?

—Gouda Abdel-Khalek, Minister of Supply,
Government of Egypt, 2012[40]

Food rations are as old as civilization. In ancient Mesopotamia between five thousand and four thousand years ago, the families of semifree laborers received rations amounting to about sixty quarts of barley grain and two to five quarts of cooking oil per month, along with four pounds of wool annually. Foremen received the same rations as lower-level workers. Women received about half the men's ration of barley and children about one-third, along with their own rations of oil and wool. From time to time, regular rations of wheat, flour, bread, fish, dates, peas, and cloth were distributed as well.[41]

Millennia later, the economy of ancient Egypt was also being fueled by public distribution of food rations. In 1152 B.C.E., workers constructing royal tombs in an area of Thebes known as the Place of Beauty began complaining that they were not receiving their full monthly food rations, which were their chief means of subsistence. "We are impoverished," they announced to the authorities. "All the supplies for us that are from the treasury, the granary, and the storehouse have been allowed to be exhausted . . . make for us a means of keeping alive." The entire crew of tomb builders ended up walking off the construction site and staged a sit-in of sorts behind the temple of Tuthmosis III. The next day, in a brazen act of civil disobedience, they moved their sit-down strike inside the temple of Ramses II, where large stocks of grain were stored. The authorities finally delivered the men their rations, six weeks late. But distribution continued to be sporadic and inadequate. Several rounds of labor–management wrangling and old-fashioned dirty politics later, reports the historian John Romer, "Quite suddenly the proper quotas of rations began to reach the village again, and now for the first time, a number of workmen . . . were put to checking and distributing the rations as they arrived at the village, doubtless to ensure a fair distribution."

Another half century passed, with Thebes descending into much tougher economic times and fresh struggles over food rations erupting. Allotments were not lasting the workers' families the full month, apparently; men were known to spend the last night of each month at the grain stores in order to get their share first thing the next morning. According to Romer, "The grain rations seem to have dwindled to the point where each month's delivery was awaited with the bright-eyed intensity of the truly hungry." In the summer of 1102 b.c.e., the workers went out on strike yet again.[42]

In the years since World War II, public food distribution has resumed in Egypt. Indeed, during the past half century, the Egyptian government has been managing one of the most comprehensive and thoroughly haggled-over food subsidy/ration systems in the world. The American observer Harold Alderman wrote in the 1980s,

On almost any street corner in Cairo one can buy a *tamaya* or *falafel* sandwich for a few cents. This daily fare is a microcosm of the government's involvement in food pricing. The fava beans in the sandwich are subsidized. The oil in which they are fried is subsidized. The bread is subsidized. The tea one might have with the sandwich is subsidized, as is the sugar used to sweeten it. Furthermore, the sandwich will probably be wrapped in a newspaper that is likely to contain a speech or an editorial on the subsidy system.[43]

In Egypt, food-policy makers have very little room to maneuver. The country has to be sustained by only one-tenth of an acre of cropland per person: imagine living for a year on a sixty-by-seventy-foot postage stamp of ground sown with wheat, rice, maize, lentils, beans, vegetables, cotton, animal forage, and date palms. That per-person endowment of cropland is one of the smallest in the world.[44] Virtually all 82 million Egyptians, along with almost all agricultural lands, are squeezed into just 5 percent of the nation's total land area, most of it in a five- to ten-mile-wide strip running along the Nile River and fanning out at the Nile Delta. It's as if the entire population of the United States and all of our agriculture were clustered within thirty-five miles of the Mississippi River and its delta. To keep everyone fed, Egypt has had to become the world's number one importer of wheat, and it imports a large share of most other required foods as well. Food security naturally ranks near the top of the nation's concerns. The government stockpiles food and has developed a vast PDS aimed at delivering adequate, low-cost food to every resident of the country who needs it. Specific features of Egypt's public food distribution system have varied through the years, but it has strived for universal coverage, and its centerpiece has always been wheat in the form of flour or bread. Egyptians, the world's biggest bread consumers, eat an average of almost a pound per person daily.[45]

The modern era of food rationing in Egypt began with temporary programs put in place during World War II to address scarcity and inflation. The initial program provided subsidized sugar, vegetable oil, tea, kerosene, cotton cloth, and other necessities. Food subsidies persisted in response to postwar inflation and by the 1960s had merged into a system that also subsidized transportation, housing, energy, soap, and even cigarettes. In the wake of the country's 1967 war with Israel, ration cards were reintroduced to ensure access to food in the face of accelerated inflation and a cutoff of U.S. food aid. The ration-card program swelled in the 1970s to cover eighteen items, including rice, dry beans, lentils, frozen fish, and meats. Then, in January 1977, at the urging of international lending agencies, the government of President Anwar Sadat announced deep cuts in food subsidies. The cuts triggered bloody riots across the country. Ironically, the price increases that prompted what came to be known as the "bread riots" of 1977 did not include Egypt's number one food, *aish baladi* (loosely, "village bread," with *aish*—"bread"—also meaning "life"). Government officials believed the cuts would affect only upper-class consumers when they announced stiff increases in the prices of premium *fino* bread, refined flour, rice, tea, gasoline, and cigarettes. The majority of people saw things differently. The two days of riots, in which approximately eighty people died and more than eight hundred were injured, forced the government to restore and expand subsidies and reduce prices of food rations. With continued growth in volume, by 1981 the PDS had swelled to as much as 20 percent of all national government expenditures. Alarmed at the expense, the government began dropping items from the subsidy system—gradually and quietly, to avoid a repeat of 1977—but continued to heavily subsidize *baladi* bread. Shops selling large stacks of the bread seemingly can be found on any city street or country road in the country. And today, as in the past, anyone can buy up to twenty of the ultracheap pocket-style loaves at any shop. Most buy that full daily allotment, and one in four consumers say it's not enough. But in some rural areas the great majority of families make their own bread from subsidized flour. Meanwhile, ration shops called *tamweens* sell subsidized goods that require a ration card, including rice, sugar, oil, flour, and tea.[46]

Unrest swept Egypt once again in 2008, when global prices of wheat and other grains skyrocketed. Some bakers found themselves dispensing their products through protective steel cages. In one incident, eight thousand people were attacked by police with tear gas after they blockaded the main highway between Cairo (the capital) and the Mediterranean coast. The protest was prompted by a government decision, in the face of shortages and inflation, to deliver wheat flour only to bakeries and not through ration shops. People of the local community, predominantly fishers, were outraged by the lack of access to flour, as they were accustomed to making their own style of bread, one better able to withstand long fishing trips than is the standard type offered by bakeries.[47]

In a diplomatic cable dated April 16, 2008, later unearthed by Wikileaks, Frank Ricciardone, the U.S. ambassador to Egypt, summarized interviews that his embassy conducted following bread riots in the industrial city of Mahalla that had resulted in three deaths, at least a hundred injuries, and forty-nine arrests. He wrote, "Many Egyptians acknowledge that the fundamental unspoken Egyptian social pact—the people's obeisance in exchange for a modest but government-guaranteed standard of living—is under stress, and the poor feel this most acutely." The government responded to the unrest by going into full damage-control mode. Ricciardone wrote, "Six months ago, economic cabinet ministers openly discussed phasing out food and fuel subsidies in favor of transfer payments to the very poor. That initiative now seems to be off the table."[48] The ration-card system, which by then was providing rice, sugar, tea, vegetable oil, and sometimes flour, was expanded once again. Families were allowed to add new children to their quota. And "splits," which enabled adult children moving out of the home to obtain their own ration cards, were again permitted. By 2012, 63 million Egyptians had gained access to the ration system, an expansion of more than 40 percent in four years.[49]

In the months leading up to the 2011 revolution that finally overthrew the government of President Hosni Mubarak, officials were again making plans to phase out universal food subsidies. Then, just a week before protests against political repression erupted in Tahrir Square, high officials reversed field and began stressing that Egypt's food-ration system, with its broad coverage, was to serve as an important bulwark against the kind of rebellion that had just rocked the nation of Tunisia. According to Ikhwan Web, the Muslim Brotherhood's official English website, "Trade and Industry Minister Rashid Mohammed Rashid ruled out a 'Tunisia scenario' in his country over the economy because Egypt distributes 64 million ration cards covering the vast majority of Egyptian people who have been isolated from the global market in times of crisis." As the Mubarak government lurched toward its end, overwhelmed by a revolution that trumpeted the slogan "Bread, Dignity, and Social Justice," officials put on hold any plans to cut subsidies or rations.[50] But by then it was too late. Unrest over food was starting to look like a rerun of 1977 and 2008. *Baladi* bread at the subsidized five-piaster price was hard to come by; the day before rebellion exploded in Tahrir Square, Saeed Qaoud, an unemployed cement worker, attempted to immolate himself in front of the ruling National Democratic Party office in Suez to protest being denied a ration card. It became widely accepted in the media that although a variety of political and economic forces had driven people into the streets, frustration over unaffordable or unavailable food was a major contributing factor in the nationwide protests.[51] Their eyes on Tunisia and Egypt, governments throughout the Arab world moved to beef up their food-subsidy and distribution systems. As Samer Shehata, professor of Arab politics at Georgetown University, told *In These Times* at the height of the 2011 uprising, "In authoritarian contexts, all protest is political, even if it's protest that is supposedly about 'bread and butter' issues." When shortages of subsidized cooking fuel hit in early 2012, the government considered issuing ration stamps to low-income households that could be used along with their food-ration card to obtain filled butane cylinders.[52]

In Egypt, as in so many countries, economic growth at the top of the economy had proved an ineffective means to secure access to basic needs at the bottom. Through the 1990s, market liberalization helped accelerate the growth of Egypt's economy, but with few benefits trickling down. Following even more sweeping market-oriented changes that started in 2004, the country's growth accelerated. Not long before the Mubarak regime's collapse, the United States, the IMF, and the World Bank had recognized Egypt as a "top reformer."[53] The PDS hung on throughout, like the old family car that runs badly and is the subject of constant complaint but somehow still gets used. Nadine El-Hakim, a senior program officer for the World Food Program in Egypt, was clear on this point in a 2012 interview when she twice asserted, "Egypt's public distribution system is untouchable."[54] The International Food Policy Research Institute has singled out the *baladi* bread subsidy as especially important for providing "a relatively effective means of transferring benefits to the poor, particularly the urban poor, helping to protect them against shocks that may arise from the ongoing economic reform process in Egypt." But, warns Monal Abdel-Baki, an economics professor at the American University in Cairo, we should not expect cheap food alone to keep people satisfied. Granted, she told me, "people will erupt in protest if their food security is threatened"; however, her research shows that, with Egyptians' food supply having been made relatively secure, "many have become frustrated because they cannot afford the refrigerators and air-conditioners that they see others buying. Simply meeting people's nutritional needs? This is not what makes people happy, and it cannot bring stability."[55]

The PDS is also plagued by inefficiency. A recent survey found 20 percent of *baladi* bread and other rationed commodities going to more affluent households in urban areas; in rural areas the figure was closer to 40 percent. Meanwhile, the monthly quota of sugar available at the local *tamween* is often enough to last the average household just nineteen days. Rice and tea rations are good for half of the month, on average.[56] In some villages, the *tamween* opens for fairly regular hours throughout the month, while in others the operator doesn't even have a permanent location—when he receives his stock from the government, he just rents storefront space and sets up shop for a day or so. People depend on word of mouth to let them know the shop is open so they can make their purchases while the stock lasts. Quality varies. *Baladi* flour (derived from 60 percent imported wheat, 30 percent Egyptian-grown wheat, and 10 percent maize, as cheap filler)[57] can be be very poor ("a total mess," one customer told me) for months and then be much better for a while; furthermore, the quantity of flour in the quota has fallen as the number of people served by each shop increases. Cooking oil is of high quality in some places and so bad in others that people trade it away for smaller quantities of better oil. The most impoverished end up with the worst oil.[58]

Taheya is a weaver who lives with her family of seven in a village called Harannia, south of Cairo. She is an expert baker herself and makes as much of the household's bread as she can. Asked to compare the bread she makes with the product from the bakery, she shakes her head. "It is not even a question to ask. The *baladi* bread is inedible!" She thinks the flour used by the public bread shops is adulterated, and that their butane-fired conveyor ovens "don't do a good job." But

Taheya's family has to eat the subsidized bread in addition to what she bakes, she says, because her flour quota at the *tamween* is never close to sufficient. "I would bake all of our bread if I could," she says, "but that would require a hundred and fifty kilograms of flour each month." Giving a what-can-I-say shrug, she adds, "We eat a lot of bread." [59]

Disparaging the aesthetic qualities of *baladi* bread is something of a national pastime, but the nutritional consequences of a monotonous diet based mostly on bread and other cheap foods are serious. With a 100 percent–irrigated agriculture and a sunny, mild climate, Egypt grows a highly diverse array of crops, yet many Egyptian families cannot afford a similarly diverse diet. One result is that 25 percent of all women suffer from iron-deficiency anemia. In 2008, the Ministry of Health started a pilot program for fortifying *baladi* flour with iron and folic acid. That treats a single symptom of a highly unfair food economy but does nothing about the causes.

In the low-income areas where people depend most heavily on food subsidies, one hears constant complaints about lines at bread shops; hour-long waits are common in some places, and shops close when supplies run out. Rationing by queuing is billed as a good way to target goods toward low-income groups, but the queues at *baladi* shops are not very effective at doing even that. Many families, for example, opt to pay extra for home delivery. Wealthier people can pay others to stand in line for them. Sometimes poor people arrive before sunup, get a prime spot in the queue, and then sell the spot to someone with more money. People say they are also unable to buy as much flour at the *tamween* as they used to. Bread and flour shortages allegedly occur because significant portions of the subsidized wheat and flour that should be used for making five-piaster bread are instead being sold by millers and bakers on the open market at a healthy profit. Furthermore, many *baladi* bread shops are not located conveniently for the people who most need them: in all cities, they tend to be concentrated more in well-to-do than in poor neighborhoods.[60]

Unauthorized markets are common. Twenty-three percent of all urban households sell off a portion of their daily bread allotment to others, and surveys show that *baladi* flour distribution has gaping holes, with 30 percent of the total flour that enters the system leaking out again. Leakage is 25 percent for subsidized sugar and 28 percent for cooking oil.[61] One man's story, told in a *USA Today* article, serves to explain why so many are calling for reform of Egypt's subsidy system:

> In one poor district of Cairo, a government official in charge of a public bakery shows his paycheck: After 20 years in his position, he earns about $55 a month, including supposed bonuses. "I have to steal—how would I survive without stealing?" the official, a father of eight, told The Associated Press. He admitted that he regularly sells a portion of his bakery's subsidized wheat on the black market. The government provides a ration of wheat to state-run bakeries at a subsidized price of about $1.50 for each 110-pound sack. The wheat is supposed to produce bread that sells for less than one cent per loaf. But many bakeries sell some of it to private bakeries at up to $37 a sack. Part of the difference, the bakery employees pocket. But part is needed to pay off the host of government inspectors—from the police, the Supply Ministry, the city government and local councils—each of whom demands his own fat bribe. "I just have to give bribes to most of them or they would file fines or close the bakery," said the official, whose bakery receives 68 sacks of subsidized flour every day.[62]

Experience with targeting food subsidies only at the lower income brackets in India and Egypt has shown that efforts to remove middle-class people from the ration rolls always end up eliminating poor people as well, a kind of collateral damage. There is also a good political reason not to try to purge the lists: when the next economic earthquake hits, it will be best to have erred on the side of inclusion, because "protests over food price increases rarely consist of the poor alone."[63] With those considerations in mind, the focus in Egypt today is on eliminating errors of exclusion—extending coverage to low-income consumers, while not worrying so much about affluent free riders. A smart card that's been deployed to extend access in seven regions of the country has had mixed success. One problem is that some people who were unused to dealing with electronic payment asked *tamween* shopkeepers for help and ended up disclosing their passwords, creating obvious opportunities for exploitation.[64]

In the interim government that was set up after the overthrow of Mubarak, improving the *baladi* bread distribution system became the responsibility of Gouda Abdel-Khalek, the minister of supply and internal trade. Sitting in his office in early 2012, Abdel-Khalek stated that Egypt was becoming increasingly self-sufficient in food, partly by increasing wheat production to the point of supplying more than half of its needs. But there remained the problem of leakage of wheat and flour from the food system, he said, and a full overhaul was necessary to eliminate incentives for cheating. Under the plan he was proposing, the government would continue to stockpile imported wheat, along with wheat it would buy from Egyptian farmers at 19 percent above the market price. It would then sell that grain to millers on the open market, rather than at the current subsidized price. Mills would sell their flour to bakeries at market price as well. Each morning, bakeries would deliver bread to retailers at the market price, but the shops would then sell it to the public at the usual five-piaster subsidized rate. The government would make up the difference. That might be done by issuing every household a smart card that could be used to credit the bread shop's account for the price difference when the bread is bought. Subsidies thus would be more narrowly aimed—only at farmers and consumers. If wheat and flour were not sold cheaply to millers and bakers, Abdel-Khalek reasoned, they would have no incentive to sell on the side because there would be no profit in it, and more *baladi* bread would be produced.[65] But restructuring a system that had coexisted so comfortably with a thoroughly corrupt economy for so long would not be easy. To start with, it was necessary to deal with resistance from the food industries, interest groups, tycoons, and bureaucrats who benefited from the old, leaky system.

As in India, some in Egypt have argued that the government should junk the current food-distribution system completely and simply give people below the poverty line a subsidy in cash, to spend as they like. This would be accompanied by elimination of food subsidies, something that Western nations and international development agencies have long been urging Egypt to do, even at the risk of further radicalizing the citizenry.[66] According to Abdel-Khalek, who is an economics professor as well as a government minister, "Every World Bank mission that comes to town tells us that we should convert to a cash-transfer system. Fair enough; that's just the ABCs of economics. Sure, it's most efficient. But we are dealing with lives here, not textbook situations." And the reality of life in Egypt, he says, is that a cash subsidy would be neither workable nor acceptable to the intended recipients.[67] Having lived through a succession of food-price shocks over the years, including the 30 percent spike of 2008, Egyptians simply don't want the government to shift the burden of price increases onto their shoulders. A household survey in 2010 that asked low-income people their preferences received a loud-and-clear answer: only 2 percent said they would be willing to give up their food-ration cards in exchange for a straight cash benefit, and just 5 percent would want to see *baladi* bread distribution ended in favor of a cash-assistance program.[68]

What worries people is not so much the steady march of inflation as the frequent wild week-to-week price swings, says Taheya, the home bread baker in Harannia. She explained, "I would be concerned about a cash system. Look at cooking oil. Its price moves up and down so much you'd never know whether or not you could afford to buy it. I have more confidence in the current system."[69] Altef, a farmer from Minia, farther south, said he would not want to see a cash transfer substituted for subsidies either: "At the ration or bread shop, quantities are assured. I'd rather buy *baladi* bread and rations as I do now." Even if the government promised to raise cash payments annually to keep up with to the cost of living, Altef told me, "I would not trust such a promise."[70] Grassroots aversion to a cash-support system is backed up by the economist Hamdi Abdel-Azim, who has predicted, "If the government decides to apply this program, the result will be an increase in inflation rates," with the price of bread rising as much as sixfold almost immediately. With such food inflation, the small cash subsidies planned for low-income Egyptians would be next to useless.[71] Another economist, Karima Korayem of Al-Azhar University, firmly believes that the Egyptian PDS should not be replaced by a cash-payment system. She reached that conclusion for four reasons: the chief objective of the PDS is specifically to prevent hunger, not to raise overall living standards;

in-kind subsidies are preferable for people like those in the Egyptian
target group who live in "absolute poverty"; with high food inflation,
governments of low-income countries like Egypt cannot afford to raise
cash benefits by enough every year to keep everyone fed; and people
receiving cash benefits would have to spend them in a dysfunctional
economy that already places much more power in the hands of owners
than of workers and consumers.[72]

As Egypt looked to the future after the seismic political changes of
2011–12, on one issue there seemed to be no doubt: the food subsidy
and distribution system would endure. In February 2012, Korayem,
like everyone in Egypt, was speculating on how the recently elected
parliament, in which the Muslim Brotherhood's political party held
the most seats, would approach governing the country. She said she believed the new leaders would be extra careful to sustain food security,
noting, "Governing is a big responsibility. If you don't do it right, you'll
lose at the next election. But if people feel they've become better off,
you'll win. Therefore, the Brotherhood should work to do two things:
level out income distribution and reduce poverty. After all, isn't that
what Islam is about?"[73] After the election of the Brotherhood candidate Mohammed Morsi to the presidency in June, fellow senior party
member Waleed al-Haddad was very specific about the ranking of food
issues in what he called Morsi's hundred-day plan: "No. 1 is security,
No. 2 traffic, No. 3 fuel, No. 4 the waste, No. 5 bread." To track progress
on those issues, two young Egyptians created a "Morsi Meter" website
that indicated whether each of sixty-four promises had been addressed
or achieved. According to the site, a little over halfway through his first
hundred days, Morsi was making progress on only six of his thirteen
promises in the "bread" category.[74]

With Egypt's future hanging in the balance, others were less optimistic about the incoming government's policies. In a Cairo cafe,
Marian Fadel, a labor activist, stressed to me that "Bread, Dignity, and
Social Justice" was more than a mere slogan and that none of its three
demands was negotiable. "The ball is in Parliament's court now. The
people have no vote in what happens, so if horrible decisions are made,
we will return to the streets," she told me. And whatever direction the
country takes in coming years, she said, the working people of Egypt

will have to keep pressure on the government. "We are not going back," she declared. "We will *never* go back." [75]

RATIONING THE HARD WAY

Iraq has postponed the planned purchase of 18 F-16 fighter planes from the United States this year and diverted the funds to feeding the poor, an official said on Monday, amid growing protests that have been inspired by the uprisings in Egypt and Tunisia.

—Agence France-Presse, February 15, 2011 [76]

The humble potato has become the symbol of a new revolution sweeping Cuba. The vegetable has been eliminated from the thick brown ration books that Cuban nationals relied on for nearly 50 years to purchase government-subsidized groceries, part of the socialist country's attempt to ensure equal access to such staples as rice, beans and cooking oil. If this is the beginning of the end for Cuban ration books . . . the implications for the future of the struggling country's economy are huge.

—The Globe and Mail, November 12, 2009 [77]

In August 1990, Iraqi troops under the command of President Saddam Hussein invaded Kuwait. Almost immediately, at the urging of the United States, the UN Security Council adopted Resolution 661, imposing sanctions and blocking virtually all international trade. With supplies diminishing, the government of Iraq quickly established a PDS to provide basic necessities to all households. But in the years following the U.S.-led war that drove Iraqi forces from Kuwait, sanctions continued to hamper Iraq's ability to sell oil and buy food, and hardship further intensified. In 1995, Security Council Resolution 986 created the Oil-for-Food Program, and the flow of food through the PDS grew somewhat, but the PDS remained in place. The World Bank has concluded, "During the sanctions period, the Public Distribution System played a crucial role; by making transfers to households and by injecting food into local markets, the PDS helped Iraq avoid a humanitarian crisis." [78]

During the subsequent 2003 U.S. invasion and the almost nine years of military occupation that followed, Iraq's population remained vulnerable to hunger. With a whopping 70 percent of their food supply imported, Iraqi citizens continue to depend on public procurement and distribution of large food stocks to serve as a buffer against global price fluctuations. According to the UN World Food Programme (WFP), the country's food-ration system is "the largest public food program operating in the world today." Most upstream activities are carried out by the government, while the private sector handles distribution and retailing. Fifteen percent of Iraqi citizens still have problems getting enough food, and another 32 percent would immediately become food insecure if the PDS were terminated. The food system has, in the words of WFP, "prevented famine."[79] And it is not just the poor but the entire country that has felt the PDS's impact. The World Bank observed in 2005 that "the actual role of the PDS goes far beyond providing a safety net for the poor. Whether or not it was intended as such, . . . many better-off Iraqis see the system as a general entitlement and a mechanism to transfer natural resource revenue directly to citizens"—they see it, that is, as a way of distributing a portion of the nation's oil-derived wealth in the form of food, as was done under the Oil-for-Food program (which, in turn, finds an analog in the Alaska Permanent Fund).[80] And Iraq's PDS is so large that even in the absence of direct price controls on food, its provision of cheap or free food significantly suppresses prices of commodities being sold on the open market.

Rations are distributed to consumers through 45,000 licensed "food and flour agents" throughout Iraq. Each recipient pays just 250 dinars (about 21 U.S. cents at official exchange rates) for a monthly basket of goods. Before it was cut back in 2010, the PDS ration contained nine kilograms of wheat, three of rice, and two of sugar, along with 500 grams of tomato paste, 250 grams of tea, 250 grams of milk for adults plus almost two kilograms for children, a liter of cooking oil, 250 grams of soap, and 500 grams of detergents. There are no rations for fresh vegetables or fruit because people typically buy fresh produce with cash at local markets. In 2010, tomato paste, tea, milk for adults, soap, and detergent were officially dropped from the ration. Unofficially, various other items have been dropped as well: recipients often receive only two or three of the five listed items at a time. In one month in 2007, 46 percent of ration-card holders received no flour, 73 percent no rice, and 75 percent no cooking oil. The WFP observes, "The PDS is very effective in reaching the poor and guaranteeing a minimum standard of living, but it accomplishes this goal in a very costly and inefficient way—absorbing 21 percent of government revenue." But there's not much choice, because "there are no other large-scale safety nets functioning in Iraq which could accomplish this goal if the PDS were eliminated."[81]

The American invasion and occupation stretched and finally tore the PDS safety net. According to Usama Rekabi, who heads the Baghdad office of the relief and development organization Mercy Corps and directs its food distribution, "2006 was a critical year because of sectarian violence and the many waves of displacement that resulted. Many people had to flee their homes suddenly, losing all their documents, including identity cards and ration cards." In areas where large numbers of internally displaced persons lived, says Rekabi, "we did not see famine conditions; however, people were struggling just to fill their stomachs. They could not maintain nutrition." Nevertheless, he says, sometimes people decided they'd rather go hungry than eat the invaders' rations: "In the province of Diwaniya down south, where there had been a bitter battle between U.S. forces and militias in 2005, WFP shipped in supplies of cooking oil. But the people absolutely refused to accept the oil when they saw the labels and realized that it had been produced in America."[82]

In Iraq, as in India and Egypt, there have been calls for scrapping the PDS and replacing it with a cash-transfer system. But the size of the benefit being proposed—a small bundle of Iraqi dinars worth only $5 to $10 per month—is far less than what would be needed to buy the amount of food the PDS provides. In the WFP's view, any reduction in benefits would very likely be exacerbated by food inflation and could trigger widespread hunger among poorer Iraqis. Even among the well-off, "the political ramifications could be destabilizing," according to the WFP. Rekabi says, "When Prime Minister Maliki announced a few years ago that the PDS would be abolished, I am sure the greedy local shopkeepers were happy. If that had happened, they would have doubled their prices as soon as they heard the news. And everyone would have blamed the government for the fact we could not buy enough food." To be effective, the cash transfer would have to be large enough to permit Iraqis to continue buying the same quantities of goods today, and be indexed to inflation to allow them to do so tomorrow. That would probably increase, not reduce, government expenditures.[83]

Many Iraqis complain about the quality of some of the foods they receive, and, as in Egypt, people are known to sell part of their ration, using the proceeds to buy food on the open market. Another similarity to Egypt: when pollsters asked whether they would prefer to receive cash in lieu of commodity rations, only 5 percent of respondents said they would. Rekabi says the PDS retains near-universal support even though only a minority of families still depend on it for survival. He explains, "Today, the PDS has become less important for the majority of people. They are more concerned with the poor electricity, water, and sewage service, with housing, and especially with the unemployment situation. However, for those living under the poverty line— that's 15 percent of Iraqis, according to the Ministry of Planning, but I think it's much higher—the PDS is a very high priority."[84]

With the idea of a cash transfer highly unpopular, the World Bank has recommended targeting food rations more directly at the poor, reducing the range of products distributed, increasing the role of the private sector, and streamlining food procurement. The World Bank further urged that rationed goods be made less attractive and convenient in order to push more people into the private market, despite the higher cost, or that the PDS be converted into a food-for-work program. Another idea was to require all cardholders to present documents proving their low income, as a way to persuade the non-poor to opt out of the system voluntarily "out of pride and patriotism."[85] Only one of those measures has been adopted: the number of items distributed by the PDS was reduced.

By 2010, the United States and international agencies were still urging Iraq to overhaul the system in order to stimulate its economy, but local protests stalled any action. In the six months leading up to the political protests that rolled across North Africa in early 2011, the PDS, along with public utilities and other services, was faltering badly— something that, in Iraq, means that the government itself is faltering—

and it appeared to be only a matter of time before Arab Spring protests would erupt in Baghdad. In Diwaniya province on February 5, 2011, protesters carried small packets of sugar and lamps that burned rationed oil to symbolize their demands for full food rations and electric service; police fired on the crowd, killing one and injuring four. This incident and others like it—at one, banners read, "It's a fodder ration, not a food ration" and "We are sitting on billions of barrels of oil, but we can't find anything to eat"—prompted a member of Parliament to warn, "Iraq is boiling and it could blow up at any moment." It was at that point that Maliki promised to pay for expanding the PDS by postponing a major F-16 order.[86]

In late 2011, with the full pullout of U.S. troops just a couple of months away, WFP officials made new, concrete proposals to strengthen the PDS. In a meeting with the Anbar Provincial Council, officials offered to "procure, package, and deliver" rice, sugar, and vegetable oil to Ministry of Trade warehouses "for a certain portion of the population"; help manage the PDS supply chain through "procurement, packaging, shipping, pipeline management, warehouse management, monitoring, etc."; and help "improve the tracking of commodities and monitoring (i.e., electronic chips and bar codes on packages, SMS messages between warehouses, food agents, beneficiaries and central control authority and other methods.)."[87] No one talked about getting rid of the food ration.

Usama Rekabi, whose job it is to help ensure that Iraqis continue to have enough to eat, complains that too many people are unemployed and don't like having to depend on the PDS. But he's able to be somewhat philosophical about the country's predicament: "We've been through the Iran war, Desert Storm, the sanctions, the invasion, the occupation, the sectarian fighting. . . . It's only natural that we'd see the future as unstable. But all we need is a door to knock on. If we see an opportunity for work and a better life, we will grab it."[88]

Another example of rationing under siege is provided by Cuba. Before the revolution that swept the dictator Fulgencio Batista from power in 1959, the nation of Cuba had relatively high average food consumption, but extreme inequality of economic power meant that most poor people suffered badly from malnutrition. But three years after the revolution, the Communist government found itself facing a different problem: an increasing capacity of people to buy food and a falling supply. The U.S.-imposed embargo was partly to blame, but there was more to it than that. In a 1985 article, Medea Benjamin and Joseph Collins described the sequence of events that made food rationing necessary:

> The primary goal of the revolutionary leadership was to ensure that no one in Cuba would go hungry. Viewing inadequate income as the fundamental reason why people were undernourished, the government set into motion policies designed both to boost the earnings of the poorer half of society and to enlarge the share of their earnings they could afford to spend on food. Above all, the government sought to generate fuller employment and to ensure the poor a greater share of the national wealth. Job opportunities soared on the newly created state farms and government construction projects (roads, schools, clinics, office buildings and housing). The poorest workers won substantial wage increases and poor farmers benefited from the new government's sweeping agrarian reform. The new government also sought to enable low-income households to spend more of their earnings on food. Basic social services were made free for everyone. Included were not only schooling, medical care, medicines and social security but also water, burial services, sports facilities, even public telephones. The government lowered the charges for electricity, gas and public transport that had eaten up so much of working people's earnings.

As an immediate result of these economic policies, people could afford to eat more and better food, and they did. That drove up prices, prompting the government to impose price controls and take charge of wholesale distribution. But demand continued to outstrip supply, and hoarding and speculation touched off even worse inflation. Benjamin and Collins continue, "What was amounting to rationing by income flew in the face of everything the revolutionary leadership stood for.

They might have opted simply to make certain basic staples available to the poor at low prices (and thus to create different diets for the rich and the poor). Instead they decided to institute a ration system for all Cubans covering most important food items."[89]

Starting in March 1962, each Cuban household received a ration book called *la libreta* that permitted the purchase of a specified quantity per family member of each item on a list of goods. As in wartime Britain, each household registered with a specific shop to provide the goods. And as in Iraq, the food-ration system evolved during an era of U.S. government sanctions. By the 1970s, despite the continuing embargo and persistent food shortages, childhood malnutrition had been almost completely eradicated in Cuba, and improvement in public health indicators continued through the 1980s. That was achieved in spite of the fact that there had been no major improvements in food production—true, agricultural output had risen 50 percent since the revolution, but then so had the island's population. It was thanks to *la libreta* that hunger was eradicated.[90]

As national production of individual commodities fluctuated over the years, different items moved on and off *la libreta*—and all too often some of the listed items failed to appear in the shops. Foods forming the consistent core of the ration included rice, beans, cooking oil, meat, lard, sugar, salt, and coffee. Fruits and vegetables on the list would vary by season and supply. Children received a generous ration of fresh milk, and people doing heavy manual labor, such as cane cutters at harvest time, were provided extra rations. For families in rural areas, home production could make up a share of the diet equal to or greater than that from the ration. Because *la libreta* involved strict quantity rationing rather than more flexible rationing by points, the most common complaints involved situations in which an individual family would receive insufficient rations of some items and too much of others. Benjamin and Collins found a common response was what they called the "gray market": the technically illegal but widespread practice of swapping rationed food between families to satisfy varying needs and preferences. Farmers' markets free of price controls were legalized in 1980, but the foods they sold were so expensive that they were out of reach for most people. Furthermore, the farmers who were meant to sell in the market were largely displaced by brokers, creating a situation that fed speculation better than it fed people. The government attempted to crack down on the markets but found that the more effective approach was to open state-run markets for nonrationed foods, although these also were expensive places to shop.[91]

In their article "Is Rationing Socialist?" Benjamin and Collins offered this analysis of the debate over rationing in Cuba during that decade:

> Those who favor the elimination of rationing argue that its egalitarian basis thwarts the development of socialism. For them, the fundamental principle of socialism is "to each according to his or her work." Those who work harder and better should earn more. But, this argument continues, rewarding greater productive effort and accomplishment is futile unless more and more desirable things are offered to the workers to buy. And that is exactly what rationing, which guarantees the same goods to all, works against. Rationing, then, is not a socialist but a communist form of distribution (to each according to his or her need), for which Cuba is not yet sufficiently developed. Those, however, who favor continued rationing agree that under socialism, unlike the more evolved stage of communism, goods are distributed according to work. And they agree that the parallel market is necessary to help motivate people to work. But they contend that it should be used only to distribute those goods that are rare, scarce, or of superior quality. Here, for them, socialism distinguishes itself from capitalism. "In capitalist countries the supply of all products is governed by the law of supply and demand," an official of the national planning agency stated. "In our society only a minimal part of our total supply of products is controlled by this economic mechanism, and only after having satisfied the basic needs of the entire population."[92]

Other socialist societies have had similar problems in making up their minds about rationing's place within socialism. For theoreticians of the Chinese revolution, Karl Marx could be counted upon to approve or disapprove of rationing, depending on the situation. In the mid-1950s, during the early years of China's food-ration system, officials in Beijing played down its egalitarian aspects, because uniformity of consumption would reduce the people's incentive to work and produce. Then, in the late 1950s, during the Great Leap Forward, egalitarianism was a high priority, true communism was thought to be within shouting distance, and the rationing system was advertised as promoting the goal "to each according to his needs." But soon official thought had swung back to another view of Marx's—that it will take a very long time to eliminate inequality and that meanwhile development of society's productive forces must take priority.[93] The ration coupon nevertheless persisted as a central feature of China's economy until 1994, well into the country's adoption of a market economy. The Russian people experienced food rationing during World War I, and in 1928, under the still-new Soviet government, the country adopted a comprehensive system for rationing food and other consumer goods. That system did not last long and was phased out completely by 1934 after debates over production incentives similar to those that would later occur in Cuba and China. Rationing returned in 1941 in response to critical wartime shortages, but in the post–World War II period consumption was handled through a complex combination of markets that the Ukrainian-born economist Aron Katsenelinboigen classified as "red," "pink," "white," "gray," "brown," and "black," to indicate varying degrees of legality and market versus government control.[94]

Cuba lost a crucial lifeline when the Soviet Union collapsed in 1990, ushering in what the Castro government termed the economy's "Special Period." GDP plunged 30 to 40 percent within three years; Soviet aid, including provisions of fertilizers and pesticides, was cut off and its sugar purchases plummeted; the U.S. trade embargo remained in place; and the island's agricultural production took another hit. As a result, the amount of food provided by *la libreta* had to be cut. Yet even by the end of the 1990s, rationed foods were still providing the average Cuban's diet with 61 percent of its calories, 65 percent of vegetable proteins, 36 percent of animal proteins, and 38 percent of fats.[95]

Economic liberalization slowly spread through many areas of the Cuban economy during the Special Period. People in more than one hundred occupations were allowed to operate privately, spending of U.S. dollars was permitted, state farms were divided up into smaller cooperatives, and farmers' markets were legalized and expanded. A boom in urban agriculture and agroecological production methods (necessitated by the cutoff of agricultural chemical imports) provided a larger and more varied array of foods, especially fresh produce.[96] And, as always, diets were supplemented with foods bought through illegal markets. Despite the huge burden it placed on the government's budget, the routine cheating it inspired, and its frequent failure to deliver, *la libreta* remained "a near sacred document to every Cuban household," to quote one observer, and therefore stayed more or less intact well into the twenty-first century.[97] And despite deep dissatisfaction with the quantities and quality of food provided by *la libreta*, Cuba continued to see very low rates of malnutrition and was celebrated for having infant mortality rates and other health indicators that ranked it among the nations of the global North. Nevertheless, the opening of the economy introduced risk, uncertainty, and rising inequality, making many Cubans very nervous.[98]

Starting in 2000, the economy improved somewhat with help from oil-rich Venezuela and its Bolivarian Revolution, but suffering increased with the global economic crash that began in 2008. Cuba continues to import 80 percent of its food, and today seven out ten Cubans have lived their entire lives eating rationed food. The government under Raúl Castro, who succeeded his brother Fidel as president in 2008, has taken several actions to stimulate agricultural production, including land redistribution, increases in prices paid to farmers, and legalization of some private sales. The government began to remove items from the food ration and reduce quantities of items that remained, and an editorial in the Communist Party newspaper *Granma* called for *la libreta* to be abandoned altogether. Protein became a special concern, with monthly allowances of high-protein foods remaining small: in 2009, 230 grams of ground red meat mixed with soy; 460 grams of chicken (more often than not, "ground mystery meat, mixed with a large amount of soy paste," known as "*pollo con suerte*, or chicken with luck")[99]; 460 grams of fish with the head (or 316 without the head); ten eggs; and varying quantities of dry beans and sausage.[100]

The daily ration of one liter of milk per child up to the age of seven, one of the most prominent symbols of the revolution, remained intact. Cubans estimate that the monthly ration by itself would feed a person for twelve days. It is possible to buy additional quantities of some foods in the ration shops at an escalating price in a kind of increasing block tariff arrangement. Foods that have been dropped from the ration are still available, but in nonrationed stores at high prices. Vegetables are available in farmers' markets at state-controlled prices, but they are still expensive. By growing a few vegetables and raising a few animals, rural families can eat somewhat better, and urban farming continues to flourish.[101]

Everyone in Cuba complains about the ration, but no good alternative is on the horizon. In 2011, seventy-two-year-old Enriqueta Domínguez told Agence France-Presse that she and her neighbors desperately needed protection against the inflation that was once again sweeping world food markets, saying, "The *libreta* is Cuba. Without it, many Cubans would face starvation."[102] National Public Radio (NPR) in the United States reported this scene from Havana: "Edenia Rivera is picking up her family's monthly allotment of 6 pounds of rice per person at the Vedado bodega. The rice is shipped to Cuba from China. She says she would 'die' without the subsidized food. Rivera buys a pound of rice each day for her family and says she doesn't have the extra 40 cents it would cost at market prices. 'I hope they never take the ration book away,' she says."[103]

COULD CONSUMPTION CEILINGS RETURN?

It should be obvious that a business-as-usual model is not an option, for either human health and well-being or a sustainable environment. Once this fact is appreciated, we can get on with discussing the alternatives— to minimise regret for future generations.
    —Garry Egger and Boyd Swinburn, *Planet Obesity*, 2010[104]

In the United States, a staggering four thousand calories' worth of food is available per person, yet the government, out of necessity, operates one of the largest food-assistance programs in the world: the

Supplemental Nutrition Assistance Program (SNAP, formerly known as the food-stamp program). Here, however, rising hunger and rising obesity have coexisted for years. That seeming paradox fits a global pattern. As societies become more affluent, the rate of overconsumption of food, and therefore of obesity, tends to rise even faster than income, so by the time a country achieves a comfortable standard of living it has already overshot the optimal level of food intake. There appear to be no exceptions to this; the market, in other words, does not seem to contain any mechanism to balance prosperity and food consumption.[105] Is it possible that food rationing could ever be employed as a remedy?

Most present-day food-security systems ration a portion of the food supply and leave individual consumption otherwise unrestricted. Rationing to improve nutrition would have to be more like the U.S. and UK systems in the 1940s or of Cuba today.[106] Although, as Mark Roodhouse puts it, "In Britain during World War II, we were rationing food scarcity, while in America you were rationing plenty," both countries rationed the total supply of certain foodstuffs, imposing consumption ceilings as well as floors. Rachel Davey, currently the director of the Centre for Research and Action in Public Health at the University of Canberra, thinks rationing could and should be initiated for the sake of health. In a 2004 paper, Davey observed, "We have tried asking people to eat fewer foods of poor nutritional value, but when these foods are advertised and promoted so widely, our poorly funded entreaties have had little effect." Therefore, she wrote, stronger measures may be needed:

> It is not inconceivable that some form of food rationing and portion size control may be required in the future if the dramatic rise in obesity continues. This could be achieved through the supermarkets, as most of the food that we consume in the home is purchased at a relatively small number of food outlets. All of the big supermarkets produce an item by item breakdown of goods purchased on the till receipt. It is possible in theory to estimate most of one's average food consumption each month.[107]

In other words, we would adopt wartime-style consumer rationing. Similarly, the Norfolk Island carbon-trading plan, although voluntary, would limit food consumption. There are also proposals for upstream rationing. In a 2011 article in the *New England Journal of Medicine*, Kristina Lewis and Meredith Rosenthalin proposed a cap-and-trade policy to limit quantities of unhealthful food components such as saturated fats, sugar, and sodium that are included in products being sold by the food industry. They wrote, "Reliance on individual incentives and wellness programs, though politically expedient, probably won't overcome the forces behind poor nutrition. Given the alternative approaches, we believe that capping and trading certain food ingredients is worthy of consideration." Furthermore, "cap and trade would not directly limit consumer choice and would avoid the direct taxation of products—approaches resisted by the U.S. public."[108] People in the global North have shown that they will accept rationing of the entire food supply in response to externally induced shortages, and a small minority have considered the possibility of carbon rationing to stave off global ecological crises. But it is difficult to grasp how a mandatory program for weight reduction or nutritional improvement, as advocated by Davey, Lewis, and Rosenthalin, could overcome the almost instinctive public resistance that is likely to greet it.

Many climate watchers are urging a reduction in agriculture's carbon footprint, and that could be another impetus for food rationing. It has been suggested that for one class of food in particular—meat—rationing by quantity could have a beneficial climate impact. Through release of carbon dioxide, methane, and nitrogen oxides, as well as destruction of vegetation and desertification, global livestock production has been estimated to make an annual contribution to atmospheric warming equal to that of 7.3 billion tons of carbon dioxide—an astonishing 18 percent of total human-caused emissions. Worldwide meat consumption is about 100 grams per person per day, but high-consuming populations eat about ten times as much meat as low-consuming populations. Anthony McMichael of the Australian National University and his colleagues in Australia and Britain came up with those estimates of emissions from livestock raising, and that led them to recommend a "working global target" of 90 grams of animal protein consumption per day per person, shared as equitably as possible, in the spirit of contraction and convergence. Were meat consumption to be equalized, people in the global South would be able to double their average intake, whereas the average resident of the North would face a 60 percent average reduction in meat eating. In the pursuit of such goals, reductions in greenhouse-gas emissions and obesity rates would tend to reinforce each other.[109]

McMichael and his co-authors acknowledge the political difficulties that would be faced by any attempt to achieve complete equality in this especially sensitive sector of the human diet, but they stress, "Privileged groups in high-income countries (including the UK) have already shown willingness to reduce their consumption of animal foods, apparently in relation to the risk of cardiovascular disease."[110] Australia's National Health and Medical Research Council, they note, recently issued revised National Dietary Guidelines that include a recommendation that Australian men cut their red meat consumption by 20 percent on average. And of course many people around the world already have reduced meat consumption or have gone vegetarian in response to environmentally destructive and often cruel factory-farm methods of livestock production. Still, voluntary cutbacks have not had a significant impact thus far on the meat industry's emissions.

If in the struggle to hold down greenhouse-gas concentrations, high-emitting countries manage to make the recommended cuts of 60 or 80 percent in their total emissions, a 60 percent cut in meat eating might turn out to be one of the easier parts of that transition— easier than, say, cutting back on home heating or transportation. A much smaller demand for grain-fed animal products could help reduce the land area devoted to corn, soybean, and other soil-damaging feedgrains while putting an end to factory farming of animals and the waste, pollution, health threats, and human exploitation for which the industry is notorious. Nevertheless, such a deep reduction in meat production and consumption might be difficult to achieve through any means other than rationing. A far-fetched idea? Maybe so—and McMichael himself believes that meat consumption could continue to decline over future generations without rationing—but we know for a fact it's not impossible, because less than seventy years ago it was a way of life in some of the very North American and European countries where, according to McMichael and many others, much lower meat consumption will be required in the future.

Public distribution of food rations appears to have become a permanent feature of economies not only in India, Egypt, Iraq, and Cuba, but in a wide variety of countries on every continent. With world per-capita grain production continuing to fall, the world's soil and water resources degrading at alarming rates, and food prices often rising much faster than those of other goods, it is easier to imagine that more countries will adopt rationing—of subsidized food only or of total food supplies—than to imagine that food rationing will disappear.

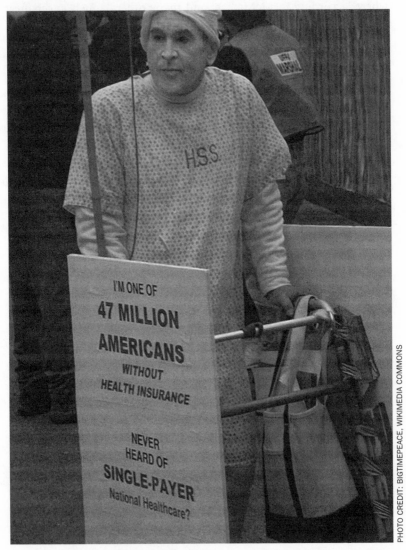

The sign reads:

I'M ONE OF
47 MILLION
AMERICANS
WITHOUT
HEALTH INSURANCE

NEVER
HEARD OF
SINGLE-PAYER
National Healthcare?

Supporter of a single-payer health care plan demonstrates at an April 4, 2009, "March on Wall Street" in New York City's financial district.

6

PAINFUL QUESTIONS, ELUSIVE ANSWERS

We will never have an acceptable answer to the question: how much money should we spend to save someone's life? And we will probably never resolve our inconsistencies about the values we place on saving identifiably ill patients versus saving statistical lives through preventive care. But moral dilemmas do not lose their relevance simply because they are irresolvable. Instead, their irresolvability indicates their continued relevance. We must never stop debating the price of life. And we must never stop arguing about how much to spend on health care.

—Peter Ubel, *Pricing Life:*
Why It's Time for Health-Care Rationing, 2000 [1]

Rationing is certainly the third rail of American politics.
—Leonard J. Nelson III, 2011 [2]

In the early days of Ronald Reagan's administration, Mary Ann Baily served as a staff economist on the President's Commission for the Study of Ethical Problems in Medicine and Biomedical and Behavioral Research. The commission's assignment was to study inequity in America's health care system, and in 1983 Baily helped write its report "Securing Access to Health Care." Reflecting on that experience soon after the work was completed, Baily applauded the fact that the final version of the report "directly addresses the issue of limits on care" and "explains why it is in our interest to limit the health care we receive to the care that is worth its cost, rather than to receive all care that would be of any possible benefit." However, she noted, "nowhere in the report does the word *rationing* appear." Instead, the commissioners preferred to use terms like "allocation" and "elimination of waste." In fact, Baily was asked to remove the word "rationing" from the title of the section that she wrote for the report.[3]

Baily went to her dictionary, looked up "allocate" and "ration," and pointed out, "Both of these definitions are about apportioning supplies out to particular persons; but the word *ration* emphasizes equity in the face of scarcity, whereas *allocate* carries no overtones of either scarcity or equity. If the commissioners think that it is important to recognize that all resources are scarce, and if they think that health care resources should be allocated in accord with an equity principle, then the term *rationing* is an appropriate term." She also objected to the use of the euphemism "waste": "Like *rationing*, the word *waste* has emotional overtones; but *rationing* sounds negative and generates controversy, whereas *eliminating waste* sounds positive and generates support. Thus, in debates about cost control, it can be tempting to phrase proposals in terms of 'eliminating waste' rather than 'limiting services to those which are worth their cost' or, even more inflammatory, 'rationing care.'" But, she predicted, policy makers could not hide behind words like "allocate" and "waste" for long; people know rationing when they see it.[4]

But do we? Today, there is still widespread disagreement on what constitutes rationing in the world of medicine. In the United States, there has long been near-universal agreement that spending on health care is too high and growing too fast. To date, almost all policies aimed at restraining that growth have been designed explicitly to prevent non-price rationing, and so far, spending has not been controlled. Health care, which accounted for 7 percent of GDP in 1970, has ballooned to 18 percent of GDP today. And with new, more costly medicines and medical procedures being developed every year, the industry's share of the economy will continue to expand.[5]

That mammoth system is able to provide millions of Americans with a vast array of treatments from which they might benefit, while at the same time failing to provide adequate care to millions of other people because they lack sufficient money and insurance. Does that mean we are already rationing care? Or will rationing begin only when we adopt a national policy that limits all patients' access to certain types of treatments in order to make other, more effective treatments available to everyone? And if there is such a thing as a right to health care—and most of us today believe there is—then how could we tolerate any policy that denies beneficial treatment to anyone, whatever the size of the benefit?

In Baily's view, the health care debate, stuck on such seemingly insoluble questions, is getting nowhere. Three decades after her experience on the President's Commission, Baily is feeling, as she puts it, "pretty despondent." She recalls that, in preparing to give a talk on rationing in 2011, "I looked back, reviewing the discussion over the past thirty years, and I became very unnerved. Everything I have written on this subject since the presidential commission is still totally relevant!"[6]

Yet it's not really surprising that we have a hard time agreeing even on the terms of the debate. As we search for a fair way in which to share scarce, increasingly costly medical resources—with their immediate, highly visible impacts on our well-being and survival—there may be no solution that will satisfy anyone very much. Compromises are essential. But in health care, more than in any other part of our economic lives, compromise can seem just plain wrong. Is there any way to guarantee all Americans' right to health care without letting the medical industry drain off a bigger share of our increasingly scarce resources every year?

NOT YOUR TYPICAL COMMODITY

An American medical economy that exceeds the entire GDPs of all but four of the world's nations could, one would think, provide health for everyone. But millions of Americans go without adequate care. (The 2012 announcement that growth in health care spending had slowed to 4 percent per year in 2009–10 led to great celebration. But growth was down from the 7 percent rate of 2004–6 largely because of the recession and the ensuing loss of health insurance for many. Even a 4 percent rate would double the size of the health economy in twenty years, and without systemic change that rate of growth could not extend health security to the currently uninsured part of the population under the system now in place). Few (if any) would argue that we, as individuals or as a society, should spend escalating sums year after year in order to have access to every possible medical service we might want. As Baily puts it, "Believe me, you don't *want* to have everything you want."[7] Everyone on all sides of the health care debate agrees that expenditures must be reduced, yet no one, it seems, wants to deny any individual the right to all the medical treatments they want and can pay for.

Defenders of purely profit-driven medicine use the word "rationing" strategically, pretending that it looms out there somewhere in a grim future when we will not be able to buy unlimited medical treatment. It often emerges as an all-purpose scare tactic. In his failed campaign to pressure the U.S. Supreme Court into declaring the 2010 Patient Protection and Affordable Care Act (PPACA) unconstitutional, Governor Rick Scott of Florida repeatedly (and erroneously) charged that the law would trigger explicit rationing of services.[8] During the 2011 congressional shoot-out over the federal budget, Michael Cannon of the libertarian Cato Institute was asserting that House Budget Committee chair Paul Ryan's proposed privatization of Medicare would "protect seniors from government rationing" at the very same time that the Congressional Budget Office was predicting that Ryan's plan would *necessitate* rationing. Two years earlier, in the heat of the debate over the health care overhaul that would eventually become PPACA, not even "rationing" seemed to be a scary enough term. Sarah Palin, the former governor of Alaska, supplied the bill's opponents with their most alarmist talking point yet when she charged that, if it were passed, "the sick, the elderly, and the disabled" would have to "stand in front of Obama's 'death panel'" to learn whether they would be eligible for treatment.[9]

While there is almost unanimous agreement that medical rationing is not something to be desired, there is no consensus at all about what constitutes rationing. When medical economists discuss rationing, they generally have in mind a definition something like this concise one offered by Alan Maynard in the journal *Health Policy*: "Rationing takes place when an individual is deprived of care which is of benefit (in terms of improving health status, or the length and quality of life) and which is desired by the patient."[10] To deprive people of beneficial care sounds heartless indeed; it's no wonder so few public figures want to be associated with rationing health care. But there are two things to consider about Maynard's definition. First, the size of the benefit is not specified: to deny any treatment with a benefit greater than zero, no

matter how small, is to ration. Second, depriving a patient of beneficial treatment, however undesirable it may seem, already happens all
the time. (As Baily notes, "Rationing slipped in under the radar before
radar was invented.")[11]

As we sort through the conflicts over limits on medicine, we will
consider rationing of treatments that are scarce in an absolute sense
(like organ transplants) as well as those that must be made scarce intentionally because of limits on the size of the medical system as a
whole. We will also compare explicit rationing with rationing that is
strictly implicit—denial of beneficial treatment that is justified to the
patient and to society as being something other than rationing.[12]

Of course, as with food, water, and energy, the most pervasive form
of implicit rationing is the limitation of access according to ability to
pay. In the U.S. health system, access to care depends on insurance
status, income, and eligibility for government programs. Under such
a system, one portion of the population is "deprived of care which
is of benefit," while another portion is not. At the other end of the
spectrum—in, let's say, the fictional nation of Rashonia—everyone has
access to the same range of medical treatments, but some treatments
for certain conditions are explicitly denied to all. As we will see, most
real-world health care systems lie somewhere between those of America and Rashonia: there is no nation that provides unlimited care for
everyone, and no nation explicitly bans specific beneficial treatments
altogether.

Of course, rationing of all sorts of goods by ability to pay often
goes unrecognized as rationing. But in health care, the picture is pulled
even further out of focus by differential access to insurance. When the
health care debate was boiling over in 2009, Uwe Reinhart, an economics professor at Princeton University, wrote, "One must wonder
where people worried about 'rationing' health care have been in the last
20 years. Could they possibly be unaware that the United States health
system has rationed health care in spades for many years, on the economist's definition of rationing?" He cited a long list of studies showing
that people without insurance regularly do not make needed visits to
the doctor; that eighteen thousand people die prematurely every year
for want of timely health care; that uninsured Americans receive only

43 percent as many dollars' worth of medical care as their privately insured compatriots; that uninsured middle-class families pay higher prices than those with insurance; and that "uninsured victims of severe traffic accidents receive 20 percent less health care than equivalent, insured victims and are 37 percent more likely to die from their injuries."[13]

The prospect of medical rationing raises knottier questions than the rationing of food, water, energy, or greenhouse emissions.[14] The first problem is that medical needs vary enormously. People of a given age, sex, and activity level have fairly predictable requirements for water, calories, protein, etc., and it's a fairly simple matter to declare that all humans have a right to this or that quantity of food and water. Even with energy consumption, for which needs vary more widely among people and households, it's usually possible to set reasonable upper limits beyond which consumption is considered to be excessive. But requirements for medical care are anything but uniform. We differ in our genetic susceptibility to disease; we are exposed to very different sets of diverse health hazards over a lifetime; we may go for ten years without even setting foot in a doctor's office and then suddenly be struck down by an accident or disease that requires weeks or even years of costly treatment. It is not possible to specify a fixed quantity of lifetime medical treatment to which every citizen is entitled and which no one may exceed. As we will see, deciding how to proceed fairly under such conditions is difficult indeed.

Second, what we call "health care" is a conglomeration of many diverse products and services. Good water is good water; foods are freely interchangeable; and while fuels differ they can be compared easily in a nonmonetary currency such as energy content or carbon emissions. But for someone who needs dialysis, a ration coupon stating, "Good for one cardiac bypass surgery, two rounds of chemotherapy, and twelve office visits" would be useless. Much of the wrangling over medical rationing has focused on how to decide the value of widely varying treatments in terms other than money.

Third, when we try to determine what constitutes "fair shares for all" in health care, we're shooting at a moving target. Medical research is constantly creating new necessities. Many highly touted technological advances may address non-life-threatening conditions, while others may provide only marginal improvements in the length or quality of life, yet most can be shown to confer a measurable benefit. If a treatment can benefit a patient, doctors have a duty to use it: it officially becomes a basic need, as much a need as water. Medical technologies cannot be uninvented; those that prove to do more good than ill (no matter how small the difference between the good and the ill) will accumulate in the doctor's arsenal. To deny any one of them to a patient is to ration it.

A final difference lies at the heart of today's struggles over health care. When faced with tough decisions on food, water, and energy, societies can resort to an easy (if often unfair) way out: let the market decide where the commodity will go. But rationing by price works very poorly in the medical economies of wealthy nations. For one thing, these are purchases nobody really wants to make. They arise not from consumer preferences but from dire necessity, and we patients need protection against costly overtreatment as much as we need assurance of necessary treatment. Even though she is an expert in medical economics, Baily says she is "scared to death" of having to go to the emergency room herself. There, she says, the patient is utterly vulnerable: "I have no idea how to control all those things a hospital staff might decide to do to me." As a result, a medical professional makes our purchasing decisions for us. And price does not influence those decisions in the way it would in a "normal" market, because in most cases it is an insurance company or the government that pays the bulk of the cost, not the individual. With prices excused from their enforcement duties, the market spins out of control. And with fantastic profits out there to be made, the medical industry has every incentive to keep that market spinning.

In their 2005 book *Can We Say No? The Challenge of Rationing Health Care*, Henry Aaron, William Schwartz, and Melissa Cox observed that in the United States we appear to have little trouble accepting that millions lack adequate health coverage, while "in a strange exercise in mental compartmentalization, limits on care for those with good health insurance or enough money to pay seem strange and unthinkable." They argue that putting limits on medical products that have small benefits will not degrade the overall health system; on the contrary, by freeing up resources, such rationing could improve overall access to effective care. They further argue that "intelligent rationing, informed by solid research on the medical results of various procedures and people's evaluation of those results, will increase social welfare. And, if rationing averts misconceived efforts to lower health care spending for vulnerable populations or to reduce spending on medical research, it can improve overall health as well."[15]

EARLY MEDICAL RATIONING

Before wrestling with the question of how to impose limits on health spending, it is useful to examine how the medical profession handles rationing of resources that are in absolute shortage, with no good alternative treatments at hand: health care's version of siege rationing.

In the early 1920s, for example, when Frederick Banting and Charles Best discovered how to use insulin for the treatment of diabetes, they suddenly faced a huge public demand but were able to produce only a very limited supply of the drug. There was no model to follow in deciding how to ration insulin, so the decisions were mostly ad hoc. Banting decided to use two-thirds of the supply for treating his own patients and distribute the rest through two hospitals, one of them a hospital for children. Within those venues, it was reported, "emotional, political, and personal appeals often influenced who received treatment." Among a number of prominent recipients was the daughter of the U.S. secretary of state.[16]

In the years 1942–44, the newly discovered antibiotic penicillin was rationed within the United States and by the U.S. military overseas. Low output from manufacturers and heavy combat demand meant that the supply available for civilian use was severely limited. The Roosevelt administration's Committee on Medical Research decided that penicillin prescribed for civilians should be part of a clinical research program conducted by an agency called the Committee on Chemotherapy (COC). Word was getting around that penicillin was a "miracle drug," and COC members evaluated the accelerating requests for it from across the country on a case-by-case basis. Criteria were strict:

only illnesses caused by bacteria known to be sensitive to penicillin and resistant to sulfonamide (the standard treatment at that time) would be treated, and only if doing so would "yield information useful to the war effort." Lawyers advising the COC warned that "humanitarian considerations" should not play a part in decisions when a case would not advance the medical research program or contribute to the war effort. COC chief Chester Keefer followed that advice to the letter.[17]

The rationing effort was dogged by media frenzies. Breathless reports in the New York press about a sick toddler named Patricia Malone prompted the U.S. surgeon general to have four hundred thousand units of the drug sent to her doctor, overriding the COC's authority. Newspapers also trumpeted the case of Marie Barker of Chicago, who suffered from bacterial endocarditis, an infection of the heart. Doctors were not sure at that time whether penicillin would be effective in curing endocarditis (as they later learned, it is not), and COC had determined that the disease did not qualify for treatment because it was "of no military importance." In news stories, Keefer was often portrayed as "heartless and insensitive." For his part, the penicillin czar grumbled, "What I should like more than anything else is to keep my name out of the papers."[18] He lost much sleep during that period because he was constantly awakened in the wee hours by desperate phone calls, including ones from a U.S. senator and the secretary of state, pleading on behalf of favored patients—many of whom had diseases such as cancer or lupus that are not treatable with antibiotics of any kind. Keefer also had to deal with rogue physicians who requested penicillin for approved purposes but then used it to treat endocarditis patients. That, in effect, denied penicillin to patients with diseases for which the drug had proved highly effective. But the COC adhered faithfully to the rules it had laid down and kept almost total control over the penicillin supply. David Adams, who wrote the history of the penicillin-rationing episode, explained that "bureaucratic administration lay at the heart of the program of wartime penicillin rationing" to permit "authority figures to depersonalize judgments." The result, Adams concluded, was that the COC's handling of penicillin "provides an excellent case study of the equitable and efficient distribution of a scarce medical resource."[19]

In 1946–47, the UK's Medical Research Council used the newly discovered antibiotic streptomycin in clinical trials to treat tuberculosis.
Streptomycin was still very scarce in Britain, so doctors used a lottery
to determine which patients would receive the treatment and which
would unknowingly join the unlucky control group. Denial of a known
effective treatment would normally have been controversial, but the
short supply of streptomycin limited the total number of patients who
could be treated, and pure chance was viewed as the fairest and most
scientifically valid means of allocating the drug. The study became fa-
mous as the first randomized drug trial. Commemorating its fiftieth
anniversary, the science historian P. D'Arcy Hart observed, "In the era
of the slogan, 'fair shares for all,' the suspicion of favouritism was to
be avoided" and that random allocation relieved doctors of making
wrenching personal decisions.[20]

If experiences with scarce drugs in the 1940s provide good examples
of how to ration, the first clinical use of kidney dialysis demonstrated
how not to do it. When in the early 1960s Belding Scribner and co-
workers at the University of Washington developed a workable method
for using hemodialysis to treat end-stage kidney disease, they set up the
Artificial Kidney Center in Seattle to treat patients as part of a clinical
trial. Because there were only enough machines and personnel to treat
a tiny fraction of eligible patients, rationing immediately became necessary. In 1961, a group of citizens was asked to form an Admissions
and Policies Committee responsible for selecting patients to be treated
at the center. They were provided "no moral or ethical guidelines save
their own individual consciences," according to Shana Alexander, who
wrote an explosive story on the committee for *Life* magazine. The committee included "a lawyer, a minister, a banker, a housewife, an official
of state government, a labor leader, and a surgeon"—all local citizens.
Many years later, in admiration of the work of the group he termed the
"God Squad," the medical ethicist Albert Jonsen called the committee
"faceless, impersonal, unmoved by tragedy, almost terrorist in aspect."[21]

Doctors advised the committee against recommending for treatment either children (because of the misery it would cause them) or
people over forty-five (because of their poorer prospects). Otherwise,
the group was on its own. At the committee's first meeting, members

decided on the criteria they would use: "age and sex of patient; marital status and number of dependents; income; net worth; emotional stability, with particular regard to the patient's capacity to accept the treatment; educational background; nature of occupation, past performance and future potential; and name of people who could serve as references." It went without saying that under those criteria in that era, male patients would rise inevitably to the top of the list. And despite Jonsen's praise, the list was not immune to manipulation from outside. David Mechanic, now director of the Institute for Health, Health Care Policy and Aging at Rutgers University, confirmed that one day he was having lunch in Seattle with the center's chief nephrologist (presumably Scribner) as plans were made to allow a friend of the state of Washington's senior senator—and a major promoter of the state medical school—into the dialysis program as a "research subject," sidestepping the God Squad.[22]

When hemodialysis vacancies became available, the Admissions and Policies Committee would be provided with a list of candidates to fill them. In one typical case, they were given five names to consider for two open slots. Alexander reconstructed portions of their deliberations based on the memories of the participants. This is an excerpt:

HOUSEWIFE: If we are still looking for the men with the highest potential of service to society, I think we must consider that the chemist and the accountant have the finest educational backgrounds of all five candidates.

SURGEON: How do the rest of you feel about Number Three—the small businessman with three children? I am impressed that his doctor took special pains to mention this man is active in church work. This is an indication to me of character and moral strength.

HOUSEWIFE: Which certainly would help him conform to the demands of the treatment . . .

LAWYER: It would also help him to endure a lingering death . . .

STATE OFFICIAL: But that would seem to be placing a penalty on the very people who perhaps have the most provident . . .

MINISTER: And both these families have three children too.

LABOR LEADER: For the children's sake, we've got to reckon with the surviving parents' opportunity to remarry, and a woman with three children has a better chance to find a new husband than a very young widow with six children.

SURGEON: How can we possibly be sure of that? . . .

However casual their dialogue might sound, committee members agonized over the grim choices they had to make. The minister told Alexander, "I do have reservations about the moral aspects, the propriety of choosing A and not B for whatever reason. I have often asked myself—as a human being, do I have that right? I don't really think I do. I finally came to the conclusion that we are not making a moral choice here—we are picking guinea pigs for experimental purposes. This happens to be true: it also happens to be the way I rationalize my presence on this committee." He added, "In this situation our function is to take the pressure off the doctors." The state official told her, "We have forced ourselves to make life-or-death decisions on a virtually intuitive basis. I do have real faith in the ability of kindly, conscientious, intelligent people to do a good job guided simply by their instincts, but we ought not to go on this way." The surgeon made what may have been the most revealing comments: "You know, at our committee's first meeting we seriously discussed selecting candidates by drawing straws. We were going to make it easy on ourselves by having a human lottery! Frankly, I was almost ready to vote for the lottery idea myself. In the practice as a surgeon, the responsibility of making life-or-death choices faces me practically every day, and I can tell you this: I do sleep better at night after deciding on one of these committee cases than I sleep after deciding a case of my own."[23]

Researchers looking back at the Seattle experience wrote in 2005, "The committee's decisionmaking process reflected the values and biases of White, middle-class Protestant American society: the committee chose patients most like themselves," and such biases were not lost on the public even in the early 1960s. When Alexander's story appeared, it touched off a heated controversy, which led the committee to formalize the process further, limiting criteria to those that were meant to indicate patients' psychological capacity for tolerating and sticking with what was a grueling lifelong regimen of spending three nights a week, twelve hours a night, attached to the machine at the clinic.[24]

BEYOND TRIAGE

Not long after those early attempts to ration modern medical technology under conditions of absolute scarcity, the development of organ transplantation created a whole new set of ethical difficulties. At times and in places where there have been neither bans on organ selling nor well-enforced allocation systems, the market has taken over, with often shocking results.[25] Buying and selling of human organs is strictly banned in most of the world today. Instead, most countries require allocation of organs through waiting-list systems such as the United Network of Organ Sharing (UNOS) in the United States. For a kidney or a pancreas, a patient's time on the waiting list is the primary factor, with some weight given to urgency and probable outcome, while for hearts, urgent need is more important than waiting time. For lung and liver transplants, the three criteria are treated as equally important. Criteria to be avoided are spelled out by the American Society of Transplantation's statement of ethics: "A patient should not be excluded from consideration for a transplant solely on the basis of gender, race, ethnicity, religion, mental capacity, social status or financial background."[26]

Such biases can creep into the process nevertheless, even when no one intends them. There are large racial disparities, for example, in waiting time for kidney transplants. Along with socioeconomic factors, physicians' judgment, and geographical location, one factor widening the disparity is the lower degree of immunological matching between black American kidney patients and available kidneys when compared with white American patients. Closeness of match is one of the criteria used in selecting recipients, because closer matches lead to lower rejection rates. In the mid-1990s, when black patients were waiting twice as long as whites for kidney transplants, Peter Ubel and his colleagues conducted three versions of an opinion survey. In one, members of the general public were asked if they approved of antigen-matching rules that would improve transplant outcomes overall by 5 to 10 percent but would mean that black patients had to wait twice as long for a kidney as would whites. In the second version, a different set of subjects was asked the question, but with one difference: they were told (inaccurately) that it is white patients who must wait twice as long because of antigen matching. With both versions of the question and whatever the race of the respondent, there was overwhelming disapproval of antigen matching if it caused racial disparities. Subjects in a third group were also asked about their opinions of antigen matching, having been informed of the same small improvement in outcome, but this time there was no mention of race. Instead, they were told that matching would cause people with blood types B and O to wait twice as long for a kidney as those with types A and AB. This time, respondents were significantly more likely to approve of antigen matching as a criterion.[27] Therefore, a transplant policy that affects people of different races differently is widely considered to be wrong, whereas a policy that discriminates against a group of people on the basis of blood type (a trait no more under a patient's control than skin color) appears to be thought of more like a lottery. In such ways, we take positions on allocation that may appear inconsistent to a purely logical observer, but those positions show clearly that most of us have a very strong, and admirable, desire to avoid racial discrimination.

Other disparities in organ transplantation are purely economic. Among almost five thousand organ transplants done in the United States in 2003, fewer than 1 percent of recipients lacked health insurance, but 17 percent of donors had no coverage.[28]

Another common type of situation calling for rationing is a drug shortage. Despite the boom in the development and marketing of pharmaceuticals, Philip Rosoff of Duke University Medical School writes that "unanticipated and critical drug shortages have become a constant and a way of life for hospitals in the United States," thanks to sporadic manufacturing difficulties, financial troubles, and problems in distribution networks. When a hospital or region faces sudden scarcity of a drug, there is currently little choice beyond "distributing the dwindling supply of the drug on an ad hoc, first-come-first-served basis." Rosoff points out that it obviously would be better to plan ahead and develop "ethically defensible and fair distribution systems." He argues, "The foremost criterion for giving one patient access to a scarce drug over another should be demonstrable evidence of a superior clinical therapeutic effect in the selected patient. This is the theoretical and practical underpinning of evidence-based medicine." Based on such considerations, if the available supply of a drug could treat a larger number of people effectively with short courses, rather than treating one or a few people with a long or indefinite course, then the larger number should be treated. "However," Rosoff continues, "it would be unfair to remove a person from preexisting treatment with a scarce drug in favor of someone who has not yet initiated treatment, unless there are very good reasons to do so," such as a known lack of benefit or looming death. Such "tragic choices" should be approached "with a maximum of compassion." [29]

The most interesting questions raised by Rosoff deal with what should be done when a drug shortage has passed: "Do the institution and its prescribers simply return to their prior way of practice, prescribing without paying heed to the evidence supporting a specific use, utilizing expensive 'me-too' drugs when cheaper generic substitutes with equivalent risk–benefit ratios are available, etc.? Or could one take advantage of a lesson that may be learned during the crisis: that medical practice can be altered without catastrophic consequences to either doctors or patients?"

Vaccine shortages arise regularly. In the case of influenza, they occur partly because of manufacturers' inability to predict precisely, months in advance, which viral strains will be most widespread the following winter. The U.S. Department of Health and Human Services recommends that in a flu pandemic, vaccine be rationed to the following groups, listed in order of priority, before any remaining supplies go to the general population:

Vaccine and antiviral manufacturers and medical personnel who are involved in direct patient contact, essential support services, or vaccination

Medically vulnerable people

Pregnant women and household contacts of immunocompromised or small children

Emergency response workers "critical to pandemic response" and political leaders

Healthy elderly people and children aged 6 months to 2 years

Emergency workers in public safety, utilities, transportation, and telecommunications

Essential government health decision makers, funeral directors, and embalmers[30]

Shortages of drugs, vaccines, and many other treatments can prompt rationing through some form of triage. Starting with the simplest triage methods used for sorting battlefield victims—identifying those who will recover without treatment, those who will die whether or not they are treated, and those whom treatment can save—a variety of methods to sort patients have evolved according to predetermined clinical criteria, with critically scarce resources being rationed among them accordingly. A calamity on the scale of the 1918 flu pandemic, in which an H1N1 strain of the flu virus infected 27 percent of the world's population, killing 3 to 6 percent, would impose some of the toughest such decisions a health system can face. It would, for example, overwhelm any national health system's capacity to supply respiratory ventilators to the large numbers of people whose lung function would suddenly become impaired. In 2007, the New York State Department of Health (NYSDH) and the New York State Task Force on Life and the Law drafted a set of guidelines for rationing ventilators during a pandemic.[31] In the procedure that the workgroup suggested, health workers would first apply "exclusion criteria" to patients. Those suffering cardiac arrest, metastatic cancer with a poor prognosis, burns on 40 percent or more of the body, or end-stage organ failure would simply not qualify for a ventilator. Age would not be an explicit criterion. Patients making it past those thresholds would be subjected to triage according to their "sequential organ failure assessment" score. Generally, that process would allocate ventilators to patients with intermediate scores; those too sick to have good prospects even if provided a ventilator and those who would probably survive without a ventilator would not get one. Patients placed on a ventilator would be scored again at 48 and 120 hours, and those who had either worsened or improved to the extent that they no longer qualified would be taken off. Crucially, personnel involved in treating patients during a pandemic would be "sequestered" from these triage decisions. The workgroup stressed that rationing of ventilators did not imply that ineligible patients would simply be shown the door; rather, they would receive appropriate treatment and palliative care. They further warned that the procedure they outlined is a make-do measure that cannot resolve larger questions of fairness, writing, "Ethically, access to health care is unequal, and no rationing system for a crisis can resolve inequities in preexisting health status that result from unequal access." But in a controversial move designed to increase the ultimate number of survivors, the workgroup decided that patients who are already in the hospital when triage is initiated will be assessed according to the same criteria as those newly arriving, with the result that existing patients' machines could be taken from them if they are needed by new patients of higher priority.[32]

Other states, including Florida, joined New York in making plans to ration ventilators, and, not surprisingly, such explicit talk of removing people from life-sustaining equipment provoked controversy—especially when the threat of a new H1N1 pandemic arose in 2009.[33] During an emergency-preparedness exercise that year, one that was partly based on the NYSDH guidelines, state health officials asked a group of New York–Presbyterian Hospital staff how they would deal with the hypothetical case of a man with cystic fibrosis in need of an appendectomy who arrives at their emergency room with his own ventilator in the middle of a flu pandemic. The guidelines say that he should be admitted for treatment but that, because he suffers from a disease "associated with high mortality," the ventilator that keeps him alive should be taken from him and provided to a flu victim. The medical professionals reportedly said they would refuse to comply with such a rule "unless given legal protection." A physician-ethicist leading the exercise said, "The issue of removing patients from ventilators was so overwhelming that it precluded discussion of further case scenarios." [34]

Every day, personnel in hospital emergency rooms are faced with urgent rationing decisions involving scarce time, space, people, and equipment. Patients tend to accept a long wait in an emergency room without objection because that's what they expect, and because they assume that people in greatest need of urgent care are being seen first. One survey asking British patients about their emergency-room experiences appeared to find a high level of trust in the staff; as one patient said of the priorities set by the medical staff under trying circumstances, "They've a good idea, haven't they really?" In Britain, patients do not normally pay for emergency-room treatment. When the surveyors asked patients about "the hypothetical notion of paying to be seen more quickly," they tended to find such a prospect unacceptable: "All interviewees raised the issue of equity; that it would be unfair on those who could not afford to pay." But interestingly, many of the same respondents who objected in principle to a payment system also said that if they had a serious complaint and were suffering pain, they would be willing to pay to move up the queue—if it didn't cost too much! [35]

CAN THERE BE SUCH A THING AS ETHICAL RATIONING IN MEDICINE?

In rationing scarce medical care, the concept of "fair shares for all" cannot mean "equal shares for all." The basic ethical questions to be answered are usually put something like this:

What priority should be given to those with the most serious or urgent conditions, as compared with those who have better prospects for a good outcome?

When should small benefits to a large number of people outweigh large benefits to a small number?

How can we choose between fair individual chances and the best overall outcome? [36]

According to John Harris, a British professor of bioethics, an even more fundamental question must be answered before addressing those three: should we *ever* give priority to one person, group of people, or type of treatment over another? His answer to that is an unequivocal "No." Citing his belief in the equal value of every human life, Harris refuses to accept the use of any human judgment at all in deciding how to ration medical care. He writes, "The principle of equal access to health care is sustained by the very same reasons that sustain both the principle of equality before the law and the civil rights required to defend the freedom of the individual. These are rightly considered so important that no limit is set on the cost of sustaining them. Equal access to health care is of equal importance and should be accorded the same priority for analogous reasons." [37]

Harris believes cost should not impose a limit on medical care offered. In cases of absolute scarcity, when there is simply not enough of a treatment to go around at any price, his principles imply that a lottery should decide who is to be treated. As we have seen, random selection can be acceptable as part of a clinical trial of an absolutely scarce drug. But, as the ethicist Mark Stein argues, rationing by lottery in other situations can easily lead to unacceptable outcomes: "Suppose that the two candidates for life-saving treatment are (1) a 20-year-old with a post-treatment life expectancy of fifty additional years and (2) an 85-year-old with a post-treatment life expectancy of one additional year. Surely, we cannot accept a theory that gives the 85-year-old an equal chance of receiving the scarce treatment." A compromise approach would be to maximize years of life saved when potential differences are large, while applying random selection when differences are small. That could be done through a "weighted lottery," in which those who would gain more years from treatment receive more lottery "tickets," so to speak, than those who would benefit less.[38] Another way to avoid rationing decisions is to go by the first-come, first-served principle. As we've seen, such rationing by queuing is used at times in distributing water and food, and it happens in clinics everywhere. But when applied in medicine it can favor the affluent, "who become informed and travel more quickly, and can queue for interventions without competing employment or child care concerns."[39]

If we are to assign priority for scarce medical resources, it is commonly suggested that it should go to those in the most desperate situations.[40] This may often seem to be the most "natural" way to proceed, thanks to an apparently universal human propensity that Albert Jonsen has named the "rule of rescue": the imperative to provide treatment first to anyone who would soon die otherwise, whatever size of the gain in length or quality of life. In coining the term, Jonson used some of the more prominent human-heart transplant recipients as examples:

> Should we encourage the development of the artificial heart? Of course we must, it is said, because it rescues the doomed from certain death. And those doomed to death are certainly quite visible individuals—Dr. Barney Clark, William Schroeder, Baby Jamey Fisk, and baby Jesse, my son, your wife, the nice man next door—rather than the invisible multitudes who may die of exposure to toxic chemicals, cigarette smoke, or radiation, or those deprived of immunization or adequate nutrition. . . . We benefit a few at cost to many. This occurs when technology assessment becomes specific and explicit. The barrier will not rise up if we let these life-and-death decisions slip by, politely unnoticed, in a general rationing or allocation policy (as the British National Health Service learned to do long ago). But if we work at explicit evaluations of single technologies, the barrier is bound to appear. I call this barrier the rule of rescue.[41]

Even if objective analysis might judge the total benefit from treating a large number of people for chronic severe pain to be greater than the benefit of prolonging a single life for a very short time, following the rule of rescue compels us to save the one life.

Others believe that it is possible to prioritize. When the philosopher Peter Singer writes, "The death of a teenager is a greater tragedy than the death of an 85-year-old, and this should be reflected in our priorities,"[42] he is making a version of the "fair innings" argument, which Alan Williams, a health economist, has described this way: "The popular folklore is rich in phrases indicating that we all have some vague notion of a 'fair innings' in health terms. Put at its crudest, it reflects the biblical idea that the years of our life are three score and ten. Anyone who achieves or exceeds this is reckoned to have had a fair innings, whereas anyone who dies at an earlier age 'was cut off in their prime' or 'died tragically young.'" Rationing medical care based on fair innings, Williams argues, would not only favor those worse off (because they have not been able to do their fair share of living), it would also give the biggest return on the care given, since younger people, once restored to health, will live more additional years on average than older people. Having argued that the "vain pursuit of immortality is dangerous for elderly people," and that, taken to its logical conclusion, the rule of rescue "means not simply that we shall all die in hospital but that we shall die in intensive care," Williams concluded,

> So I am encouraged to hope that, in the interests of fairness between the generations, the members of my generation will exercise restraint in the demands we make on the health care system. We should not object to age being one of the criteria (though not the sole criterion) used in the prioritization of health care, even though it will disadvantage us. The alternative is too outrageous to contemplate—namely, that we expect the young to make large sacrifices so that we can enjoy small benefits. That would not be fair.[43]

Responding to Williams, J. Grimley Evans, a professor of geriatric medicine, objected strongly to the labeling of whole populations of diverse people as having a lesser right to medical care simply because they belong to a certain age group: "Should we withhold health care from members of lower social classes or from black people because of the poorer average outcome of their groups? Rather, most of us would suggest that extra attention should be paid to vulnerable members of such groups to try to compensate for their disadvantage. Why should old people not be viewed similarly?" He concluded, "We should not create, on the basis of age or any other characteristic over which individuals have no control, classes of Untermenschen whose lives and well being are deemed not worth spending money on." He has been joined by many others who decry any form of "ageism." [44]

In situations of absolute scarcity that require us to choose which medical conditions, kinds of treatments, or groups of people have priority, the decision could depend on which option would save the largest number of lives. That would appear to be a straightforward and ethically sound approach, but a simple head count of deaths averted (or, more accurately, postponed) fails to take into account the length or quality of the time added to the lives that are rescued. Arguing that no one principle can be applied in all types of life-and-death situations and still lead to acceptable distribution, Govind Persad, Alan Wertheimer, and Ezekiel Emanuel of the National Institutes of Health have argued for a "complete lives system" based on multiple criteria. In addition to the "saving most lives" principle, they would include one they call "modified youngest-first," which would generally favor the young over the old but also give adolescents and young adults priority over infants. Their rationale for giving lower priority to the youngest is that "the 20-year-old has a much more developed personality than the infant, and has drawn upon the investment of others to begin as-yet-unfulfilled projects." Based on "modified youngest-first," they have constructed a graph that shows highest priority being given to the fifteen-to-forty age group. Explicitly favoring some age groups over others is not ageist, they argued, because "unlike allocation by sex or race, allocation by age is not invidious discrimination; every person lives through different life stages rather than being a single age." A second criterion would favor those with a better prognosis after treatment, since the purpose is to achieve "complete lives—those containing all stages through old age" and "a young person with a poor prognosis has had very few life-years but lacks the potential to live a complete life." Finally, when comparing cases that are very similar with regard to those three criteria, they suggest limited use of lottery methods.[45]

The complete-lives system has been criticized on a number of counts, including its devaluation of the lives of the elderly and very young children and the charge that it isn't even a system at all but rather a collection of potentially contradictory criteria that would be hard to put into practice.[46] (Emanuel went on to become health adviser to President Barack Obama, serving during the contentious health care debate of 2009–10. Based on his role in writing the complete-lives proposal, Emanuel was referred to by opponents of the health care bill as Obama's "Rationer-in-Chief.")[47] Joining a published debate on the complete lives system, Sadath Sayeed, a practicing pediatric physician, worried that "the psychological task of implementing any rationing scheme that transparently privileges some human lives over others is not only daunting to someone in my position, it risks devastating relationships built on trust between those asked to do the rationing and those forced to bear the loss." In that, he wrote, "the space between tidy academic paper arguments and the untidy world of clinical practice remains vast." He also expressed concern about applying such formal principles to impoverished people in poor countries: "There can be no denying that, in such places, resources are frighteningly scarce, but there also can be no denying that our complacency towards first-order issues of social injustice contributes to their ongoing scarcity."[48]

ROUGHLY JUST

When we move from rationing absolutely scarce goods like ventilators in the midst of a pandemic to rationing resources in the broader health care system—where treatments are theoretically abundant but limitations are imposed by budgets—even more vexing questions arise. In a country with universal health coverage, rationing based on some kind of cost-benefit analysis, either explicit or implicit, is inevitable, since no country has an unlimited health budget. In America, just about any drug or procedure is theoretically obtainable for a price, whatever its cost-benefit ratio or total cost to the country. Coverage is not universal, so we ration by providing more or less unlimited treatment for some groups of people and denying certain treatments to others.

In a system likes ours, asks Leonard Fleck, a philosopher and medical ethicist, what should we do with a medical product like the left ventricular assist device (LVAD), a kind of booster pump that is implanted in the chest and attached to the heart? Being fitted with an LVAD costs about $200,000, and it could benefit two hundred thousand Americans per year. Are we as a society willing to pay $40 billion annually to give each of those people one to two years of added life? Former vice president Dick Cheney became a prominent LVAD recipient in 2010, and he followed that up with a heart transplant less than two years later. Fleck points out that because so many people have either inadequate health insurance or none at all, "there are at least a hundred million Americans who would have zero chance of getting on a heart transplant list if they had the same need as Cheney. That same hundred million would not have gotten the LVAD either." Of course, the number of heart transplants is limited by supply. But if we decide to pay whatever is necessary to provide an LVAD to everyone who would benefit, what would we then do about the totally implantable artificial heart, which—when fully developed and provided to all patients who could benefit—could cost the nation more than $100 billion per year? [49]

Faced as we are with the inexorable advance of technology, Fleck asserts that "we do not really have the practical option of allowing everyone to decide whichever way they wish for themselves when it is a common pool of resources from which all must draw (and we are trying to fairly limit access to that pool of resources). We need some agreed upon rule, some shared understanding of what might be fair. This is where we are practically compelled to invoke a fair process of rational democratic deliberation." The results, he adds, will be only "roughly just," but "rough justice is morally preferable to the routine, arbitrary, hidden, subjective, irresponsible, and uninformed allocation injustices that presently pepper our health care system." [50]

Long, sad experience tells us that publicly raising the subject of rationing a costly, low-benefit medical commodity is unlikely to prompt the kind of "rational democratic deliberation" Fleck recommends. In view of the public outcry that typically greets any explicit discussion of rationing, many have recommended "implicit rationing" as an alternative. Implicit rationing occurs, for example, when firm budget ceilings are set and then hospital staff and doctors are left to figure out how to stay within the budget. In the United Kingdom, implicit rationing "is carried out by doctors who are aware of the resources available and who ration by telling patients that they cannot help them, rather than explicitly stating that resources are not available."[51] In applying so-called bedside rationing, doctors use their judgment in deciding that a particular treatment is not right for a patient. Cost-effectiveness is not supposed to play a role in that decision, but until a device is developed for reading doctors' minds, it will be impossible to know to what extent they weigh costs against benefits. But whether or not cost is taken into account, the logic of the decision as explained to the patient is always in purely medical terms. Patients may be told that it would be futile to pursue further treatment without the nature of the futility explained. Such a system has been described as being easiest on both the doctor and the patient: "Explicitly to confront individuals with the fact that because of scarce resources they will not receive health care which they need will make them more unhappy than believing that there is no clinical option but to take what is offered. This distress will be compounded if they discover that other patients deemed more worthy of resources will receive treatments denied them."[52]

The other rationale for implicit rationing is that the explicit version is just too politically hot to handle. David Mechanic put it this way in a much-cited 1995 article published in Britain: "Implicit rationing, despite its imperfections, is more conducive to stable social relations and a lower level of conflict. It is doubtful that tough systems of explicit rationing can be maintained, except during crises such as war, without focusing conflict and destabilizing the medical care system. Explicit rationing is also likely to confront government and the political process with unrelenting agitation for budget increases." Public discussion of rationing also tends to rouse disease-specific advocacy groups to action, and they can be a potent, less-than-objective influence on resource allocation. Mechanic expressed confidence that doctors and patients together can usually make good decisions if it's done within known budget boundaries: "once the boundaries are set, more is gained by muddling through than by trying to establish all the rules beforehand."[53]

Bedside rationing can be regarded as a relatively benign form of lying. And like any kind of lying, everyone knows it happens, most know it is necessary at times, but few want to talk about doing it. Peter Ubel and David Asch once conducted a survey of general internists in which they asked about situations that, according to standard definitions, are clear examples of bedside rationing: for example, recommending a hypothetical colon cancer test that costs $100 and detects 90 percent of malignancies, rather than one that costs $400 and detects 95 percent. They asked the doctors they surveyed whether or not they (1) viewed such choices as appropriate, (2) viewed them as examples of rationing, and (3) believed that "physicians should never ration medical care." Those doctors who did not take the absolute position against rationing tended to form their views on whether a given hypothetical medical decision was right or wrong independently of their views on whether or not the decision involved rationing. On the other hand, the doctors who opposed all rationing tended to identify medical choices that they supported as not being cases of rationing, while labeling those with which they disagreed as rationing.[54] That implies that two physicians who are in complete agreement on the specific treatments that would be appropriate for a particular range of patients could nonetheless be in complete disagreement about whether the actions they endorse or reject would constitute bedside rationing.

Critics of implicit rationing argue that it is nothing but a semi-transparent ruse for denying care without explanation. Len Doyal, a British medical ethicist, writes, "There is nothing new about the idea that because patients may find certain types of information distressing, they should not be told it. Yet any benefit derived from deception will be sustained only while patients are kept in ignorance."[55] With patients finding easier online access to medical information every day and asking their physicians a lot more questions, it is becoming harder to keep people in the dark about the benefits and costs of treatment. Explicit rationing gives doctors the advantage of being open and honest with-

out asking them to act as advocates for their patients while simultaneously trying to make objective decisions on rationing their treatment.

A 1996 survey of British physicians found many of them unhappy
with the bedside rationing then common in their system and looking
for someone else to set explicit priorities. Here are some of their comments, as published in *Social Science and Medicine*:

> I don't see rationing being an important part of my role. . . . If
> you are . . . the patient's defence lawyer . . . I don't see how you
> can be the judge as well.

> We were pleased with this black list [of nonfunded
> treatments]; for a change somebody decided for us, we
> could . . . blame them.

> I don't want to be involved [in rationing] on a day to day basis.
> I'm quite happy to implement it, if somebody said to me,
> "There are no tattoo removals or in vitro fertilization services
> available in your area." That wouldn't particularly worry me.
> I would say to the patient, "I'm sorry I can't refer you for this."

> I think the government should come clean and tell the public
> exactly what it can and what it can't have with this health
> service . . . they should carry the flack for it. They are the
> sitting ducks, not us.

> I don't think it [rationing] can, or should be, slipped in
> through the side door, and instituted by compliant GP's.
> I think if it is going to occur on any major basis, it should
> be public.[56]

If rationing is to be done explicitly, it requires an explicit cost-
benefit calculation. In searching for objective criteria that people who
hold differing views can agree upon (at least theoretically), health
economists long ago developed formulas for computing "well years" or

"quality-adjusted life years" (QALYs). One year lived in perfect health is valued as one QALY, while one year lived with a health impairment is given a value between zero and one QALY: the worse the impairment, the smaller the value, with being dead valued at zero. In this way, a medical treatment given to some number of people can be valued by the number of QALYs it provides to the population. To take a highly simplified example, if a drug is predicted to extend the lives of one hundred people for an average of four years each but at only 80 percent of perfect health, it will give an increase of $100 \times 4 \times 0.8 = 320$ QALYs. This gives economists a way to conduct cost-benefit analyses. If the cost of treating each person with that drug (and thereby giving each person an additional 3.2 QALYs) is $8,000, then the cost per QALY is $2,500. If a different drug also adds four years of life but at only 60 percent of good health and costs only $3,600 per patient, then its cost per QALY is just $1,500. With an unlimited budget, the first drug will provide a greater total benefit, but if there is a ceiling on total expenditures more people will benefit and more QALYs can be "produced" by approving the second drug. (For example, with a spending limit of $500,000, the first drug could treat 200 people and add 640 total QALYs to their lives while the second would treat 333 people and add 800 QALYs.) But whatever the size of the budget, one can still debate whether it is desirable to value one person's year of life more than another's and whether it is better to give fewer people a higher quality of life or give more people a lower quality of life. Furthermore, who gets to decide the value of a year lived with, say, chest pain from a heart condition or without sight or hearing versus a year lived in bed on a ventilator? In the opinion of many, the whole concept is so badly flawed that no one should be allowed to make such decisions.[57] Finally, a QALY calculation is based only on averages, whereas the number of life-years that an individual patient might gain from the treatment could range anywhere from zero to far higher than a calculation based on averages suggests.[58] Still, systematic yardsticks are necessary, and the QALY provides one way of demonstrating why low priority should be given to, say, an extremely costly chemotherapy for a specific cancer that extends life for an average of two weeks. Yet it is widely recognized that if

QALYs and other yardsticks are used, they must be used in conjunction with other considerations.[59]

Some recoil at the very idea of using cost-benefit analysis for human health. John Harris has long campaigned against its use. With the following scenario, he sums up his argument that our own individual preference for having a longer life, whatever its quality, tells us nothing about how to prioritize the situations of different people:

> Suppose that Andrew, Brian, Charles, Dorothy, Elizabeth, Fiona and George all have zero life-expectancy without treatment, but with medical care, all but George will get one year complete remission and George will get seven years' remission. The costs of treating each of the six are equal but George's operation costs five times as much as the cost of the other operations. It does not follow that even if each person, if asked, would prefer seven years' remission to one for themselves, that they are all committed to the view that George should be treated rather than that they should. Nor does it follow that this is a preference that society should endorse. But it is the preference that QALYs dictate.[60]

That course is dictated because treating George alone would cost less than treating the other six people, and the total gain would be seven years of life rather than six. But if you believe, as Harris does, that every life is equally worth extending or improving, then all seven people should be treated, whatever the cost, the length of life extension, or the degree of improvement. He is plain about that when he writes, "Among the sorts of disasters that force us to choose between lives is not the disaster of over-spending a limited health care budget!"[61] That argument tends to frustrate policy makers. When Harris urged in the *Journal of Medical Ethics* that in vitro fertilization (IVF) be provided to all British women who have fertility problems and who request the procedure (not just the twenty-three- to thirty-nine-year-olds who were given preference because they stood the best chance of having a successful outcome), members of Britain's National Institute for

Clinical Excellence, responding to Harris in a subsequent issue of the journal, threw up their hands. "This is the point, of course," they wrote, "where Harris leaves the real world and enters a parallel—value and cost free—universe. For if the NHS (or any other healthcare system in the world) were to go along his route, and provide everything anyone wanted, it could consume almost the entirety of a nation's gross domestic product with nothing left for any other form of public (or, for that matter, private) expenditure." [62]

Unlike bedside rationing, explicit rationing, whether based on QALYs or other criteria, is transparent and wide open to public debate. But rationing done out in the open can be an uneven process. If a disease has big corporations, awareness groups, and glamorous celebrities publicizing it, treatments for it may be approved and provided while other, equally beneficial treatments may be denied. The experience of trying to put explicit rationing into practice in two places—the United Kingdom and the state of Oregon, both of which I will now discuss—has demonstrated how hard it is to convince a society to acknowledge its own limits.

THE NATIONAL HEALTH SERVICE

Britain's universal, publicly funded medical system, the National Health Service (NHS), was created soon after World War II. A British public battered by more than a decade of austerity welcomed the NHS as "an egalitarian oasis in a class-ridden society," viewing it the same way they had the rationing of food and gasoline during the war. The NHS was designed so that the family doctor served as the gatekeeper to virtually all medical care. Those first-line doctors referred patients to hospitals for specialty care when necessary. Hospitals, in turn, operated on fixed annual budgets; there was no fee-for-service system. Specialists were employed by hospitals on a salaried basis. For many years, up until the 1990s, "British hospitals were semi-feudal enterprises, ruled largely by a peerage of senior specialist physicians, called 'consultants' [who] parceled out the meager rations allotted through the health district." Since the early 1990s, the NHS has oscillated between more austere and more generous budgets, implicit and explicit rationing, and lesser and greater freedom to obtain private care outside NHS.[63]

Among American observers, especially those opposed to universal health care, the most frequently discussed feature of the NHS is the infamous waiting list. Before explicit rationing was introduced, the system had to fall back on implicit rationing by general practitioners and rationing-by-queuing in hospitals. People needing emergency treatment almost always got it in time, but others might wait for months to receive less urgent medical care. In 1999, more than 1.2 million Britons were on hospitals' inpatient waiting lists, and hundreds of thousands were waiting three, six, or more months for outpatient care. Those numbers have since been cut substantially, but there are still many people waiting weeks or months for surgery or other kinds of treatment.[64]

The UK government attempted to install a form of explicit rationing in 1999 with the creation of the National Institute for Clinical Excellence (NICE), a group of experts tasked with advising the NHS on how to allocate its resources in deciding which treatments to provide. NICE's job was to make nonbinding recommendations to Primary Care Trusts, which at that time oversaw NHS hospitals and doctors in each locality. In practice, the trusts usually followed NICE's recommendations. To provide treatments for which NICE had given a thumbs down would have created budget problems, and to refuse ones that NICE had approved tended to provoke an outcry in the community. NICE used QALY-based evaluations in making its decisions.[65] But surveys indicate that most Britons, like most people in other countries, view QALY maximization as less compelling than either the rule of rescue, the plight of people with multiple health conditions (who have fewer QALYs to gain), or the "sense of personal worth and security of afflicted patients."[66] The public tends to make those preferences known, sometimes loudly, and those preferences have enjoyed support from the corporations that stand to lose out on big profits when NICE rejects a drug or other treatment. Industry lobbying has at times pushed NICE into approving new drugs, and those decisions, by sapping resources, have forced less visible rationing elsewhere in the system.[67] Steven Pearson and Michael Rawlins wrote in *JAMA*, "Some critics have pointed out that NICE's approach to using cost-effectiveness, although touted as a mechanism for making difficult decisions to limit the approval of new technologies, has in fact led to the approval for funding, at least for some indications, of most new drugs and devices. NICE has thus been called a 'golden goose' for the pharmaceutical industry."[68] Of 387 recommendations NICE issued between 2000 and 2010 regarding specific treatments, only forty—twenty-two of those for very costly new cancer drugs—were negative.[69]

Although the group's high degree of expertise and political independence has won it much respect, NICE has come under fire for turning down applications for drugs to treat diseases such as late-stage Alzheimer's disease and late-stage kidney and breast cancer.[70] In such cases, neither its tendency to approve the great majority of drugs nor its technical reputation could immunize NICE against charges that it denied people lifesaving treatments.

In 2008, the NHS caused a stir by denying treatment for macular degeneration to eighty-eight-year-old Jack Tagg, a former RAF bomber regarded as a hero of the 1982 Falklands war. The NHS said the guidelines handed down by NICE would permit treatment only after Tagg had gone blind in at least one of his eyes. More than 120 doctors mailed £5 checks to Prime Minister Tony Blair to prod him into ordering that Tagg be treated. Tagg's primary care trust finally yielded to pressure and approved the injections to save his sight, claiming that it was all a misunderstanding over the patient's right to appeal. Tagg was unimpressed, declaring, "I'm pleased but I want free treatment for all." Then in 2012, NICE recommended that the NHS not provide the drug abiraterone for late-stage prostate cancer, citing the estimated price tag of £63,200 per QALY. The highest cost per QALY of any drug recommended by NICE up to that point had been £50,000. The head of the Prostate Cancer Charity lamented the NHS decision, noting, "Abiraterone can increase the amount of time a man with advanced prostate cancer has left to live by an average of about four months and in a very human currency, this may give him the chance to walk his daughter down the aisle or see the birth of a grandchild." For some patients, there were alternatives. Two private insurers said they would cover the drug, and hundreds of patients received abiraterone treatment funded by the Cancer Drugs Fund, a pool of government money set aside to pay for cancer treatments that NICE had rejected as providing too little benefit for their cost.[71] The creation of that fund in 2010 was one of several measures that together undermined NICE's ability to apply cost-effectiveness analysis. In late 2010, the government announced that by 2014, NICE would be completely stripped of its authority to decide whether new medicines are cost-effective and could no longer make recommendations on that basis. The institute would be limited to evaluating drug use guidelines and safety.[72]

While it has been rare for British doctors to urge NICE publicly to deny companies' applications for new drugs, they do seem more willing to ration on the basis of patient characteristics. When medical authorities in Suffolk decided, as a cost-cutting effort, not to accept obese people for joint surgery, a survey of physicians across the country found that 39 percent agreed with the decision. Doctors are not supposed to discriminate against patients with conditions such as obesity solely because they see them as "self-inflicted," but the NICE guidelines did allow for denial of treatment if "lifestyle factors" would render the treatment ineffective. And Suffolk authorities believed that obese people would face higher risks and poorer results from surgery. The same doctor survey found 96 percent wanting "an open debate on rationing in the NHS in order to clear up confusion about the subject."[73]

In addition to curtailing NICE's power to reject new drugs, the Conservative government that came into power in 2010 moved to put more power in the hands of doctors, indicating a distinct shift away from controversial explicit rationing and back toward implicit, bedside rationing.[74] If Britain is pulling back from explicit rationing, what are the prospects for reining in medical costs in the United States? Even if Americans had to make only mild sacrifices, the authors of *Can We Say No?* predict that "they would likely be perceived as more painful, because Americans have never experienced the denial of services long familiar to the British." Furthermore, it's "hard to imagine" a U.S. system that would not allow patients who can afford to pay for care to do so. As a result, "Just as the well-to-do can buy superior education for their children in private schools, they are likely to be the principal users of medical-care safety valves to buy more or better health care, contributing to the development of two-class health care, with a higher standard for those with the means to 'buy out' of constraints."[75] As it happens, Americans have been testing just such a two-tier system for almost two decades, in Oregon.

THE OREGON HEALTH PLAN

On July 1, 1987, the Oregon state legislature stopped providing Medicaid funding for transplant operations in order to free up money that could extend preventive and prenatal care to needy families, because the redirected money would help many more people than those awaiting transplants. Five months later, seven-year-old Coby Howard died of leukemia. He had been denied Medicaid funds for a bone marrow transplant that could have saved his life, and he died before his mother could raise enough money to make a cash deposit on the operation.[76] The controversy that erupted around Howard's death was one of many factors that pushed Oregon to seek a way to provide medical coverage for every state resident and to pay for it by deciding rationally which treatments to cover and which to reject as unnecessary.

In 1989, the state legislature passed a bill that required employers to provide health insurance plans for all employees, and it extended Medicaid coverage to all residents living below the poverty line, through the Oregon Health Plan (OHP). By including the two provisions, the bill's lead author, the state senate president John Kitzhaber, a physician, was aiming for universal medical coverage. But only the Medicaid portion of the plan received federal clearance, and that happened only in 1994, after prolonged, heated debate. And thanks to strong opposition from business interests and the ascendance of a Republican majority in the state legislature in 1994, the employer mandate never went into effect. Extending Medicaid benefits to hundreds of thousands more people without a huge increase in funding could mean only one thing: rationing. Kitzhaber was elected governor that same year, largely on the strength of his health plan's popularity, but the demise of his initial dream of universal coverage tarnished the Oregon plan right from the start. Rationing medical care was one thing, but rationing it only for Medicaid recipients did not look good. Nevertheless, the OHP became "the first public insurance program to ration medical care explicitly, systematically and openly" in the United States, according to an article in the *Canadian Medical Association Journal*, and remains the only one to have done so.[77]

The method was supposed to be simple: rank all treatments from highest to lowest priority; estimate how many of those treatments the state could afford to pay for, starting at the top of the list and working down; and draw a line on the list below which no treatments would be paid for. From 1989 until the plan went into effect in 1994, state officials worked to produce a reasonable and acceptable list and line that would satisfy the federal government, because Washington must approve each state's plan for spending Medicaid funds. The original ranking, arrived at solely by means of QALY-based cost-benefit calculations, produced numerous irrational results. For example, highly effective surgical procedures to treat otherwise fatal conditions, including ectopic pregnancy and appendicitis, were ranked lower in priority than less crucial items like dental caps and splints for temporomandibular joint disorder. When that first version of the list came under heavy attack, the Oregon State Health Commission (OSHC) took another run at it. They started by sorting treatments into seventeen broad categories. The categories were ranked by priority, and then items within each category were ranked. Both ranking steps were based solely on treatments' net benefits, ignoring their costs. Finally, OSHC members, relying, in their words, on "subjective collective judgment," did some rearrangement, moving items "by hand" either higher or lower on the list. In making those decisions, officials considered the numbers of people who would benefit, the relative values that society placed on different treatments, and cost-benefit calculations.[78]

To inform the public about the development of the plan, dozens of meetings were held throughout the state. People attending the meetings tended to be members of the middle and upper classes, however, rather than people eligible for Medicaid. That meant that the members of the public who discussed the plan and offered recommendations tended not to be those who would be covered by it. Some critics, such as Claudia Landwehr of Goethe University Frankfurt, charged that, because most average citizens had no medical training and therefore were not in a position to rank lists of conditions and treatments based on medical logic, "Oregon's health leaders used citizen participation mainly strategically in order to gain support for reforms."[79]

The list and the line were published with the provision that they would be adjusted every two years to take into account changes in the federal and state Medicaid budgets, medical technology, and costs. But as it turned out the list and line did not impose strict, explicit rationing after all. The state economy was in good shape at the time; there was enough money in the budget to cover the most necessary treatments; most of the services that were excluded were of marginal benefit to relatively small numbers of people; and many patients with covered conditions were moved out of Medicaid and given the financial support needed to join managed-care plans, where they could be subject to implicit rationing. By 1997, the state had managed to extend health coverage to six hundred thousand additional residents, and the percentage of uninsured people had dropped by one-third. In stepping back from hard-nosed cost-benefit analysis at the beginning and making subsequent adjustments to the list by hand, Oregon health officials were able to avoid making many unpopular decisions while still expanding coverage. The system even saved a little money: over the first five years, savings to the state's Medicaid budget were estimated at 2 percent more than what would have been the case under the former system. Rising prescription drug costs added strain, but for the most part the legislature tried to ensure that enough money went to the OHP (with a portion of the money coming from a new cigarette tax), in an effort to avoid more Coby Howard fiascos. The character of the OHP changed in 1997, when the federal government insisted that Oregon keep the cutoff line fixed within the priority list—that is, rather than defunding some treatments when money was tight, the plan would be forced to defund people by dropping them from coverage altogether.[80] A 2001 analysis saw the Oregon system as illustrating "the political paradox of rationing," which was that "the more public the decisions about priority setting and rationing, the harder it is to ration services to control costs."[81]

In 2004, Oregon voters made matters worse by rejecting a tax increase that was needed to sustain the OHP's Medicaid coverage. After that, the number of people eligible for the plan plummeted. Enrollment was frozen until 2008, when a lottery was held to add three thousand new beneficiaries. Ninety thousand people entered the lottery.[82] Kitzhaber became governor again in 2011, with health care still one of his top priorities. In February 2012, the legislature passed a bill to reorganize and strengthen the OHP, but a bill backed by Kitzhaber that would have created a health insurance exchange for individuals and small businesses—another attempt to universalize coverage—remained stalled.[83]

More than two decades after Coby Howard's death, health care in Oregon remains controversial. In 2008, as Springfield resident Barbara Wagner entered the final stages of lung cancer, her oncologist recommended a course of Tarceva, an expensive drug that had been shown to add a few months to the lives of about 8 percent of late-stage cancer patients who took it. The OHP declined to pay for the treatment, citing the low probability that it would help, as well as its often toxic side effects. A media furor over the state's action brought Tarceva's manufacturer, Genentech, to the rescue. Thanks to the pharmeceutical company's largesse, Wagner received the treatment at no cost, but she lived for only a short time after starting the Tarceva course. The news media that had earlier fulminated over the OHP's denial of supposedly "life-saving" treatment had by then quieted down, and little was made of the story's sad, all too predictable end.[84]

Jennifer Fisher Wilson, a science reporter writing about the Oregon plan in 2008, noted, "Some people who lived through the trials of implementing the OHP believe that no state—no matter how innovative—can do it alone. They feel that lasting reform is impossible without significant leadership at the federal level and changes to the rules that govern public programs, such as Medicaid and Medicare."[85] But that puts pioneering states in a chicken-and-egg situation. Oregon in particular was frequently held up as a bugaboo by both sides during the intense national debate leading up to passage of the PPACA. The bill was signed into law by President Barack Obama in March 2010 over the objections not only of conservatives but also of progressives, who argued that the new law was a wholly inadequate substitute for a national single-payer health plan with universal coverage. Indeed, in the spring of 2012, when it appeared that the Supreme Court was about to overturn the PPACA, the House Progressive Caucus prepared to introduce a new single-payer bill that, unlike the PPACA, would have guaranteed coverage for all and therefore would not have needed the highly controversial provision at the center of the PPACA that required all Americans to have private insurance or else pay a fee (which the Court redefined as a tax when it surprised many by largely upholding the PPACA in July 2012).[86] While the PPACA still left many millions uninsured and relied on the customary approach of rationing according to ability to pay for treatment or obtain insurance, a single-payer law providing for universal coverage, like it or not, would have created the need for nonprice rationing.

The earlier furor over phantom "death panels" had seen to it that the PPACA contained no provisions for limiting treatment. The law nonetheless did provide for the establishment of a nonprofit corporation called the Patient Centered Outcomes Research Institute (PCORI) that would conduct "comparative effectiveness research." The legal scholar Leonard Nelson III notes,

> Perhaps in response to concerns about rationing, PPACA expressly precludes the Secretary of the Health and Human Services from relying solely on comparative effectiveness research to deny coverage or from using PCORI-sponsored comparative effectiveness research "in a manner that treats extending the life of an elderly, disabled, or terminally ill individual as of lower value than extending the life of an individual who is younger, nondisabled, or not terminally ill" [or] "with the intent to discourage an individual from choosing a health care treatment based on how the individual values the tradeoff between extending the length of their life and the risk of disability."[87]

In other words, it was considered acceptable to compare the effectiveness of various treatments as long as the information was not used to preclude payment for treatments that cost too much while providing very small benefits. Instead, the PPACA is designed to reduce costs by the more palatable strategy of improving efficiency and eliminating waste. The medical industry has made similar moves. In 2012, a coalition of nine medical specialty boards, coordinated by the American Board of Internal Medicine Foundation (ABIMF), began urging that a wide range of diagnostic tests be used much less often and that patients challenge doctors who recommend unnecessary tests. As usual, conservative groups such as the Heritage Foundation cried foul, claiming that the initiative was just another covert attempt to introduce rationing. In response, ABIMF's president argued, "In fact, rationing is not necessary if you just don't do the things that don't help."[88] Mary Ann Baily comes close to concurring, saying that eliminating unnecessary spending on diagnostic tests would free up money that could be used to address today's lack of care for uninsured and underinsured Americans. She believes "we could get very close to eliminating what I'd call 'harsh rationing' simply by rearranging how money is spent."[89]

But while elimination of overtesting and overtreatment has long been needed in American medicine and could bring significant savings, there is no guarantee that waste reduction alone will bring health care spending under control. Even if all waste were eliminated, medicine would still occupy an outsized share of GDP; spending growth would soon swamp any efficiency gains; a large share of gains from waste elimination could not be banked but would have to be spent to fill the needs of those who are currently underinsured and undertreated; and, despite claims to the contrary, waste elimination is probably just as difficult to achieve as reductions in beneficial services, because an enormous, politically influential industry depends on both for its hefty profits.[90] The authors of *Can We Say No?* conclude, "Eliminating inefficiencies in the system can provide brief fiscal relief, but rationing of beneficial services, even to the well-insured, offers the only prospect for sustained reduction in the growth of health care spending."[91]

Leonard Fleck believes it is not individual selfishness but a broken political system that has blocked all attempts to build a rational health system. "From what you see on TV, you'd think all Americans are irrational and irascible," he says, but his research experience shows otherwise. "We conducted a community dialogue project in seven Michigan communities, with thirty to fifty people of all ages and walks of life in each place. We spent twelve evenings, two hours each evening, asking them some hard 'values' questions. In all of those meetings, there was not a single incident of disrespect." In contrast to the histrionics of the national health care debate, this process consisted entirely of face-to-face encounters in which everyone was fully aware of the rules and expectations. There were no news media involved and nothing at stake politically. "No one was thinking, 'What position should I take to increase the chance that the politicians I most hate will be defeated?' " says Fleck. He and his colleagues presented dialogue participants with a range of scenarios: "We asked if they would deny their possible future selves things like artificial hearts or various drugs to treat terminal cancer. In many situations, they said they would decline treatment for themselves in order to protect resources for future generations." [92]

RATION TECHNOLOGY?

It has long been recognized that the most powerful force driving up medical spending is the relentless advance of technology for profit. Back in 1990, in the pages of that paragon of research the *New England Journal of Medicine*, David Callahan—co-founder of the Hastings Center, a bioethics nonprofit in Garrison, New York—urged that we "ration medical progress." He wrote, "It is impossible to meet every human need merely by pursuing further progress. In this pursuit, we redefine 'need' constantly, escalating and expanding it." [93] Callahan has continued to push for the idea of restraining medical technology and, in doing so, has had to contend with the widely held notion that technology always improves efficiency and that, instead of increasing spending, it saves money. Although the federal research establishment, the medical industries, and advocacy groups all claim that research is one of the best means of reducing the cost of medical care, he points out that total health care expenditures have risen in almost perfect parallel with increases in research spending from 1975 into the 2000s. Studies have indeed shown that technology accounts for the bulk of health care cost increases, and there is little evidence to support the idea that the fruits of research lead to reductions in total costs at the hospital, the doctor's office, or the pharmacy. On the contrary, Callahan writes, "New technologies often make possible the treatment of earlier untreatable conditions, adding fresh expenditures to the system. . . . Even though unit costs of individual technologies may decrease over time, that outcome usually results in a larger number of people using them," pushing total costs constantly upward.[94]

Mary Ann Baily is far from alone in finding Callahan's position "exasperating."[95] She believes in society's ability to discriminate among technologies and use those that improve health at lower cost while rationing others. She argues that many technologies, like the tuberculosis vaccine that made the more expensive iron lung unnecessary, do lower costs. "But," she admits, "the way our system works today, it is set up to pay for cost-raising technologies," too. It should be possible to support the use of cost-lowering technologies and still agree with Callahan's contention that "when the research imperative acts as a moral bludgeon—turning a moral good into a moral obligation and then into a call to arms—to level other values in the name of reducing suffering, it goes too far." To resist that imperative, Callahan has suggested that we "come to see health care as being like fire, police, and defense protection—a necessity for the public interest rather than a market commodity."[96]

In taming technological progress, we have a few—but only a few—examples. The British medical establishment, for example, takes a wait-and-see approach to approving newly developed treatments. That avoids wasting resources on drugs and procedures that later turn out not to have significant benefits.[97] A longer, more extensive testing phase in the United States would be costly to drug companies but would on balance conserve resources and avoid creating excessive demand for questionable treatments. Corporations involved in medicine, especially drug companies, routinely attempt to justify their manipulation of intellectual property protection and the exorbitant prices they charge by arguing that they pay for costly research and development of new products. That would suggest that tougher patent requirements and tight price controls would be an effective way of curbing runaway technology-driven costs. Callahan would like to see just that: "a presidential declaration of immediate price controls on drugs, devices, hospital charges and those of all medical vendors, and parallel imposed cuts in the fees of medical specialists." But he is realistic, admitting that "price controls will not be put in place, not now and possibly not ever. That reality means we are stuck with a range of cost control ideas and proposals that will take years to put into place and at least a decade to bear real fruit."[98]

Callahan also recommends shifting resources from end-of-life care to preventive medicine. In response, Baily warns, "Preventive medicine does not always save money either; in fact, preventive technologies also are often cost-raising." Experts have even begun to discuss a need to ration preventive care.[99] If pursued with the goal of lowering expenditures, however, it has been shown that preventive care can succeed. Cuba, a country that achieves a high average level of health, spends 96 percent less money per person on medical care than the United States. This has been done largely by extending preventive services at no cost to patients. Hospital facilities are no-frills affairs reminiscent of U.S. hospitals in the 1950s, and costly, high-tech, low-payoff treatments are rationed very simply: they aren't available. But, maintain many Cubans, demand for such treatments is low thanks to the preventive health services.[100]

GREEN MEDICAL RATIONING?

In view of the formidable opposition faced by any attempt to ration medical services for budgetary reasons, it may seem absurd even to mention the possibility of medical rationing in the interest of environmental sustainability. But it is still worth pondering Western medicine's enormous ecological impact and what could be done about it. The sheer scale of medicine gives it a heavy footprint. As of 2007, the U.S. health care sector had an estimated greenhouse impact equal to that of 546 million metric tons of carbon dioxide; 80 percent was the result of carbon dioxide release and the rest was caused by release of methane, refrigerants, and other gases. That amounted to 8 percent of total U.S. greenhouse-gas emissions, with the largest contributors being hospitals and the prescription drug industry.[101] The fact that medical care, which made up 16 percent of the U.S. economy in 2007, was producing 8 percent of greenhouse-gas emissions indicates that it has a smaller greenhouse footprint per dollar generated than the transportation and construction sectors, among others. But with medicine's dollar input and output continuing to grow at a breakneck pace, such comparisons with dirtier industries should provide no comfort—and no rationale for saying that medicine is anywhere close to "green enough" or that such unrestricted growth should not be curbed.

Restraints on hospitals and the pharmaceutical industry could bring the largest improvements. Hospitals consume approximately twice as much natural gas and electricity per square foot as the average commercial building.[102] They generate eight to forty-five pounds of solid waste per inpatient daily, seven days per week, and each pound contains three times as much plastic as household trash. As the proportion of that waste being incinerated decreases due to concerns about toxic emissions, the proportion going into landfills increases. High levels of water pollution from pharmaceutical manufacturing, disposal of unused drugs, and bodily elimination of intact pharmaceutical compounds into sewage systems is now well established. In 2008, the Associated Press reported, "A vast array of pharmaceuticals—including antibiotics, anti-convulsants, mood stabilizers and sex hormones—have been found in the drinking water supplies of at least 41 million Americans." In an effort to hold down prices, pharmaceutical companies have turned increasingly to ingredients manufactured in countries with lower labor costs and more lax environmental regulation, creating severe pollution problems for farms and villages situated close to drug factories.[103]

Shrinking the medical economy is necessary if we are to tackle the ecological as well as the economic crisis. Money spent is a solid indicator of ecological damage done. For example, the British medical system's much smaller per-capita contribution to climate change is precisely proportional to its lower level of spending. The National Health Service, which accounts for only about 7 percent of that country's economy, accounts for about 3 percent of total greenhouse-gas emissions, far below medicine's 8 percent share of U.S. emissions. Still, data show that when the NHS spends £1 on a hospital inpatient, it generates greenhouse-gas emissions equal to an astonishing 376 kilograms of carbon dioxide—eight times the emissions produced when the same sum is spent on an outpatient at a clinic.[104] Assuming that similar disparities in greenhouse-gas impact exist in the United States, rationing of costly high-tech tests and treatments in hospitals could have a much larger ecological benefit than would rationing of out-patient services.

The NHS has set a goal of reducing its carbon footprint 34 percent by 2020 and 80 percent by 2050, and we are seeing calls for "green" rationing in America's medical establishment as well.[105] Proposals to use rationing of medical care as a way of protecting the atmosphere, land, and water would face the same generally hostile reaction that greets all mentions of rationing in the U.S. health system, but that's not to say that it should not be done. Such efforts are imperative for many reasons, and they should be made part of any comprehensive effort to reverse destructive growth overall.[106]

7

SLOWING DOWN WITH THE JONESES

The fact that the earth's atmosphere cannot safely absorb the amount of carbon we are pumping into it is a symptom of a much larger crisis, one born of the central fiction on which our economic model is based: that nature is limitless, that we will always be able to find more of what we need, and that if something runs out it can be seamlessly replaced by another resource that we can endlessly extract. . . . Climate change is a message, one that is telling us that many of our culture's most cherished ideas are no longer viable. . . . So when the Heartlanders react to evidence of human-induced climate change as if capitalism itself were coming under threat, it's not because they are paranoid. It's because they are paying attention.

—Naomi Klein, 2011[1]

It is not a matter of whether we ration but of how. When resources seem generally plentiful, rationing goes largely unrecognized. In other times and places, food, water, and medicine are rationed in one way for some people and in another way for others. We have probably not seen the last of the national crises that make formal rationing necessary for a time. But what are the chances that one day we will see rationing as part of a plan for *preventing* crises? Such a policy may be followed in only one country or region but, guided by the principle of "fair shares for all," why couldn't it represent the idea of justice for people everywhere and in future generations? If it is decided democratically to ration resources on a fair-shares basis, what would be the consequences? Would it be possible to do so within any of the world's existing economies? Or would it be more likely to follow rather than cause profound economic transformations? Only by actually making serious attempts to limit total production and consumption, and to do it fairly, will we get full answers to those questions. For now, however, there is still much to be learned from experience.

A Simplex time clock for recording the working hours of employees.

EXPERIENCE SHARED

It should be stressed, at the risk of repetition, that rationing of household consumption in itself is not a means for limiting total resource use or ecological footprint. Rather, it makes sense only as part of a broader systemic approach to limiting resource consumption and ecological damage. As we've seen, it has been adopted reluctantly when civilian production is curtailed to conserve resources for war, or when production or imports of essential resources are cut off; it has been used by governments attempting to stabilize their nations' food prices and prevent hunger in the face of a chaotic agricultural economy; it often serves as a final step in the complex process of dividing up scarce water resources; and it is an inevitable, built-in feature of the medical industry. Nonprice rationing, however, should not be advertised as a first step toward curbing overconsumption. A decision to place a firm ceiling on fuel consumption or carbon emissions, for example—or to put any such limits on the economy while barring any offsets, safety valves, or other fudge factors that undermine those limits—would be the first move, and limits on production and consumption would follow only afterward.

Rationing by queuing, the most hands-off alternative to rationing by price, can work for a short time in some situations, but public resentment tends to build fast, especially if basic necessities are at stake. Though lotteries—the "choice not to choose"—already have been used for some goods, they cannot deliver proportionally.[2] They still might prove the lesser evil when what is being rationed—a course of a very scarce drug, a work visa, a cabin during hunting season, or a place in a military draft, for example—cannot be divided up. But for necessities required by everyone on a daily or monthly basis, lotteries obviously wouldn't be very helpful.

When informal rationing becomes unacceptable and explicit rationing by quantity takes its place, public aversion has to be balanced by firm "fair shares" principles, which have shown consistently strong appeal. In most cases, the closest thing to fair shares is equal per-capita shares. There are areas in which this is clearly not the case, however: food rationing when caloric requirements differ greatly; energy rationing when some homes are insulated very poorly or people live varying distances from their workplaces; and of course, as always, the rationing of medical care. An equal-shares allocation generally does not require much explanation or defense. But it can be very difficult to find a politically acceptable way of allocating resources unequally. That is one of the chief reasons that attempts to ration medical care have faltered.

If there is a "siege motive" for rationing or if it is part of a strategy to prevent runaway inflation, it tends to meet with broad public acceptance, as when calls for formal gas rationing to replace gas lines swept the United States in 1979 or when food was rationed in Iraq in response to UN sanctions. But if rationing is seen as something other than a last resort, especially if it is to be deployed preemptively (as has been attempted on Norfolk Island for emissions reduction), it meets stiffer challenges, to say the least.

Both theory and experience show that, with rationing, it is often a case of in for a penny, in for a pound. Or maybe a better metaphor would be the Whack-A-Mole game: when demand for one good is suppressed, it pops up for nonrationed goods and may need to be restrained. That is part of the reason rationing expanded in World War II economies. The wartime experience also shows that consumption is more easily limited if there are firm limits on numbers of grades, models, or styles of products available or even manufacturing specifications that improve quality and durability.

Rationing is also more readily tolerated when it is applied to tangible, inanimate commodities than when it targets the characteristics of individuals or groups—especially when biological functions are involved. Rationing of energy consumption in order to reduce greenhouse-gas emissions, difficult as that can be, would probably be less politically toxic and far more effective than reducing emissions through rationing of human reproduction (for which voluntary restraint does work). Our antipathy toward rules that apply to the human body is also among the reasons that medical rationing creates such a furor. It's also why rationing of meat or food in general would be highly controversial but still might be imagined as part of an effort to limit humanity's ecological footprint, while it would probably be pronounced dead on arrival if promoted as a means to prevent obesity or improve general health.

Long experience with wartime rationing under price controls and with subsidized food-ration systems in Egypt, India, Iraq, Cuba, and other countries shows that a universal policy is more politically acceptable than one that targets only low-income families. Any means-tested ration begins to resemble a "handout" to the vulnerable—more so if it is explicitly designated as an income supplement or even provided in the form of cash—and creates a two-tier system. Total consumption is limited only if a system not only provides a floor but imposes a ceiling on consumption of certain foods as well. In those situations, there is always strong pressure for a "safety valve" that makes some food available on the market for those who can afford it. Thus, there was no quantity rationing of bread and potatoes in wartime America and Britain or in the farmers' markets of Cuba or Iraq. Foods nominally "off the ration" are instead rationed by the individual's ability to pay—or, if prices are controlled, by queuing. Similar two-tier arrangements are common in rationing of residential water and electricity in developing countries and of medicine in countries like Britain that have both universal and private health care systems. Proposals to permit trading of ration credits for energy and greenhouse-gas emissions also move away from an egalitarian arrangement toward one that is two-tiered. Any time a system evolves into two (or more) distinct tiers, it accommodates the desire for higher consumption by those who can afford it but weakens the fair-shares principle, and that tends to undermine broader acceptance. When rules apply equally to everyone, even the most powerful, they draw far stronger public support. That was fully recognized during World War II and can be seen today as well—in San Antonio, for example, where people with big lawns and punishing water bills get little sympathy, or in Egypt, where you can't (legally) go into a *baladi* bread shop and buy fifty pieces at once, no matter how rich you are.

Rationing of pollution—most prominently, greenhouse-gas emissions—is a special case, because demand for the "commodity" being rationed is negative. It is probably more useful to handle carbon rationing as a point-rationing scheme for gasoline, diesel, electricity, etc., in which we would pay two prices for the energy: one in money and one in points, the latter denominated in pounds of carbon. That is how it would work in various plans put forward in Britain. Household carbon rationing would be different from other point-based systems, however, because wartime points had no intrinsic value, positive or negative. Many consumers living under a carbon-rationing system, like those who lived under point rationing in the 1940s, would want more energy or other goods than they are allowed to have. But while printing more ration stamps would not have increased the quantities of food or gasoline available during the war, issuing additional carbon credits would make more fossil energy available, increasing consumption and emissions (assuming depletion has not yet created absolute scarcity). There would always be powerful, relentless economic pressures to issue more credits, just as Europe has seen pressure to raise the cap on its carbon-trading scheme. Rationing is hard enough to manage when dealing with scarcity; using it to deal with abundance could face even stiffer challenges.

Rationing always requires the setting of priorities and quotas, and that is the focus of political struggles. With the progression from straight to point rationing and then to the systems of expenditure rationing that were studied in the 1940s but never carried out, flexibility and convenience increase. With the creation of a parallel currency often comes pressure to reintroduce market mechanisms that can adjust ration quotas to demand. That in effect creates a connection between the ration currency and the regular monetary currency, which would lead to some of the same problems that rationing is meant to curb in the first place. Markets recognize demand only when it's expressed through purchases; they cannot "see" actual wants, much less needs.[3] So permitting ration credits to be bought and sold, as has been suggested for emissions schemes, might be neither as robust nor as fair as proponents of personal carbon trading predict. Upstream carbon trading has certainly gone far from smoothly.

Finally, long experience in rationing has shown that ensuring fair shares on the national or international scale requires clear, consistent, firm (but democratically determined) procedures for allocating resources, while consumer rationing draws stronger support when decisions are made locally within overall limits. We also have to accept that public debates over how to ration will always be messy affairs—as is illustrated most prominently by struggles over medical care but is also obvious with rationing of food, water, and energy.

FAIR'S FAIR

It is widely assumed that rationing, like any attempt to restrain consumption, will always be fiercely resisted, because people are maximizers at heart and put their own desires ahead of concerns about the good of society. Rationing would probably always fail were it not for the high value we place on fairness; the "carrot" of fairness compensates for the "stick" of consumption controls.

Fairness is not considered to be a factor in the marketplace, at least in the theoretical market, where every participant is highly knowledgeable, behaves rationally, and acts only out of self-interest; furthermore, no one player is powerful enough acting alone to influence the market.[4] Supply, demand, and prices find an efficient equilibrium point at which no further change can make any participant in the economy better off without making another worse off. Under those assumptions, rationing by price is the optimum guide to distribution. Over the past thirty years, extensive research nonetheless has asked what would happen if we set aside some or all of those assumptions, especially since none of them has been shown to be very reliable anyway.

Such research has demonstrated that, in economic transactions, people often act as if they have a variety of other motives, including a strong desire for fairness, accompanying the desire to acquire. Economic models that attempt to incorporate fairness use different mathematical means of accounting for it, based on concepts such as "inequity aversion" and "reciprocal fairness."[5] In a common experimental game, subject A is given an actual sum of money, say $100, and asked to share some portion of it—any amount between $1 and all $100—with subject B, with the stipulation that if subject B rejects the offer, neither subject gets any money. In that game, a large majority of A's tend to offer something close to an even split, even though they could probably have gotten away with offering a much smaller share. They do so even if they know there will be no subsequent round of the game in which B could retaliate for an unfair split.

In another kind of study, a group of Swiss economics students were recruited as research subjects and told about a bottled-water vendor who set up a stand at the top of a steep hiking trail and decided to raise his prices dramatically on an especially hot day. The students were asked to compare his price-rationing system with other kinds of systems: auctioning off the bottles, holding a lottery, or enforcing rules such as "first come, first served," "weak people first" (giving priority to children, pregnant women, and the elderly), and "government distribution" (election of representatives who decide how to distribute the water). The runaway winner was "weak people first," considered the fairest method by 54 percent. "First come, first served" attracted 16 percent, while price rationing and auctioning, the two methods based on ability to pay, were favored by a combined 18 percent. Almost no one thought that holding a lottery or leaving the decision to the judgment of elected policy makers was fairest. (An "equal shares" option would have been difficult to execute and was not included.) From the combined popularity of "weak people first" and "first come, first served," both of which tend to favor those who need the water the most (the former because of their physical condition, the latter, it is inferred, because of their willingness to pay a price in time and effort by lining up for it), the researchers concluded that "institutions taking account of the 'need' of a person are considered to be fairer than others."[6]

Yochai Benkler of Harvard Law School summed up the results of a wide range of fairness and cooperation studies:

> In experiments, almost one third indeed behave as . . . selfish *homo economicus*. But more than half act cooperatively. Many are active reciprocators [who] respond kindly and cooperatively to cooperating others and punish, even at a cost to themselves, those who behave uncooperatively. Others cooperate unconditionally, whether because they are true altruists or solidarists, or because they simply prefer to cooperate and do not measure what others are doing. The overarching finding, however, is clear: in no human society studied under controlled experimental conditions have people on average behaved as predicted by the standard economic model.[7]

The fact that human beings tend to act fairly in their daily economic transactions has not created anything like a fair economy in practice, however. The routine functioning of the existing economy rewards unfair behavior, whatever the personal preferences of producers, sellers, or consumers. Benkler warns against replacing the now-dominant economic "mantra," which he characterizes as "the market will take care of it all," with the similarly passive notion that "social cooperation will take care of it all." He urges instead that we build public institutions specifically for "the pursuit of democratically-adopted public goals" that advance fairness.[8]

If demand is quantified by adding up people's expenditures on various kinds of goods and services (as economics typically calculates it), then the greater the consumption, the greater the satisfaction. But it is becoming increasingly clear that relative consumption is also important—that is, the scale by which we measure the satisfaction we derive from our own consumption depends on others' level of consumption. Although evidence for this phenomenon is building, it is far from a new idea. In his 1909 book *The Theory of the Leisure Class*, the legendary economist and social critic Thorstein Veblen wrote,

> the standard of expenditure which commonly guides our efforts is not the average, ordinary expenditure already achieved; it is an ideal of consumption that lies just beyond our reach, or to reach which requires some strain. The motive is emulation— the stimulus of an invidious comparison which prompts us to outdo those with whom we are in the habit of classing ourselves. Substantially the same proposition is expressed in the commonplace remark that each class envies and emulates the class next above it in the social scale, while it rarely compares itself with those below or those who are considerably in advance.[9]

Because the so-called Veblen effect runs in only one direction— with the lifestyles of wealthier classes influencing less wealthy classes— it creates "cascades" in which increased consumption by one class leads to increased consumption by all classes below it. That is why Veblen argued that society's richest segment, which has no higher class to emulate, sets the standard for consumption by everyone else. And the top class is always in a position to expand its own consumption, presenting everyone else with a moving target. When Veblen effects are at work, especially if there is a large gap between the rich and everyone else, consumption cascades ensue. Statistical evidence shows that such cascades do occur in the real world.[10] The success of fair-shares rationing in controlling consumption is due in part to the fact that it brings the biggest reductions at the top of the economy, helping stop such cascades before they can start.

Consumption is made possible by income, and the influence of relative income on people's satisfaction can be stronger than that of their absolute income. For example, an average gain in neighbors' incomes of $1,000 can have about the same negative effect on one's sense of well-being as does a loss of $1,000 in one's own income; it has been noted that such influences can alter the impact of income taxes or consumption taxes. Taxes decrease our take-home pay or decrease the quantities of goods we consume by making them more costly, but that may not necessarily make us feel worse; some evidence shows that if similar levels of taxation decrease the incomes and consumption of people around us, we generally don't mind.[11] While rationing during World War II reduced people's satisfaction when they could not get as much meat or gasoline as they wanted, they were partly compensated by the fact that consumption by everyone else, no matter what their income, was similarly limited.

It has been predicted that in a low-consumption economy people would look to increases in "social capital" to compensate for reductions in material wealth. In contrast to material consumption, there are apparently no Veblen effects when it comes to social capital. In fact, while others' increased wealth makes us less satisfied with our own economic position, seeing those around us build better social relationships makes us more, not less, satisfied with our own personal networks.[12]

So how is the inner struggle between our desire for fairness and good social relationships on the one hand and our predilection for competitive consumption on the other related to a third phenomenon: the failure of voluntary restraint to bring down total consumption? In that, we fail in times of scarcity as consistently as we do in times of abundance. Twentieth-century wartime experience has demonstrated the inadequacy of voluntary measures for holding down consumption or prices. Voluntary restrictions also have faltered repeatedly during peacetime shortages: urban water use, the 1970s gas crisis, traffic congestion, carbon emissions, drug shortages, and many others.

Our immersion in an economy and a culture dedicated to profit through consumption—and now corporate promotion of pale green products and practices that don't cut into those profits—are largely responsible for the failure of voluntary restraint. But an increasingly solid body of research is exposing an additional reason: voluntarism suffers from built-in negative feedback. It seems that when people voluntarily act in what is generally considered a morally correct way, they are much more likely to follow up those good deeds with selfish or otherwise immoral behavior. The usual explanation for this reversal is that we tend to regard "good" actions or even thoughts as providing us with a degree of "moral license." The license to act badly may be created, according to Anna Merritt, Daniel Effron, and Benoît Monin of Stanford University, by the belief that one "can commit bad deeds as long as they are offset by prior good deeds of a similar magnitude"—a concept they characterize as a kind of "moral bank account." [13]

A look at the results of a few of these studies shows how consistently we tend to claim moral license. In one case, experimental subjects, all Canadian university students, were asked to sit alone at a computer and select $25 worth of items that they would like to purchase from an online store. Some were presented with a store that sells predominantly "green" products, others with a store selling predominantly conventional products. In performing subsequent unrelated experimental tasks, the green-shopping group exhibited significantly higher degrees of greed and dishonesty.[14] In another study, groups of students were shown pictures of various foods and asked to rate them on the basis of desirability. One group was shown four types of organic fruits and vegetables, one was shown four types of desserts, and one was shown four foods regarded by the researchers as neutral (oatmeal, rice, mustard, and beans). When subsequently asked if they would volunteer their time to assist in another, unrelated research project, subjects who had been asked to rate the organic foods offered to give significantly less time than did those in the other two groups. And after reading stories about various moral transgressions committed by others, another group of subjects who had been exposed to organic food expressed harsher judgments of others than did groups shown other kinds of food. The subjects who were shown organic food were drawn at random from the same pool as those shown other kinds of food; therefore, the researchers did not conclude from these results that people who prefer organic food are less moral. Rather, they concluded, simply thinking about a responsible act such as eating organic food appears to confer some degree of license to behave less responsibly afterward.[15]

In yet another experiment, students at Northwestern University were asked to write a brief story about themselves and were given a list of nine words to include in the story. Some were given a list of words describing positive traits, others were given negative words, and still others were given neutral words. When they were subsequently asked to play the role of a factory manager who has been asked to reduce emissions of a pollutant, those who had written about themselves using positive words were willing to spend less money to install pollution-control filters than were the others.[16] Finally, consider the students at a "major East Coast university" who were also divided into "license" and "control" groups. Members of the license group were asked to imagine doing three hours per week of community service and then asked whether they would rather teach homeless children or improve the environment. After that, they were told to imagine that they were now at a mall and should choose between buying a utilitarian item (in this case, a vacuum cleaner) or a luxury item (a pair of designer jeans). The control group was given the shopping question without being asked anything about community service, and 28 percent of subjects chose the designer jeans, while 57 percent of license-group members chose the jeans. So, concluded the study's authors, a person who had declared the mere intention of doing voluntary good works was twice as likely to indulge in a luxury purchase. Significantly, when the study was run again with but a single change—the hypothetical community service was not voluntary but rather a penalty for having committed a traffic violation—the license group showed no greater inclination to buy the luxury jeans than did the control group. In this case, members of the license group apparently did not feel they had made a deposit into their moral bank account.[17]

Even those who avoid the temptation to assume moral license and are consistently ethical and responsible run the risk of encouraging adverse behavior by others. Monin and colleagues have noted that people who act against prevailing negative behaviors ("moral rebels," as they call them) usually suffer "intense backlash from their peers," even when they act instinctively, without seeking approbation or trying to set an example. In explaining this sort of backlash, they observe, "Rebels may think that they are only taking a stand against the status quo, but bystanders who did not take that stand can take this rebellion as a personal threat. This suggests that the root of resentment may be that the rebel's choice implicitly condemns the perceiver's own behavior and that this potential reproach shakes the perceiver's confidence in being a good, moral person." [18]

Despite the tendency of isolated voluntarism to be self-limiting, we need more, not fewer, incentives for spontaneous green behavior. The solution may be to provide psychological and social "cover" for those who are already motivated to act responsibly so that they will not be viewed by either themselves or others as being outside the mainstream. If society as a whole is practicing some degree of restraint—the most obvious mechanism for that is, of course, comprehensive rationing by quantity—it may make it easier for individuals to go even further on their own.

THE PERILS OF INEQUALITY

Before inequality could develop, there had to be surpluses. Human pre-agricultural societies were egalitarian because they all faced scarcity. Groups could not afford to allow anyone to grab more than a fair share of resources because there was barely enough, or sometimes not even enough, to go around as it was; greedy members had to be kicked out of the group. But when raising crops and livestock made it possible for communities to accumulate surpluses of food and other goods, so-called aggrandizers could get away with more resource-grabbing because they could take more and still leave sufficient supplies for the rest. And a ratchet effect followed. Growing inequality provided aggrandizers a greater capacity to dominate and exploit others, widening the wealth and power gaps further. There is evidence from a range of such societies in transition that the aggrandizers did not return benefits to society but used their power only to enrich themselves. The problem has remained with us ever since, with powerful individuals, states, and corporations doing the grabbing.[19] A future world facing scarcity across many fronts, like a hunter-gatherer society, might no longer be able to tolerate such aggrandizers.

The rapid growth of inequality in America's economy is obvious and widely discussed, but no forceful action has been taken to reverse it. Those who are content with this lack of action argue that poverty can be cured without worrying about the accumulation of wealth by a few individuals at the high end of the income curve. In their view, to address inequality explicitly is to validate simple envy. But income and wealth inequalities not only push societies toward overconsumption through Veblen effects, they also are corrosive in other ways. Robert Frank, an economics professor at Cornell University, has observed that "U.S. counties with higher earnings inequality have significantly higher median house prices, personal bankruptcy rates, divorce rates, and average commute times. Total hours worked, both across countries and over time within countries, are also positively associated with higher income inequality." People in countries with greater inequality also tend to enjoy less leisure time and suffer poorer health. Frank disagrees with those who say actions to reduce inequality give policy weight to envy, observing that such actions "are no more an endorsement of envy than effluent fees are an endorsement of pollution."[20]

In the early 1990s, several economists took note of a statistical phenomenon that, based on standard economic models, stands out as a sharp paradox: although residents of richer countries tend to be happier than residents of poor countries, the steady increase in average real income that has occurred over time in richer countries has not brought an increase in overall happiness or well-being. Therefore, concluded Richard Easterlin, a University of Southern California economics professor whose name has become attached to the paradox, "raising the incomes of all" will not "raise the happiness of all." The reason appears to be related to the Veblen effect. As society becomes materially richer in the aggregate, it takes a higher income every year just to keep up and maintain the same level of happiness. But as more people manage to increase their income, it becomes harder for anyone to achieve greater happiness.[21] Especially influential is the average income or consumption level of the people living in one's own locality. Analysis of U.S. national data suggests that the erosion of happiness is to some extent a result of trying to keep up with the Joneses; researchers note that "people appear to be giving up leisure, to allow their friendships to suffer, and to work more, perhaps in an attempt to mimic the material living standards of their neighbors." Overall economic growth may worsen the situation. Studies of average income levels in countries worldwide show that more rapid economic growth is linked to a reduction in average happiness.[22] Wealthy nations may be happier on average than poorer ones, but the rapid growth that can carry a nation from poverty to affluence can also eat away at its citizens' sense of well-being.

LESS WORK, ANYONE?

Hugh Rockoff, who probably knows more about the twentieth-century rationing experience in America than anyone, worries that when future emergencies strike, as they are certain to do, "we don't seem to be prepared to handle them. The emergency management agency, it seems to me, should be prepared to move in with food and fuel, and a rationing system after the next hurricane disaster or the next bunch of forest fires. Is it?" Nevertheless, he does not foresee rationing ever again being used except as a short-term crisis-management tool.[23] Economists' dismissals of rationing usually focus on the inevitable cheating and leakage or on practical feasibility. But economists, politicians, and executives also know all too well what would happen if prices were controlled and demand for goods was intentionally suppressed in a twenty-first-century capitalist economy. Businesses would produce less, with permanent stagnation and chronically high unemployment the probable results. It's for this reason as much as any other that publicly raising the question of curbing growth or uttering the dread word "rationing" in the midst of a profit-driven economy has been compared to shouting an obscenity in church.[24]

But even if imposing limits on production and consumption were to knock jobs out of the economy, it would be only the latest of many such blows. Stagnation and unemployment already plague economies worldwide, and they result not from a failure of consumers to consume but from economies' inherent tendency to overproduce. Businesses accumulate capital faster than they can profitably invest it, with booms and busts the all-too-familiar results. For a time in the mid-twentieth century, U.S. and world economies seemed to have found the route to permanent growth and prosperity through Keynesian cooperation among capital, government, and organized labor, which dampened business cycles. But in the 1960s, as the economists Paul Baran and Paul Sweezy argued, the long boom then in progress was an aberration, largely the result of two unusually strong doses of economic stimulus: World War II (with several follow-up wars, hot and cold, and a relentless military buildup) and the automobile industry. But the normal tendency of mature capitalist economies toward stagnation had not gone away, they insisted. In fact, the continuing concentration of economic power into smaller numbers of larger corporations was exacerbating the original malady of overaccumulation. The kinds of firms that had begun to dominate advanced economies, they stressed, are more like monopolies than idealized competitive businesses and did not behave as economics textbooks say they should.[25]

A common rebuttal of Sweezy and Baran's analysis by free-market economists is that fierce competition among corporations, even large ones, keeps economies stimulated. After all, haven't Google, Facebook, and Amazon been thriving and hiring even as they slugged it out for control of the world? Or is all of that just another bubble with no material foundation, one that can generate plenty of transitory profit but little prosperity?[26] Economic growth has indeed sagged as monopoly power has grown over time. In the United States, the number of manufacturing industries dominated by four or fewer companies has risen from about 25 percent of industries in the 1980s to 40 percent today. The top fifty retail firms had 22 percent of the entire market in 1992; they have 33 percent today. Writing in 2011, John Bellamy Foster, Robert W. McChesney, and R. Jamil Jonna contend,

> This is anything but an academic concern. The economic defense of capitalism is premised on the ubiquity of competi-

tive markets, providing for the rational allocation of scarce resources and justifying the existing distribution of incomes. The political defense of capitalism is that economic power is diffuse and cannot be aggregated in such a manner as to have undue influence over the democratic state. Both of these core claims for capitalism are demolished if monopoly, rather than competition, is the rule.[27]

Accumulated wealth that can find no place to be invested in production of necessary goods and services has to go somewhere—much of it, according to Sweezy and the economists who have followed his lead, into ever more elaborate mechanisms of sales and marketing aimed at stimulating demand domestically and internationally; increasingly sophisticated technology to support advertising and marketing; state ventures (primarily the military-industrial complex); or, more and more in recent years, what has come to be abbreviated as FIRE (the finance, insurance, and real estate sector, a source of increasingly catastrophic bubbles). Companies have kept their workforces as small and "lean" as possible and pushed hard both for international free-trade agreements that allow them to shift capital and jobs around the world in search of greater returns and for laws that restrict the rights of organized labor. Jobs are often talked about as if they are businesses' gift to society, an argument typified by that favorite comment of bloggers and talk-show callers that "no poor man ever gave me a job."[28] It's true that employees are extremely costly and that substituting technology for human power whenever possible is a reliable way to increase profitability. The result has been huge strides in productivity—that is, wealth creation per worker—that have provided businesses huge payroll savings and boosted their profits, but at the cost of accelerating the drive toward overaccumulation and stagnation. And crucially, higher productivity has not been rewarded with higher pay for workers.[29]

If long hours simply enrich employers, then a large share of productivity gains could be converted into leisure without hurting workers' incomes. With more people working, but for fewer hours per year, a low-demand economy need not have high unemployment.[30] That would help free working people not only from exploitation but from pointless consumption as well; André Gorz, among many others, has observed that consumerism is not created by the consumer but is produced by the economy:

> The dominated worker engenders the dominated consumer, who no longer produces anything he needs. The producer-worker is replaced by the consumer-worker. Being forced to sell the whole of his time—his whole life—he perceives money as the entity that can redeem everything symbolically. If we add that working hours, housing conditions, and the urban environment are all obstacles to the flourishing of individual faculties and social relations, and obstacles to the possibility of enjoying one's non-working time, then we can understand why the worker, reduced to a commodity, dreams only of commodities.[31]

Reductions in working time are also essential to sustainability. In the view of Juliet Schor, a Harvard economist, "it is difficult to imagine a globally ethical, timely, and politically feasible resolution to the global ecological crisis in which populations in the North do not reduce the number of hours worked per capita," and that will mean overcoming incentives inherent to the labor market that push employers to extract longer work hours from employees.[32] Taken together, studies on inequality, happiness, work, and growth suggest that firm limits on economy-wide consumption and production, accompanied by a closing of the gap between rich and poor, would improve overall well-being. Interventions that restrain consumption society-wide while reducing inequality of consumption would dampen economic activity but could also increase overall satisfaction and well-being. But the way existing economies work, the economic pie must still keep growing to ensure that the narrow slice going to lower-income households will keep them above subsistence level. If scarcity or environmental concerns dictate that growth has to be restrained, then some other means of ensuring fair distribution will be needed.

Herman Daly and other ecological economists have envisioned a steady-state economy that would employ a combination of market and nonmarket mechanisms to ensure that consumption of resources and disposal of wastes occur at a necessarily low, relatively constant level—a level that would degrade the ecosphere slowly enough to allow humanity to thrive for the long term.[33] The Europe-based "degrowth" movement has taken a similar view but also stresses the necessity for an initial rapid shrinkage of much of the world economy before it can arrive at a sustainable steady state.[34] Both approaches envision differential degrees of restraint or shrinkage among and within nations; consumption by affluent people and nations would contract, while at the same time many of the world's impoverished people would gain access to all of the basic necessities as well as a decent quality of life. For consumers, this would almost certainly mean nonprice rationing. Although it is hard to see how capitalist economies could function under such restrictions, most proponents of this approach do not explicitly view capitalism as an obstacle to be overcome.[35]

An economy that contracts in a fair and orderly way, out of respect for ecological limits and basic human needs, will have to be very different from a traditional economy that's just stuck in an old-fashioned recession. Running a computer model for forecasting changes in the Canadian economy through 2035, Peter Victor of York University in Toronto compared a business-as-usual scenario with a degrowth scenario in which public policy and productive forces are explicitly directed toward sustaining a high quality of life for all instead of enriching just a few. His results showed how a negative-growth economy could actually lead to deep reductions in unemployment, poverty rates, and overall debt. Greenhouse-gas emissions would also decline steeply, by as much as 80 percent.[36]

But is there any capitalist economy that could tolerate the kinds of restrictive egalitarian policies that Victor suggests would be needed? Isn't growth the engine of capitalism? Going another step beyond the steady state or degrowth vision is the idea of "ecological revolution"— or, phrased more gently, "ecological civilization."[37] Its proponents agree that growth must be reversed, but they also argue that the human economy's overshoot of Earth's physical and biological limits is caused not simply by overconsumption but by the runaway pursuit of profit and accumulation of capital, which must be confronted directly. The quest to create ecological civilization is often referred to as "ecosocial-ism," although some of its advocates, most prominently John Bellamy Foster, do not use that term.[38] This approach accords with the sustain-able growth/degrowth approach on many points, but it also argues up front that, because the engine driving capitalism is the generation and acquisition of wealth and property—that is, capital accumulation—no capitalist economy can function as a steady-state economy, let alone a degrowth economy. Whether accumulation and growth, and therefore capitalism itself, are curtailed intentionally through efforts to head off crisis or grind to a halt as a result of a crisis, writes Fred Magdoff, "build-ing an ecological civilization that is socially just will not automatically happen in post-capitalist societies. It will occur only through the con-certed action and constant vigilance of an engaged population."[39]

Whether governments and economies continue with business as usual or are turned inside out by ecological revolution, they could very well find themselves dealing with inflation, stagnation, shortages of ba-sic necessities, or other threats. If rationing becomes unavoidable, the way it happens—justly or harshly—will depend very much on whether we have managed to build a more just society. Magdoff and Foster ar-gue, "An economic system that is democratic, reasonably egalitarian, and able to set limits on consumption will undoubtedly mean that people will live at significantly lower level of consumption than what is sometimes referred to in wealthy countries as a 'middle class' life-style." There could be a silver lining in that prospect, however, because "a simpler way of life, though 'poorer' in gadgets and ultra-large luxury homes, can be richer culturally and in reconnecting with other people and nature."[40]

Such a society could evolve to a point at which sufficiency for all does not have to be managed through rationing but rather happens organically. Could we even conceive of that kind of future? Gorz—who until his death in 2007 advocated a variant of ecological civilization without using that term—believed that such a future is achievable, if the goal of human labor is to fulfill the needs of those doing the work (as opposed to today's production-driven world, in which, in his words, we "consume none of what we produce and produce none of what we consume"). Arguing for the "politically subversive" idea that "production and consumption can be decided on the basis of needs," he envisioned "a form of economic management in which the aim is to satisfy the greatest possible number of needs with the smallest possible amount of labor, capital, and physical resources." The level of effort expended in production would be determined not by efficiency but by "the norm of *sufficiency*," and that norm would be defined politically, not through market relations. Although such an economy would contain less private wealth than today's economies, he believed it could create a more free society, because "the expansion of the sphere of liberty requires that the sphere of necessity be clearly delimited."[41]

That may sound utopian. But if it is, it is utopian in the sense of neither older, production-driven socialist utopias nor what has been called the "utopian economics" of Adam Smith and Alan Greenspan.[42] Rather, it would be one that, to quote the philosopher Kathleen League, "focuses on *something* (however indefinable and ineffable it may be) that is worth striving for, rather than submits to an empty void in the face of which one feels compelled to fatalistically grieve and surrender."[43]

Between now and the day when we finally create a society that can endure for the long haul—whatever it may look like—we are going to need mechanisms for managing scarcity and achieving sufficiency. The time may soon come for shouting a certain obscenity in church.

NOTES

Introduction

1. Meg Jones, "Spurred by Rumors, Motorists Top Off Tanks," *Milwaukee Journal-Sentinel*, September 12, 2001; Andrew Haeg, "Gas Gougers Strike After Terrorists," Minnesota Public Radio, September 12, 2001; Jason Collins, "Supply Fears Push Residents into Long Gas Lines," *Victoria Advocate*, September 12, 2001; "Rumors of Rising Prices Lead to Gas Lines," Associated Press, September 12, 2001.

2. E.L. Gold, "Psychologists: People Want to Act in Crisis," *Kentucky New Era*, September 13, 2001.

3. Jill Vardy and Chris Wattie, "Shopping Is Patriotic, Leaders Say," *National Post*, September 28, 2001; William Watts, "Bush: Bigger Military Needed; Economy Finishing Strong, Encourages More Shopping," *MarketWatch*, December 20, 2006.

4. Marsha Mercer, "It Really Is a New Kind of War," *Gainesville Sun*, October 8, 2001.

5. Thomas Friedman, "The Power of Green," *New York Times Magazine*, April 15, 2007.

6. Marius Luedicke, Craig Thompson, and Markus Giesler, "Consumer Identity Work as Moral Protagonism: How Myth and Ideology Animate a Brand-Mediated Moral Conflict," *Journal of Consumer Research* 6 (2010): 1016–32. PETA is the animal-rights organization People for the Ethical Treatment of Animals.

7. Vladas Griskevicius, Joshua Tybur, and Bram Van den Bergh, "Going Green to Be Seen: Status, Reputation, and Conspicuous Conservation," *Journal of Personality and Social Psychology* 98 (2010): 392–404.

8. Lillian Ross, "Spa Man," *New Yorker*, July 9, 2007.

9. Emily Bazelon, "Prius Preening," *Slate*, July 12, 2007, www.slate.com/articles/life/family/2007/07/prius_preening.htm l.

10. Benoît Monin, Pamela Sawyer, and Matthew Marquez, "The Rejection of Moral Rebels: Resenting Those Who Do the Right Thing," *Journal of Personality and Social Psychology* 95 (2008): 76–93. This phenomenon will be discussed more fully in chapter 7.

11. "Shades of Green," *Slate* transcript, July 12, 2007, www.slate.com/id/2170334.

12. Robert Kozinets and Jay Handelman, "Adversaries of Consumption: Consumer Movements, Activism, and Ideology," *Journal of Consumer Research* 31 (2004): 691–704.

13. Robert Baker, "Rationing, Rhetoric, and Rationality," in *Allocating Health Care Resources*, ed. James Humber and Robert Almeder (New York: Humana Press, 1995), 57.

14. Traditional hybrid cars with solo drivers were excluded from California's HOV lanes in 2011.

15. Ariel Hart, "HOT Lanes Pick Up Momentum, Critics," *Atlanta Journal-Constitution*, February 29, 2012; WSB, "Lawmaker Wants to Nix HOT Lanes as They Reach Record-Breaking Prices," February 29, 2012, www.wsbtv.com/news/news/local/judge-denies-defense-request-call-sneidermans-form/nK74y; Josie Garthwaite, "Access to the Car Pool Lane Can Be Yours, for a Price," *New York Times*, February 24, 2012; Associated Press, "Drivers Skip Out on Atlanta Tolls," March 12, 2012.

16. Hart, "HOT Lanes."

17. As of 2012, fourteen U.S. cities had HOT lanes in place or under construction. A Government Accountability Office (GAO) report found that installation of HOT lanes relieved traffic congestion only when it included construction of additional lanes. Building bigger roads is, of course, the conventional solution to traffic congestion—and one that inevitably turns out to be only temporary. The authors of the report worried about fairness as well, because "low-income drivers may spend a greater proportion of their income to pay to travel at preferred times or incur greater costs in travel time by choosing alternate unpriced routes. High-income drivers, who, economists generally believe, place a higher value on their time, may be more likely to pay the toll and benefit from a faster trip than low-income drivers, thus possibly generating income equity concerns." GAO came up with a seemingly wise recommendation that would simultaneously reduce emissions of pollutants and lower costs for commuters, suggesting that cities "use a portion of toll revenues for alternative transportation modes in the highway corridor, such as express bus service on HOT lanes." So far, no cities have followed that suggestion. Government Accountability Office, "Traffic Congestion: Road Pricing Can Help Reduce Congestion, but Equity Concerns May Grow," GAO Publication No. GAO-12-119, January 2012.

18. Edward Mason, "The Apologetics of 'Managerialism,'" *Journal of Business* 31 (1958): 1–11. See also Paul Baran and Paul Sweezy, "Some Theoretical Implications," *Monthly Review* 64, no. 3 (2012): 24–59.

19. Joshua Farley, "The Role of Prices in Conserving Critical Natural Capital," *Conservation Biology* 22 (2008): 1399–408. A thorough dissection of market failure can be found in John Cassidy, *How Markets Fail: The Logic of Economic Calamities* (New York: Picador, 2009). See also Raj Patel, *The Value of Nothing* (New York: HarperCollins, 2009). Patel argues that our economic problems result from the combined effects of the mispricing of almost everything and the huge imbalances of economic power that exist worldwide.

20. Amartya Sen, "Markets and Freedoms: Achievements and Limitations of the Market Mechanism in Promoting Individual Freedoms," *Oxford Economic Papers, New Series* 45 (1993): 519–41.

21. Mark Sagoff, "Should Preferences Count?" *Land Economics* 70 (1994): 127–44.

22. Quinoa is in the plant family *Amaranthaceae*, which contains another popular alternative grain, amaranth, as well as beets and spinach. (A close relative, *Cheno-*

podium album, is an often troublesome weed known to North American farmers as lamb's-quarters.) Cereal grains such as wheat, barley, maize, sorghum, and rice are in the grass family *Poaceae.* Quinoa seed does not contain gluten proteins, and it has found fast-growing demand in the gluten-free as well as the natural-food market.

23. Simon Romero and Sara Shahriari, "Quinoa's Global Success Creates Quandary at Home," *New York Times*, March 19, 2011.

24. Albert Sjoersma and Paul Schechter, "Eflornithine for African Sleeping Sickness," *The Lancet* 354 (1999): 254; Spring Gombe, "Epidemic, What Epidemic?" *New Internationalist*, November 2003.

25. Gombe, "Epidemic, What Epidemic?"

26. Farley, "Role of Prices."

27. Joshua Farley, telephone interview by author, October 24, 2011.

28. See Ananthakrishnan Aiyer, "The Allure of the Transnational: Notes on Some Aspects of the Political Economy of Water," *Cultural Anthropology* 22 (2007): 640–58; June Nash, "Consuming Interests: Water, Rum, and Coca-Cola from Ritual Propitiation to Corporate Expropriation in Highland Chiapas," *Cultural Anthropology* 22 (2007): 621–39; Ginger Thompson, "Water Tap Often Shut to South Africa Poor," *New York Times*, May 29, 2003; K. Ravi Raman, "Corporate Violence, Legal Nuances and Political Ecology: Cola War in Plachimada," *Economic and Political Weekly* 40 (2005): 2481–86.

29. Rachel Noble, Paul Smith, and Polly Pattullo, eds., "Water Equity in Tourism: A Human Right, a Global Responsibility," Tourism Concern special report, July 9, 2012, www.tourismconcern.org.uk/wet-report.html.

30. Here are just a few of the many books that do a good job of describing the terrible predicaments we face: James Gustav Speth, *The Bridge at the Edge of the World: Capitalism, the Environment and Crossing from Crisis to Sustainability* (New Haven, CT: Yale University Press, 2008); James Kunstler, *The Long Emergency* (New York: Atlantic Monthly Press, 2005); Richard Heinberg, *Blackout: Coal, Climate and the Last Energy Crisis* (Gabriola Island, BC: New Society, 2009); George Monbiot, *Heat: How to Stop the Planet from Burning* (Cambridge, MA: South End Press, 2007); John Bellamy Foster, Brett Clark, and Richard York, *The Ecological Rift: Capitalism's War on the Earth* (New York: Monthly Review Press, 2010); Bill McKibben, *Eaarth: Making a Life on a Tough New Planet* (New York: Griffin St. Martins, 2011); and IPCC, *Climate Change 2007: Mitigation of Climate Change (Summary for Policy Makers). Working Group III Contribution to the Intergovernmental Panel on Climate Change Fourth Assessment Report* (Geneva: Intergovernmental Panel on Climate Change, 2007).

31. James K. Galbraith, *The Predator State: How Conservatives Abandoned the Free Market and Why Liberals Should Too* (New York: Free Press, 2008), 164–70.

Chapter 1: The Material Equivalent of War

1. Associated Press, "Ickes Calls Drastic Cut Unjustified," *Pittsburgh Post-Gazette*, April 24, 1942.

2. Daniel Horowitz, *Jimmy Carter and the Energy Crisis of the 1970s: The "Crisis of Confidence" Speech of July 15, 1979; a Brief History with Documents* (Boston: Bedford/St. Martins, 2005), 111.

3. William James, "The Moral Equivalent of War," in *Representative Essays in Modern Thought*, ed. Harrison Steeves and Frank Ristine (New York: American Book Company, 1913), 519–33. Italics in original. James's prescription was not rationing but a mandatory public-service scheme.

4. Horowitz, *Jimmy Carter*, 37.

5. Maurie Cohen, "Is the UK Preparing for 'War'? Military Metaphors, Personal Carbon Allowances, and Consumption Rationing in Historical Perspective," *Climatic Change* 104 (2010): 119–22.

6. For a sharp departure from the usual idealization of the World War II era, see Studs Terkel's classic *"The Good War": An Oral History of World War II* (New York: The New Press, 2004).

7. Hugh Rockoff, *Drastic Measures: A History of Wage and Price Controls in the United States* (Cambridge: Cambridge University Press, 1984), 51–54.

8. United Press, "Entire World May Be Put on Rations Soon," *Toledo News-Bee*, September 21, 1917.

9. Helen Zoe Veit, "We Were a Soft People," *Food, Culture, and Society* 10 (2007): 167–90.

10. Rockoff, *Drastic Measures*, 51–54.

11. Ibid., 60.

12. "Restrict Coal in Every Household," *Lewiston Morning Tribune*, July 7, 1918.

13. Harry Garfield, cover letter to president Woodrow Wilson accompanying "Final Report of the United States Fuel Administrator," February 11, 1919.

14. Associated Press, "Hoover Insists on Food Saving," *Spokane Spokesman-Review*, September 21, 1918.

15. Veit, "We Were a Soft People." Of course, there were many other differences between Germany and the United States, and, in any case, notes Veit, the talk of pure voluntarism on the Allied side was a fantasy: "The facts that all the other major Allied Governments had imposed strict rations by the end of the war and that the American government had conscripted two and a half million men into its army rendered the comparison weaker still." It also turns out that, late in the war, the U.S. administration secretly studied Britain's rationing system as a possible model for a U.S. plan.

16. Rockoff, *Drastic Measures*, 57.

17. Veit, "We Were a Soft People." Italics in original. In those days, patriotic voluntarism was not entirely voluntary. Christopher Capozzola observed, "Americans were accustomed to private citizens' policing their neighbors' ideas and behaviors, their labor and leisure, before World War I. Yet it was only during the war—as ideas,

behaviors, labor, and leisure had to be mobilized, regulated, and governed in order to defeat the enemy—that the practices of citizen policing came to be state projects, even when they were not conducted under state auspices." Christopher Capozzola, "The Only Badge Needed Is Your Patriotic Fervor: Vigilance, Coercion, and the Law in World War I America," *Journal of American History* 88 (2002): 1354–82.

18. Christopher Capozzola, *Uncle Sam Wants You: World War I and the Making of the Modern American Citizen* (New York: Oxford University Press, 2008), 98–99.

19. Veit, "We Were a Soft People."

20. Kemp Malone, "Ration," *American Speech* 18 (1943): 128–30. *Ratiō*, in turn, is derived from *rat* ("thought"). It is also the source of the English words *ratio* (which was once spelled *ration*, rhyming with *nation*) and *rational*.

21. Elbridge Colby, *Army Talk* (Princeton, NJ: Princeton University Press, 1942), 170.

22. Rockoff, *Drastic Measures*, 127. The second motive for siege rationing—to make price controls work—was, Rockoff wrote, "usually minimized in communications with the public."

23. Associated Press, "Henderson Calls for End of Tire Waste," *Pittsburgh Post-Gazette*, September 14, 1942.

24. "Pleasure Driving Ban in Effect in East," *Victory Bulletin* 4 (1943): 553. *Victory Bulletin* was the "official weekly publication of the Office of War Information."

25. Rockoff, *Drastic Measures*, 128–29.

26. Amy Bentley, *Eating for Victory: Food Rationing and the Politics of Domesticity* (Champaign: University of Illinois Press, 1998), 21.

27. Rockoff, *Drastic Measures*, 95, 98. The War Production Board (WPB) was at the heart of the system, rationing all kinds of resources between the military and civilian sectors and "ensuring an efficient distribution of the civilian residual." WPB was to control production and distribution of essential goods and decide which of those goods should be rationed at the consumer level, while delegating management of the rationing system to the OPA. WPB also attempted to allocate production inputs into areas where shortages arose, through its Office of Civilian Requirements. See Rockoff, *Drastic Measures*, 115–16.

28. Bentley, *Eating for Victory*, 15.

29. "OPA Issues New Revised Table of Meat Rationing Points," *Victory Bulletin* 4 (1943): 480.

30. "Rationing Rules for Food Dealers Revised on Banking, Inventories," *Victory Bulletin* 4 (1943): 502; "Ration Regulations Further Simplified," *Victory Bulletin* 4 (1943): 552; "OPA Presents Specific Answers to Consumer Questions," *Victory Bulletin* 4 (1943): 410. Although I include the term "black market" in quoting others, I have avoided using it myself, because "black" is already associated far too frequently in everyday language with "bad" and "white" with "good."

31. Ina Zweiniger-Bargielowska, *Austerity in Britain: Rationing, Controls, and Consumption, 1939–1955* (Oxford: Oxford University Press, 2000), 10.

32. Zweiniger-Bargielowska, *Austerity in Britain*, 71. As in the United States, the government felt an additional incentive to ration: the threat of unrest. Intelligence

officials worried that long lines would become breeding grounds for discontent, giving citizens too much opportunity for morale-breaking conversations. They even speculated about the prospect of "peace talks being fostered in queues," according to Zweiniger-Bargielowska, *Austerity in Britain*, 77.

33. Zweiniger-Bargielowska, *Austerity in Britain*, 17–20; Katherine Knight, *Spuds, Spam, and Eating for Victory: Rationing in the Second World War* (Stroud, UK: History Press, 2007), 23, 27.

34. Bentley, *Eating for Victory*, 16–17, 28–29, 37.

35. Knight, *Spuds, Spam, and Eating for Victory*, 25.

36. M.J.L. Dols and D.J.A.M. van Arcken, "Food Supply and Nutrition in the Netherlands During and Immediately After World War II," *Milbank Memorial Fund Quarterly* 24 (1946): 319–58; see also Kenneth Mouré, "Food Rationing and the Black Market in France (1940–1944)," *French History* 24 (2010): 262–82; Frederick Strauss, "The Food Problem in the German War Economy," *Quarterly Journal of Economics* 55 (1941): 364–412.

37. Bentley, *Eating for Victory*, 4.

38. "OWI Reports on Food Supplies, Predicts Inconveniences," *Victory Bulletin* 4 (1943): 425.

39. Rockoff, *Drastic Measures*, 35. Business leaders, both those working within OPA and those in the private sector, objected; they wanted premium prices to be allowed for name-brand hosiery and other products but at the same time did not under any circumstances want grade labeling of rationed goods by a public agency. In other words, they liked the existing system under which companies themselves, not independent evaluators, told Americans about the relative qualities of their products. OPA's information director went so far as to declare that grade labeling "presents the greatest threat to American industry and our way of life that ever existed." Rockoff, *Drastic Measures*, 94–95.

40. Associated Press, "Canned Goods Hoarders Face Rationing Penalty," *Pittsburgh Post-Gazette*, January 26, 1943.

41. "Rationing of Liquor Not Necessary," *Victory Bulletin* 4 (1943): 435.

42. U.S. Department of Agriculture, *Agriculture Fact Book, 2001–2002* (Washington, DC: U.S. Government Printing Office, 2003); Bentley, *Eating for Victory*, 93. Yearly red meat consumption was as high as 160 pounds per person early in the twentieth century.

43. "OPA Amends Meat Rationing Rules: Greater Freedom Afforded for Farm Families," *Victory Bulletin* 4 (1943): 528.

44. Gaynor Maddox, "Meat Rationing Won't Starve You, Says Expert," *St. Petersburg Evening Independent*, March 29, 1943.

45. "Increased Production of Cereals Asked," *Victory Bulletin* 4 (1943): 455; Jerome Gross, "Housewives Favor Stews, Hash in Meat Rationing," *Toledo Blade*, March 22, 1943; United Press, "Ration Starts on Monday; 16 Units a Week," *Toledo Blade*, March 22, 1943.

46. Associated Press, "Shoe Rationing Effective Tomorrow" and "Byrnes Gives Reasons Behind Shoes Rationing," *Deseret News*, February 8, 1943.

47. Edith Coogler, "Rationed Shoe Sales Here Bring Surge of Shoppers," *Palm Beach Post*, February 9, 1943. By June, women were able to obtain supplemental stamps to buy safety shoes for work even if there were unspent stamps in her household. Local rationing boards made allowances for people who needed special shoes for hazardous occupations. "Shoe Rationing Rules Clarified by OPA," *Victory Bulletin* 4 (1943): 482.

48. "New Specifications to Conserve Hose," *Victory Bulletin* 4 (1943), 392; "Women's Hosiery Will Meet Quality, Quantity Needs," *Victory Bulletin* 4 (1943): 579; Rockoff, *Drastic Measures*, 135.

49. "Material for Dresses Limited by WPB Order," *Victory Bulletin* 4 (1943): 565; Rockoff, *Drastic Measures*, 115–18.

50. "400,000 Household Refrigerators to Be Released This Spring," *Victory Bulletin* 4 (1943): 393; "Restrictions Removed from Farm Machines," *Victory Bulletin* 4 (1943): 430.

51. "Paper Conservation Program Urged by WPB for Schools, Colleges," *Victory Bulletin* 4 (1943): 525; "Wartime Restrictions on Materials Challenge American Ingenuity," *Victory Bulletin* 4 (1943): 568.

52. Zweiniger-Bargielowska, *Austerity in Britain*, 46.

53. Ibid., 48–49.

54. Frances Bevan, "Rationing to End White Weddings," *Swindon Advertiser*, June 2, 2011.

55. Zweiniger-Bargielowska, *Austerity in Britain*, 50–51, 94–95. Despite attempts to ensure high quality, complaints about quality and appearance of utility clothing persisted through the war. At about the time utility clothes began gaining popularity in the early fifties, the program was abolished. In 1942, specifications for all ready-made clothes were imposed "to ensure simple, economical styles by banning trimmings such as embroidery and restricting pleats, buttons, and pockets along with width of sleeves and collars." Clothes rationing continued until 1949.

56. Bentley, *Eating for Victory*, 21; Rockoff, *Drastic Measures*, 130.

57. International News Service, "9 Shoppers Under Fire," *Reading Eagle*, August 12, 1943.

58. United Press, "Maryland Governor's Wife Will Lose Her Gas Rations," *St. Petersburg Times*, June 16, 1943.

59. United Press, "Maryland State Official Loses Gas Rations," *St. Petersburg Times*, June 13, 1943; Associated Press, "Editor Repeats Gasoline Charge," *Toledo Blade*, June 11, 1943.

60. "Two More Officials Lose Gas," *Pittsburgh Post-Gazette*, June 5, 1943.

61. Dexter M. Keezer, "Observations on Rationing and Price Control in Great Britain," *American Economic Review* 33 (1943): 264–82.

62. Zweiniger-Bargielowska, *Austerity in Britain*, 58, 81–82.

63. Jean Drèze and Amartya Sen, *Hunger and Public Action* (New York: Oxford University Press, 1991), 181–82.

64. Zweiniger-Bargielowska, *Austerity in Britain*, 10, 12, 44–45, 71, 79, 88. David Kynaston has provided a vignette that evokes the attitude of the times: "Britain in 1945. . . .

A land where authority was respected? Or rather, accepted? Yes, perhaps the latter, co-existing with the necessary safety valve of copious everyday grumbling. . . . The story of Churchill in the Blitz driving through a London slum on a Friday evening—seeing a long queue outside a shop—stopping the car—sending his detective to find out what the shortage was—the answer: birdseed. Turning the cuffs, elbow patches on jackets, sheets sides to middle. A deeply conservative land." David Kynaston, *A World to Build* (London: Bloomsbury, 2008), 58–59.

65. Zweiniger-Bargielowska, *Austerity in Britain*, 163, 169, 202.

66. Rockoff, *Drastic Measures*, 143–49.

67. "Black Market Meat Slaughterers Waste Vital Food Supplies," *Victory Bulletin* 4 (1943): 453.

68. Ibid.; "Illegal Sales of Meat Threat to War Effort," *Victory Bulletin* 4 (1943): 388.

69. Associated Press, "Restaurants Limited by Rationing," *The Telegraph*, March 29, 1943; Associated Press, "Eaters of Steak Take Note," *Deseret News*, March 24, 1943; United Press, "Food Rationing to Curtail Banqueting for Duration," *Miami News*, February 28, 1943.

70. "Extra Ration Privileges for Dieters," *Pittsburgh Post-Gazette*, March 26, 1943.

71. Associated Press, "Giving a Dinner Complicated by Meat Rationing," *Sarasota Herald-Tribune*, March 24, 1943.

72. Associated Press, "Pews Are Frozen in Georgia Church," *St. Petersburg Evening Independent*, January 26, 1943.

73. Associated Press, "Favor Rationing in Smoking Crisis," *Norwalk Hour*, January 15, 1945.

74. Bentley, *Eating for Victory* 4, 22–24.

75. "Over-Confidence Causes Tightening of Rationing," *Pittsburgh Post-Gazette*, December 27, 1944.

76. Rockoff, *Drastic Measures*, 100–108.

77. Bentley, *Eating for Victory*, 8, 146, 156.

78. Associated Press, "Food Rationing May Be Returned," *St. Petersburg Times*, October 1, 1947.

79. Bentley, *Eating for Victory*, 153, 157.

80. Rockoff, *Drastic Measures*, 133–34.

81. Zweiniger-Bargielowska, *Austerity in Britain*, 28.

82. Ibid., 81; Kynaston, *A World to Build*, 37–41.

83. Rockoff, *Drastic Measures*, 201, 206. Suppressing wages as means of holding down prices was controversial. Jefferson Cowie writes that AFL-CIO leader George Meany regarded the scheme as a "rich man's plan," noting, "If Meany had to have controls, the type he preferred were akin to the aggressive form used during World War II to ensure that prices as well as wages were held down." Jefferson Cowie, *Stayin' Alive: The 1970s and the Last Days of the Working Class* (New York: The New Press, 2010), 151.

84. Associated Press, "Food Rationing Begins in Parts of U.S.," *Altus Times-Democrat*, July 22, 1973.

85. United Press International, "Food Rationing May Solve Export Problems," *Milwaukee Journal*, July 9, 1973.

86. John Crompton and Richard Gitelson, "Consumer Reactions to the Standby Motor Fuel Rationing Plan," *Journal of Travel Research* 27 (1981): 27–36.

87. B. Dan Kamp, John Crompton, and David Hensarling, "The Reactions of Travelers to Gasoline Rationing and to Increases in Gasoline Prices," *Journal of Travel Research* 18 (1979): 37–41.

88. Associated Press, "Some Questions and Answers on Heating Oil Rationing Plan," *Argus-Press* (Owasso, MI), November 28, 1973.

89. Cowie, *Stayin' Alive*, 225.

90. Anonymous, "Shortage: Gas Fever: Happiness Is a Full Tank," *Time*, February 18, 1974.

91. "Energy: Rationing: Some Pros," *Time*, Monday, February 3, 1975.

92. Horowitz, *Jimmy Carter*, 42.

93. Russell Baker, "Is Carter's MEOW Worse than His Bite?" *Pittsburgh Post-Gazette*, April 27, 1977.

94. Anonymous, "Lessons from Rationing Debate," *Press Courier* (Oxnard, CA), May 15, 1979.

95. Associated Press, "Tourists Warned Off as California Turns to Gasoline Rationing," *Montreal Gazette*, May 8, 1979; Horowitz, *Jimmy Carter*, 53; Kevin Mattson, *What the Heck Are You Up To, Mr. President? Jimmy Carter, America's "Malaise," and the Speech That Should Have Changed the Country* (New York: Bloomsbury, 2009), 65. In late 2012, gasoline rationing by license-plate number returned to America as a response to severe shortages in New York City and parts of New Jersey in the wake of "superstorm" Sandy. The policy was characterized by business writer Matthew Yglesias as "folly," but rationing did succeed in shortening or eliminating many gas lines. Matthew Yglesias, "The Folly of Odd-Even Gasoline Rationing," *Slate*, November 9, 2012; "Bloomberg: Gas Rationing Eases Fuel Crunch in NYC," Associated Press, November 12, 2012.

96. Associated Press, "Mother's Day Phone Calls Boosted by Gas Shortage," *Ocala Star-Banner*, May 14, 1979; Horowitz, *Jimmy Carter*, 49–50. Scenes in New York and Levittown are from Andrew Tully III, "Police Placed at Corner to Prevent Gasoline Riot," *Frederick Daily Leader*, June 26, 1979; for Levittown, also see Mattson, *What the Heck*, 119.

97. George Will, "Gasoline Rationing a Messy Business," *Washington Post*, June 22, 1979; Horowitz, *Jimmy Carter*, 97; Mattson, *What the Heck*, 72, 126, 143.

98. Horowitz, *Jimmy Carter*, 88.

99. Ibid., 166.

100. Mattson, *What the Heck*, 161–65.

101. U.S. Department of Energy, *Standby Gasoline Rationing Plan* (Springfield, VA: National Technical Information Service, 1980), www.ntl.bts.gov/lib/12000/12200/12291/12291.pdf.

102. Ibid.

103. Crompton and Gitelson, "Consumer Reactions."

104. Ibid.

105. Ibid.

106. United Press International, "Rationing Coupons Shredded," *New York Times*, June 2, 1984.

107. Before the 1979 crisis, U.S. gasoline consumption for all purposes was 500 gallons per person per year. The 20 percent shortfall would have led to the imposition of a limit of 400 gallons per person per year. Had rationing been activated at that per-capita consumption level and had we stayed at that level for the next thirty years (with the rate of population increase that we actually had), 800 billion gallons would have been saved as of 2010. OREP, *Standby Rationing Plan 80–1*; data from Bureau of Transportation Statistics, "Fuel Consumption by Mode of Transportation in Physical Units," 2010, www.bts.gov/publications/national_transportation_statistics/html/table_04_05.html; for domestic gasoline production, see U.S. Energy Information Administration, "Petroleum and Other Liquids," www.eia.gov/dnav/pet/hist/LeafHandler.ashx?n=PET&s=WGFRPUS2&f=W.

108. Andy Kroll, "The Long and Warming Road," *Mother Jones*, November/December 2009.

Chapter 2: Is There a Ration Card in Your Future?

1. Fred Magdoff, telephone interview by author, October 14, 2011.

2. Christine Fall, "Will Rising Gas Prices Bring on a Mad Max Future?" AMC Film critic.com, May 28, 2008, www.filmcritic.com/features/2008/05/rising-gas-prices-mad-max-future/.

3. James Gustav Speth, *The Bridge at the Edge of the World: Capitalism, the Environment and Crossing from Crisis to Sustainability* (New Haven, CT: Yale University Press, 2008), 20, 52.

4. V. Smil, "Harvesting the Biosphere: The Human Impact," *Population and Development Review* 37 (2011): 613–36.

5. Johan Rockström et al., "Planetary Boundaries: Exploring the Safe Operating Space for Humanity," *Ecology and Society* 14, no. 2 (2009): art. 32.

6. Percentages are computed from national per-capita carbon footprints. See Steven Goldfinger and Pati Poblete, eds., *The Ecological Wealth of Nations* (Oakland, CA: Global Footprint Network, 2010), 28–34.

7. Global Commons Institute, *Carbon Countdown* (London: GCI, 2008), www.gci.org.uk/Documents/Carbon_Countdown.pdf.

8. Tadeusz Patzek and Gregory Croft, "A Global Coal Production Forecast with Multi-Hubbert Cycle Analysis," *Energy* 35 (2010): 3109–22.

9. Richard Heinberg, *Blackout: Coal, Climate and the Last Energy Crisis* (Gabriola Island, BC: New Society, 2009), 119, 126–27; Richard Heinberg, *The Oil Depletion Protocol: A Plan to Avert Oil Wars, Terrorism and Economic Collapse* (Gabriola Island, BC: New Society, 2006), 129–31.

10. Robert Hirsch, "Peaking of World Oil Production: Recent Forecasts," U.S. Department of Energy Report DOE/NETL-2007/1263, 2007. Five other predictions—by officials of Exxon-Mobil, BP, the Organization of Petroleum Exporting Countries (OPEC), Cambridge Energy Research Associates, and the investment bank UBS—foresaw either no peak or none until after 2020. Also see Robert Hirsch, Roger Bezdek, and Robert Wendling, *Peaking of World Oil Production: Impacts, Mitigation, and Risk Management* (San Diego, CA: SAIC, 2005).

11. International Energy Agency, "World Energy Outlook 2010: Executive Summary," 2010, www.iea.org/textbase/npsum/weo2010sum.pdf. A group of Swedish, British, and Australian scientists reran the IEA's analysis, using what the group said were more realistic projections of future oil recovery. They concluded that even if we pursue aggressive exploitation of nonconventional oil, total world production is already in permanent decline. See Kjell Aleklett et al., "The Peak of the Oil Age: Analyzing the World Oil Production Reference Scenario in World Energy Outlook 2008," *Energy Policy* 38 (2010): 1398–414.

12. Daniel Yergin, "There Will Be Oil," *Wall Street Journal*, September 17, 2011.

13. Kevin Timoney and Peter Lee, "Does the Alberta Tar Sands Industry Pollute? The Scientific Evidence," *Open Conservation Biology Journal* 3 (2009): 65–81; Tim McDonnell, "There's No Hiding from Tar Sands Oil," *Mother Jones*, December 15, 2011.

14. IEA, *World Energy Outlook 2010*.

15. Rebecca Rooney, Suzanne Bayley, and David Schindler, "Oil Sands Mining and Reclamation Cause Massive Loss of Peatland and Stored Carbon," *Proceedings of the National Academy of Sciences* 109 (2012): 4933–37; Robert W. Howarth, Renee Santoro, and Anthony Ingraffea, "Methane and the Greenhouse-Gas Footprint of Natural Gas from Shale Formations," *Climatic Change* 106 (2011): 679–90. The conclusions of Howarth et al. have been disputed; see Lawrence M. Cathles, Larry Brown, Milton Taam, and Andrew Hunter, "A Commentary on 'The Greenhouse-Gas Footprint of Natural Gas in Shale Formations' by R.W. Howarth, R. Santoro, and Anthony Ingraffea," *Climatic Change* (2012), doi: 10.1007/s10584-011-0333-0. And there has been a response: Robert Howarth, Renee Santoro, and Anthony Ingraffea, "Venting and Leaking of Methane from Shale Gas Development: Response to Cathles et al.," *Climatic Change* (2012), doi; 10.1007/s10584-012-0401-0.

16. Bryan Walsh, "The Gas Dilemma," *Time*, March 31, 2011; Robert Jereski, "Banning Methane Mining," *Synthesis/Regeneration* 55 (2011): 7–9. Also see Stan Cox, "Is Gas Really 'Twice as Clean' as Coal?" *Alternet*, November 11, 2010. Regarding the comparison with opposition to nuclear energy: even if disaster had not struck Japan's Fukushima nuclear installation in March 2011, there would be numerous reasons not to expand the world's nuclear power capacity. For a survey of arguments against relying on nuclear generation to fill the energy gap left by declining fossil-fuel use, see Stan Cox, *Losing Our Cool: Uncomfortable Truths About Our Air-Conditioned World (and Finding New Ways to Get Through the Summer)* (New York: The New Press, 2010), 164–70.

17. Heinberg, *Blackout*, 33.

18. David Rutledge, "Estimating Long-Term World Coal Production with Logit and Probit Transforms," *International Journal of Coal Geology* 85 (2011): 23–33; Tadeusz Patzek and Gregory Croft, "A Global Coal Production Forecast"; S.H. Mohr and G.M. Evans, "Forecasting Coal Production Until 2100," *Fuel* 88 (2009): 2059–67.

19. The indicator most commonly used to track this phenomenon is "energy return on investment" (EROI), which is usually expressed as the ratio of energy obtained to the energy expended in obtaining it. In the early twentieth century, for example, it required energy equal to that in one barrel of oil to extract one hundred barrels from the ground; therefore, the EROI was 100:1. Because the most easily acquired deposits are exploited first, EROI tends to decrease over time (but with spikes when new, easily recoverable deposits are discovered), so that today, according to some analysts, EROI for oil overall is between 20:1 and 40:1. EROI for conventional natural gas is estimated at between 13:1 and 20:1. Coal's EROI remains high, at 40:1 to 80:1. (Such estimates tend to vary a great deal, depending on the location of the source and how many factors one considers in adding up the energy costs of obtaining energy.) Any of the traditional fossil-fuel ratios tell us that only 1 to 5 percent of the energy coming out of the ground must be diverted into obtaining more of that kind of energy; that leaves large energy surpluses for running civilization, as long as there is plenty remaining in the ground to pump or mine. But, say pessimists, EROIs always decline over time, and with depletion of reserves accelerating EROI can drop rapidly. Deposits that are being explored as new sources have lower ratios: natural gas obtained by horizontal drilling and fracturing has a lower ratio than does conventional gas; the ratio is less than 20:1, possibly as low as 7:1, for "ultradeep water" oil and gas in the Gulf of Mexico; and it is less than 1:1 for oil from Canadian tar sands. Those ratios do not even account for the energy required for the infrastructure and fuel required to deliver energy to the consumer. Most important, they do not account for the much more profound ecological costs that are already being incurred in obtaining energy from unconventional fossil-fuel sources. When we do account for all costs of obtaining and delivering energy, a whole-economy EROI of at least 3:1 has been estimated to be necessary just to maintain society at a minimum level of existence. That is, when the average EROI of all currently used energy sources falls below 3:1, such a large share of the economy must be devoted to acquiring, processing, and delivering energy that there is not enough left over to maintain and power the basic infrastructure. Alternatives to fossil fuels would not provide as much surplus above that minimum as do currently used fossil fuels. EROI estimates for wind-, solar-, and nuclear-derived electricity range between 5:1 and 20:1, but to store and deliver electricity from intermittently generated solar and wind, or to substitute any source of electricity for current liquid-fuel uses, would soak up another significant share of the surplus. EROIs for biofuels are below the threshold: 2:1 for biodiesel and between 1:1 and 1.6:1 for corn ethanol. See Charles A.S. Hall, "Introduction to Special Issue on New Studies in EROI (Energy

Return on Investment)," *Sustainability* 3 (2011): 1773–77; and Charles A.S. Hall, Stephen Balogh, and David J.R. Murphy, "What Is the Minimum EROI That a Sustainable Society Must Have?," *Energies* 2 (2009): 25–47.

20. D.J. Murphy et al., "Tractors and Rollover Protection in the United States," *Journal of Agromedicine* 1 (2010): 249–63.

21. Food and Agriculture Organization, *The State of the World's Land and Water Resources for Food and Agriculture—Managing Systems at Risk* (Rome: FAO, 2011); Lee Addams, Giulio Boccaletti, Mike Kerlin, and Martin Stuchtey, *Charting Our Water Future: Economic Frameworks to Inform Decision-Making* (New York: McKinsey & Company, 2009), 5; Alan Bjerga, "U.S. Intelligence Says Water Shortages Threaten Stability," *Bloomberg Businessweek*, March 22, 2012.

22. See Stan Cox, "You Can't Buy a Better Agriculture," *Al Jazeera English*, September 5, 2011, and "The World Can't Afford to Keep Wasting Soil," *Al Jazeera English*, January 12, 2012.

23. FAO, *State of the World's Land and Water.*

24. See Stan Cox, *Sick Planet: Corporate Food and Medicine* (London: Pluto, 2008), 1–20.

25. Interview of cycle-wallahs by Priti Gulati Cox and the author, Hazaribagh-Ranchi highway, Jharkhand, India, December 21, 2011; Kuntala Lahiri-Dutt and David Williams, "The Coal Cycle: Small Scale Illegal Coal Supply in Eastern India," *Journal of Resource, Environment and Development* 2 (2005): 93–105.

26. See Herman Daly, "The Return of Lauderdale's Paradox," *Ecological Economics* 25 (1998): 21–23; and John Bellamy Foster and Brett Clark, "The Paradox of Wealth: Capitalism and Ecological Destruction," *Monthly Review* 61, no. 6 (2009): 1–18.

27. Robert Costanza et al., "The Value of the World's Ecosystem Services and Natural Capital," *Nature* 387 (1997): 253–60.

28. Daly, "Return of Lauderdale's Paradox."

29. James Brown et al., "Energetic Limits to Economic Growth," *Bioscience* 61 (2011): 19–26. Specifically, energy consumption varies with the three-fourths power of GDP; interestingly, that is the same statistical relationship that exists between metabolic rate and body mass in animals.

30. Jeff Rubin and Benjamin Tal, "Does Energy Efficiency Save Energy?" *StrategEcon*, November 27, 2007. For a thorough exploration of the problem of efficiency—encompassing not only energy but modern life in general—see David Owen, *The Conundrum* (New York: Riverhead Books, 2012).

31. For a thorough analysis, see Jesse Jenkins, Ted Nordhaus, and Michael Shellenberger, "Energy Emergence: Rebound & Backfire as Emergent Phenomena," Breakthrough Institute, February 2011, thebreakthrough.org/blog/2011/02/new_report_how_efficiency_can.shtml. Rebound and backfire are modern incarnations of the Jevons paradox, named for the economist William Stanley Jevons and his 1865 critique of efficiency, *The Coal Question*. Strangely, after demonstrating how efficiency largely undermines itself by stimulating faster economic growth, the authors of "Energy Emergence" conclude that the only way out of the trap

is to pursue even stronger growth through even higher efficiency—a conclusion that we might think of as the Nordhaus paradox, after Ted Nordhaus, the chairman and co-founder of the Breakthrough Institute. Bill Blackwater has noted the stark contrast between Nordhaus and colleagues' rigorous analysis of data in their critique of efficiency with their failure to provide any support for their pro-growth conclusion. Blackwater argues:

> The overriding problem Nordhaus and Shellenberger face is making the case that the environmental gains that come in their theory of economic growth will outpace . . . the despoliation attendant on that same growth. In practice, they hardly ever make the attempt, simply advancing this as an article of faith. The best they do is a repeated insistence that economic growth should be of the "right kind"—but what this means and how it could be guaranteed they decline to say. Their positive ideas remain on the level of simplistic wish-fulfillment.

William Stanley Jevons, *The Coal Question: An Inquiry Concerning the Progress of the Nation, and the Probable Exhaustion of Our Coal Mines,* 2nd ed. (London: Macmillan and Co., 1866); Bill Blackwater, "The Denialism of Progressive Environmentalists," *Monthly Review* 64, no. 2 (2012): 10–21; for more on rebound and backfire, see Cox, *Losing Our Cool,* 160–64.

32. Jeff Rubin, "The Efficiency Paradox," *StrategEcon,* November 27, 2007.

33. Herman E. Daly, "The Illth of Nations and the Fecklessness of Policy: An Ecological Economist's Perspective," *Post-Autistic Economics Review* 30 (2005): art. 1.

34. Ted Trainer, "De-growth—Is Not Enough," *International Journal of Inclusive Democracy* 6 (2010): record no. 4.

35. Minqi Li, "Capitalism, Climate Change and the Transition to Sustainability: Alternative Scenarios for the US, China and the World," *Development and Change* 40 (2009): 1039–61. Li assumed a 2 percent rate of efficiency improvement, which easily exceeds the historical increase of 1.4 percent per year since 1980 and the 1.4 to 1.8 percent increase projected by the International Energy Agency (IEA) up to 2050. Compare his figures of 200 to 800 gigawatts of solar and wind capacity increases with the current IEA projection that the world will add 120 gigawatts annually over the next four decades (IEA, *World Energy Outlook 2010*). Even with those wildly optimistic assumptions, Li cannot find a high-growth scenario.

36. David Orr, telephone interview by the author, August 17, 2011. Orr believes that "the gas lines in the seventies brought out a nastiness in human nature. We may just not have what it takes." In fact, if there were such a thing as an "intergalactic betting parlor," says Orr, the odds on humans having what it takes to deal with the crisis would be pretty long.

37. Fred Magdoff, telephone interview by the author, October 14, 2011.

38. Martin Weitzman, e-mail interview by the author, August 6, 2011.

39. Maurie Cohen, "Is the UK Preparing for 'War'? Military Metaphors, Personal Carbon Allowances, and Consumption Rationing in Historical Perspective," *Climatic Change* 104 (2010): 119–22.

40. Orr, telephone interview.

41. Richard Glenn Gettell, "Rationing: A Pragmatic Problem for Economists," *American Economic Review* 33 (1943): 260–71.

42. "Scalpers Spoiling the View for Yosemite's Parkgoers," *Sacramento Bee*, April 18, 2011; Marjie Lundstrom, "Scalpers Flipping Yosemite Reservations," *Sacramento Bee*, April 18, 2011. The National Park Service instituted reservations and other restrictions in Yosemite in the 1970s, when overcrowding, traffic jams, and urban levels of air pollution were threatening to ruin the park.

43. Franklin Allen and Gerald R. Faulhaber, "Rational Rationing," *Economica* 58 (1991): 189–98; Margaret Slade, "Strategic Pricing with Customer Rationing: The Case of Primary Metals," *Canadian Journal of Economics* 24 (1991): 70–100.

44. Jeremy Clark and Bonggeun Kim, "Paying vs. Waiting in the Pursuit of Specific Egalitarianism," *Oxford Economic Papers* 59 (2007): 486–512.

45. Martin Weitzman, "Is the Price System or Rationing More Effective in Getting a Commodity to Those Who Need It Most?" *Bell Journal of Economics* 8 (1977): 517–24.

46. Francisco Rivera-Batiz, "The Price System vs. Rationing: An Extension," *Bell Journal of Economics* 12 (1981): 245–48.

47. Jacques Polak, "Rationing of Purchasing Power to Restrict Consumption," *Economica* 8 (1941): 223–28.

48. James Tobin, "On Limiting the Domain of Inequality," *Journal of Law and Economics* 13 (1970): 263–77. Also see David Fleming and Shaun Chamberlin, *TEQs: Tradable Energy Quotas* (London: House of Commons All Party Parliamentary Group on Peak Oil and The Lean Economy Connection, 2011).

49. Martin Weitzman, e-mail interview by author, August 6, 2011.

50. James Tobin, "A Survey of the Theory of Rationing," *Econometrica* 20 (1952): 521–53.

51. Tobin, "On Limiting." More of Tobin's comments: "Our society, I believe, accepts and approves a large measure of inequality, even of inherited inequality. Americans commonly perceive differences of wealth and income as earned and regard the differential earnings of effort, skill, foresight, and enterprise as deserved. . . . To the extent that economists are egalitarians at all, they are general egalitarians. The reason is their belief that specific interventions, whether in the name of equality or not, introduce inefficiencies, and the more specific the intervention the more serious the inefficiency."

52. Hans Neisser, "Theoretical Aspects of Rationing," *Quarterly Journal of Economics* 57 (1943): 378–97.

53. A. Henderson, "A Note on the Theory of Rationing," *Review of Economic Studies* 15 (1947–48): 42–45.

54. Polak, "Rationing of Purchasing Power." Polak had two observations that would argue for the blanket rationing of luxuries, however: "(i) With respect to nonessentials, too, it is unpleasant (to say the least) for the person of moderate means to be able to buy almost nothing for his 'free' money, whereas a rich person can buy all he wants. (ii) It is confusing to upset a customary system of prices in

the sense that the prices of necessities are kept within limits whereas those of non-necessities rise out of any proportion. This creates an unrealistically sharp distinction between the two groups."

55. Michal Kalecki, "A Scheme of Curtailment of Consumption," *Oxford Institute of Statistics Bulletin*, June 30, 1940, 7–9; discussed in George Feiwel, "Kalecki's Ingenious Expenditure Rationing Scheme: How to Improve the Range of Economic Choice Under Trying Conditions," *Keio Economic Studies* 11 (1974): 67–87.

56. Gustav Papanek, "General or Expenditure Rationing," *Quarterly Journal of Economics* 66 (1952): 418–35; Polak, "Rationing of Purchasing Power."

57. Feiwel, "Kalecki's Ingenious Expenditure Rationing Scheme." Suppose a wealthy banker, rather than the government, wanted to buy £10 worth of coupons from a laborer under the table. The banker would most likely pay a rate higher than the face value of the coupons, say £15. The cost of those coupons, plus the £10 in cash that those coupons would allow him to spend, means that to buy a silk shirt worth £10, he would have to spend £25. That, believed Kalecki, would give the banker strong doubts about buying coupons on the black market. The laborer's family, meanwhile, would have little incentive to sell their coupons to the banker rather than to the government, because if they did so, they would no longer have enough ration coupons to be able to spend the extra £5 they'd make from the illicit sale.

58. Richard Starkey and Kevin Anderson, *Domestic Tradable Quotas: A Policy Instrument for Reducing Greenhouse Gas Emissions from Energy Use* (Manchester: Tyndall Center, 2005), 5.

59. Papanek, "General or Expenditure Rationing."

60. Cohen, "Is the UK Preparing for 'War'?"

61. Geofrey Mills and Hugh Rockoff, "Compliance with Price Controls in the United States and the United Kingdom During World War II," *Journal of Economic History* 47 (1987): 197–213.

62. Rockoff, *Drastic Measures*, 123.

63. Victor Polterovich, "Rationing, Queues, and Black Markets," *Econometrica* 61 (1993): 1–28.

64. Cohen, "Is the UK Preparing for 'War'?"

65. Rockoff, *Drastic Measures*, 140.

66. Fred Mannering, "An Empirical Analysis of Driver Perceptions of the Relationship Between Speed Limits and Safety," *Transportation Research Part F* 12 (2009): 99–106; Rune Elvik, "A Restatement of the Case for Speed Limits," *Transport Policy* 17 (2010): 196–204; Glenn Blomquist, "The 55 m.p.h. Speed Limit and Gasoline Consumption," *Resources and Energy* 6 (1984): 21–39.

67. Edgar Feige and Richard Cebula, "America's Underground Economy: Measuring the Size, Growth and Determinants of Income Tax Evasion in the U.S," Munich Personal RePEc Archive, Paper No. 29672, March 17, 2011; Internal Revenue Service, "IRS FY 2012 Budget Proposal Summary," Report no. FS-2011-09, February 2011, www.irs.gov/uac/IRS-FY-2012-Budget-Proposal-Summary.

68. Jack Gillum, "AP Exclusive: Romney Uses Secretive Data Mining," Associated Press, August 24, 2012. Associated Press, "Officials Approve Study of SF Bay Area Mileage Tax," *San Jose Mercury News*, July 19, 2012; Christine Vendel, "KC Police Hold a Treasure Trove of License Plate Data," *Kansas City Star*, July 30, 2012; Mark Smith, " 'Snapshot' Car Insurance: What's the Catch?" Carinsurance.com, October 23, 2011, www.carinsurance.com/Articles/progressive-snapshot-whats -the-catch.aspx.

69. The *Wall Street Journal* has collected articles on these and many other privacy issues on a page called "What They Know," online.wsj.com/public/page/what-they -know-digital-privacy.html.

70. Yabing Liu, Krishna Gummadi, Balachander Krishnamurth, and Alan Mislove, "Analyzing Facebook Privacy Settings: User Expectations vs. Reality," Proceedings of the ACM SIGCOMM/USENIX Internet Measurement Conference, Berlin, Germany, November 2–4, 2011, doi>10.1145/2068816.2068823; Deborah F. Spake, R. Zachary Finney, and Mathew Joseph, "Experience, Comfort, and Privacy Concerns: Antecedents of Online Spending," *Journal of Research in Interactive Marketing* 5 (2011): 5–28.

Chapter 3: Fair Skies

1. Tina Fawcett, interview by the author via the Internet, October 12, 2011.

2. Tamra Gilbertson and Oscar Reyes, *Carbon Trading: How It Works and Why It Fails* (Uppsala: Dag Hammarskjöld Foundation, 2009), 89–90.

3. Charles J. Hanley, "The American 'Allergy' to Global Warming: Why?" *Washington Times*, September 24, 2011; "Poll: Most Americans Think Devastating Natural Disasters Are Increasing," *Environmental Protection*, July 8, 2011, eponline.com/ articles/2011/07/08/poll-most-americans-think-devastating-natural-disasters -are-increasing.aspx. The increase in climate denial in polls has been primarily among self-described political conservatives.

4. Daniel Greenfield, "Politicizing Energy Independence," *Canada Free Press*, September 29, 2011.

5. Andrew Freedman, "Dueling Climate Meetings Aim to Steer Policy," *Washington Post*, March 11, 2009; James Taylor, "Public Outrage Throttles California Plan to Control Home Thermostats," *Heartlander*, March 1, 2008; Wendell Cox, "Planning Is a Tool, Not a Goal," *Heartlander*, August 1, 2003; H. Sterling Burnett, "ESA Listing Not Needed for Polar Bears," *Heartlander*, March 1, 2007; Amanda Carpenter, "Chu on Chamber," *Washington Times*, October 12, 2009; Ronald Bailey, "Carbon Rationing by Other Means," *Reason*, April 2011; "AJ," "Agenda 21: Ending Liberty in America," Noisyroom.net, July 5, 2011, noisyroom.net/blog/2011/07/05/ agenda-21-%E2%80%93-ending-liberty-in-america/1.

6. Josep Canadell et al., "Contributions to Accelerating Atmospheric CO_2 Growth from Economic Activity, Carbon Intensity, and Efficiency of Natural Sinks," *Proceedings of the National Academy of Sciences* 104 (2007): 18866–70; John Broder,

"Emissions Fell in 2009, Showing Impact of Recession," *New York Times*, February 16, 2011; Kevin Begos, "CO_2 Emissions in U.S. Drop to 20-Year Low," Associated Press, August 16, 2012; Stan Cox, *Losing Our Cool: Uncomfortable Truths About Our Air-Conditioned World (and Finding New Ways to Get Through the Summer)* (New York: The New Press, 2011), 152; Corinne Le Quéré et al., "Trends in the Sources and Sinks of Carbon Dioxide," *Nature Geoscience* 2 (2009): 831–36. Although U.S. emissions fell from 2007 to 2012, the output from U.S. coal mines was sustained, and exports of coal to Asia and Europe rose sharply. This led *New Scientist* to argue that "in reality the emissions have simply been exported." Michael Marshall, "Lowest U.S. Carbon Emissions Won't Slow Climate Change," *New Scientist*, August 20, 2012.

7. Shoibal Chakravarty et al., "Sharing Global CO_2 Emission Reductions Among One Billion High Emitters," *Proceedings of the National Academy of Sciences* 106 (2009): 11884–88.

8. Ibid.

9. André Gorz, *Ecologica* (London: Seagull, 2010), 85–90.

10. Lucas Davis, "The Effect of Driving Restrictions on Air Quality in Mexico City," *Journal of Political Economy* 116 (2008): 38–81.

11. "Beijing Starts Car Plate Lottery," CNTV News, January 26, 2011, english.cntv .cn/program/newsupdate/20110126/105041.shtml; Cambridge Systematics, *License Plate Rationing Evaluation: Technical Memorandum* (New York: Cambridge Systematics, Inc., 2007). As an alternative to a license-plate ration system, Mayor Michael Bloomberg proposed in 2008 that all cars entering the island of Manhattan be charged a congestion fee of $8, with a $21 fee for trucks. The plan, modeled partly on congestion-fee systems in London, Stockholm, and Singapore, was approved by the New York City Council but died in the State Assembly.

12. David Owen, "How Traffic Jams Help the Environment," *Wall Street Journal*, October 9, 2009.

13. Charles Raux and Grégoire Marlot, "A System of Tradable CO_2 Permits Applied to Fuel Consumption by Motorists," *Transport Policy* 12 (2005): 255–65; see also Robert Archibald and Robert Gillingham, "The Distributional Impact of Alternative Gasoline Conservation Policies," *Bell Journal of Economics* 12 (1981): 426–44.

14. Olivia Chung, "Power Rationing Strikes China Early," *Asia Times*, May 20, 2011.

15. Severin Borenstein, "Equity Effects of Increasing-Block Electricity Pricing," University of California Energy Institute Working Paper CSEM-WP-180, 2008.

16. Ibid.; California Public Utilities Commission, "How Your Electricity Bill Is Calculated," July 2010, www.cpuc.ca.gov/NR/rdonlyres/6AF20251-011C-4EF2-B99D -74CA315A4C40/0/RatesFAQ0710_3.pdf.

17. Sanjay Dutta, "Powerless and Clueless: 684 Million Indians Without Power," *Times of India*, August 1, 2012.

18. Tina Fawcett and Yael Parag, "An Introduction to Personal Carbon Trading," *Climate Policy* 10 (2010): 329–38; David Fleming and Shaun Chamberlin, *TEQs:*

Tradable Energy Quotas (London: House of Commons All Party Parliamentary Group on Peak Oil and The Lean Economy Connection, 2011).

19. Fleming and Chamberlin, *TEQs*.

20. Ibid.; Richard Starkey and Kevin Anderson, *Domestic Tradable Quotas: A Policy Instrument for Reducing Greenhouse Gas Emissions from Energy Use* (Manchester, UK: Tyndall Center, 2005).

21. Mayer Hillman, Tina Fawcett, and Sudhir Chella Rajan, *How We Can Save the Planet: Preventing Global Climate Catastrophe* (New York: Thomas Dunne, 2007), 200–201.

22. Garry Egger, telephone interview by the author, February 13, 2012. For an example of attacks on the plan, see Andrew Bolt, "Norfolk Island Green Ration Is Ludicrous," *Melbourne Herald Sun*, November 3, 2010. In Bolt's view, "global warming is just the latest cause of the closet totalitarian."

23. An example of such a nutritional rating is the "NuVal" score developed by David Katz, director of the Yale Prevention Research Center. See www.nuval.com.

24. For example, an oft-cited indicator of a food's quality and climate impact is the number of miles the food travels from where it is produced to where it is consumed. But it is possible, for example, that lamb or apples produced in New Zealand and consumed in London can have a smaller greenhouse impact than their locally produced counterparts, with equal quality. See Stan Cox, "Does It Really Matter Whether Your Food Was Produced Locally?" *AlterNet*, February 19, 2010, www.alternet.org/story/145673.

25. Will Ockenden, "Norfolk Finds a Way to Beat the Traffic," *World Today* (ABC), February 10, 2012.

26. Egger, telephone interview. In another example of voluntary carbon rationing, climate activists in several countries have formed Carbon Reduction Action Groups (CRAGs), which attempt to simulate the process of personal carbon trading. When you join a CRAG, you commit to reporting all of your purchases of air travel, motor vehicle fuel, home heating, and electricity to the group's accountant, who deducts credits from your annual quota. If at the end of the year you have exceeded your allowance, you must pay a cash fine corresponding to your amount of excess usage. Fines from the whole group go into a fund that can be spent in any of several ways or in some combination: to charity, to "green" projects, or to be divided up proportionally among members of the group who did not use their whole carbon quota. This last option would not appear to be the kind of policy that would foster the sense of common purpose that is one of the purported goals of carbon rationing. Because the scheme is administered voluntarily, there are no enforceable penalties other than banishment from the group. Groups also hold meetings to discuss each member's progress. One academic who works on climate strategies does not participate in CRAGs because "you'd just have to sit through so many of those meetings. It would be sort of like being in A.A." See, for example, "Carbon Rationing Action Groups," www.carbonrationing.org.uk.

27. James Hansen, "Carbon Tax & 100% Dividend vs. Tax & Trade," testimony given to the Committee on Ways and Means, U.S. House of Representatives, February 25, 2009. But Hansen's faith in the market is not accompanied by an equivalent trust in Congress to pass the necessary laws. In a footnote to his testimony, Hansen recounts this experience: "Two years ago I sat next to the Saudi Arabian Ambassador to the United States at a dinner. He became upset, politely, when I mentioned this concept of a carbon tax. Clearly, he understood the implications. He did not seem too concerned that it would be adopted—he probably took it for granted that fossil fuel special interests could overcome any wisdom of our law-makers."

28. Fleming and Chamberlin, *TEQs.*

29. Fawcett, interview by author; Hillman, Fawcett, and Rajan, *How We Can Save the Planet,* 202–3.

30. Colin Brinsden, "Spending Rises as Compensation Rolls Out," *Herald Sun,* July 4, 2012.

31. Starkey and Anderson, *Domestic Tradable Quotas,* 39.

32. Matthew Lockwood, "The Economics of Personal Carbon Trading," *Climate Policy* 10 (2010): 447–61. Note that adjusting for need does not make the scheme more progressive. To achieve equity, there will have to be aid. Vicki White and Joshua Thumim, "Moderating the Distributional Impacts of Personal Carbon Trading," Report to the Institute for Public Policy Research, August 2009, www .cse.org.uk/pdf/Moderating_the_distributional_impacts_of_PCT_aug09.pdf.

33. Keith Hyams, "A Just Response to Climate Change: Personal Carbon Allowances and the Normal-Functioning Approach," *Journal of Social Philosophy* 40 (2009): 237–56.

34. White and Thumim, "Moderating the Distributional Impacts."

35. George Monbiot, *Heat: How to Stop the Planet from Burning* (Cambridge, MA: South End Press, 2007), 47.

36. Starkey and Anderson, *Domestic Tradable Quotas,* 39.

37. Monbiot, *Heat,* 46.

38. Lockwood, "Economics of Personal Carbon Trading."

39. Margaret Cheney et al., "H. 385: An Act Relating to Establishing a Vermont Common Assets Trust," introduced in the Vermont House of Representatives, 2011–12 session, www.leg.state.vt.us/docs/2012/bills/Intro/H-385.pdf.

40. Ibid.; Joshua Farley, telephone interview by the author, October 17, 2011.

41. Laurence Mathews, "Upstream, Downstream: The Importance of Psychological Framing for Carbon Emission Reduction Policies," *Climate Policy* 10 (2010): 477–80.

42. Hillman, Fawcett, and Rajan, *How We Can Save the Planet,* 198.

43. Fawcett, interview by the author.

44. Tobin, "Survey of the Theory."

45. Weitzman, "Is the Price System."

46. Hillman, Fawcett, and Rajan, *How We Can Save the Planet,* 210.

47. Tobin, "On Limiting."

48. Starkey and Anderson, *Domestic Tradable Quotas.*

49. Brian Tokar, telephone interview by the author, October 18, 2011.

50. Nick Eyre, "Policing Carbon: Design and Enforcement Options for Personal Carbon Trading," *Climate Policy* 10 (2010): 432–46.

51. Starkey and Anderson, *Domestic Tradable Quotas.*

52. Steve Suppan, "Speculating on Carbon: The Next Toxic Asset," Institute for Trade Policy, Minneapolis, MN, 2010.

53. Ibid.

54. Lockwood, "Economics of Personal Carbon Trading."

55. Ibid.

56. Fawcett, interview by the author.

57. Mark Roodhouse, "Rationing Returns: A Solution to Global Warming?" *History and Policy*, March 2007, www.historyandpolicy.org/papers/policy-paper-54.html.

58. Jonathan Porritt, "Population and Climate Change," *New Internationalist*, January/February 2010; J. Kenneth Smail, "Remembering Malthus II: Establishing Sustainable Population Optimums," *American Journal of Physical Anthropology* 122 (2003): 287–94.

59. See a contentious 2008 discussion of Population Matters's views, hosted by the Bulletin of Atomic Scientists, "Population and Climate Change," April 16, 2008, www.thebulletin.org/web-edition/roundtables/population-and-climate-change; see the "PopOffsets" website, www.popoffsets.com; see criticism of PopOffsets in Vanessa Baird, "The Missing Pieces," *New Internationalist*, January/February 2010.

60. David Satterthwaite, "The Implications of Population Growth and Urbanization for Climate Change," *Environment and Urbanization* 21 (2009): 545–67; Michael Kremer, "Income Distribution Dynamics with Endogenous Fertility," *Journal of Economic Growth* 7 (2002): 227–58; Jeffrey Kentor, "The Long Term Effects of Globalization on Income Inequality, Population Growth, and Economic Development," *Social Problems* 48 (2001): 435–55.

61. Bulletin of Atomic Scientists, "Population and Climate Change."

62. See Khadija Turay, "Human Rights and Population: Politics in India During the Emergency and at the Present Moment," in *Between Life and Death: Governing Populations in the Era of Human Rights*, ed. Sabine Berking and Magdalena Zolkos (Frankfurt am Main: Oxford, 2009), citing R.H. Cassen, *India: Population, Economy, Society* (New York: Holmes and Meier, 1978).

63. R.B. Bhagat, "Integration of Demographic Issues in Sustainable Development: Reflections on India's Population Policies," *Population Geography* 24 (2002): 21–30.

64. Therese Hesketh, Li Lu, and Zhu Wei Xing, "The Effect of China's One-Child Family Policy After 25 Years," *New England Journal of Medicine* 353 (2005): 1171–76.

65. Ibid.; Laurie Burkitt and Jeremy Page, "China's Population Is Aging Rapidly," *Wall Street Journal*, April 29, 2011.

66. Tyrene White, *China's Longest Campaign: Birth Planning in the People's Republic, 1949–2005* (Ithaca, NY: Cornell University Press, 2006), 245. Trotting out the one-child policy as a kind of nightmare scenario is common in America. For example,

several months after dropping out of the race for the 2012 presidential nomination, Rep. Michele Bachmann (R-Minn.) charged in a speech that health care reform, as embodied in the Patient Protection and Affordable Care Act, would lead to a one-child policy under President Obama. L.V. Anderson, "Michele Bachmann Thinks Birth-Control Rule Will Lead to a One-Child Policy," XX Factor, *Slate*, March 8, 2012, www.slate.com/blogs/xx_factor/2012/03/08/michele_bachmann_thinks_birth_control_rule_will_lead_to_a_one_child_policy.html.

67. Hesketh, Lu, and Xing, "Effect of China's One-Child Family Policy"; Evan Osnos, "Two Children, No 'Cults': Chinese Family Advertising," Letter from China blog, *New Yorker*, July 5, 2012, www.newyorker.com/online/blogs/evanosnos/2012/07/families-reject-cults.html. The high sex ratio is not entirely attributable to the one-child policy, because it existed in prerevolutionary China as well—in older times, as a result of female infanticide. And high ratios are seen in other places, including Taiwan, Singapore, South Korea, and parts of northern India, where voluntary birth limitation has been successful.

68. Satterthwaite, "Implications of Population Growth."

69. Patrick Bond, "Climate Debt Owed to Africa: What to Demand and How to Collect?" *African Journal of Science, Technology, Innovation and Development* 2 (2010): 83–113.

70. Letter from James Hansen to Kevin Rudd, Prime Minister of Australia, March 27, 2008, www.aussmc.org.au/documents/Hansen2008LetterToKevinRudd_000.pdf.

71. Henry Shue, "Global Environment and International Inequality," *International Affairs* 75 (1999): 531–45.

72. Those failures are documented in detail in Joanna Cabello, Kevin Smith, Tamra Gilbertson, and Walden Bello, *Upsetting the Offset: The Political Economy of Carbon Markets* (London: Mayfly Books, 2009); and in Gilbertson and Reyes, *Carbon Trading*. In March 2012, a Thomson Reuters survey found that "carbon market participants are forming an increasingly pessimistic view" of the European carbon trading scheme's ability to limit emissions, let alone make money for them. Jay Maroo, "Increasing Pessimism over European Carbon Market: Survey," *Risk.net*, March 29, 2012, www.risk.net/energy-risk/news/2164696/increasing-pessimism-european-carbon-market-survey.

73. Brian Tokar, telephone interview by the author, October 18, 2011. Also see Brian Tokar, *Toward Climate Justice* (Porsgrunn, Norway: Communalism Press, 2010).

74. These cases and many others are documented in detail by Cabello, Smith, Gilbertson, and Bello in *Upsetting the Offset*; see also Oscar Reyes, "Carbon Trading: A Brief Introduction," *Synthesis/Regeneration* 51 (2010): 10–11.

75. Elisabeth Rosenthal, "Profits on Carbon Credits Drive Output of a Harmful Gas," *New York Times*, August 8, 2012.

76. Mark Schapiro, "Conning the Climate: Inside the Carbon-Trading Shell Game," *Harper's Magazine*, February 2010.

77. Gilbertson and Reyes, *Carbon Trading*, 53–54.

78. Maxine Burkett, "Climate Reparations," *Melbourne Journal of International Law* 10, no. 2 (2009), Opinio Juris Online Symposium, corrigan.austlii.edu.au/au/journals/MelbJIL/2009/29.html.

79. Ibid.

Chapter 4: . . . And Not a Lot to Drink

1. See "Cochabamba Declaration on the Right to Water," Nadir.org, January 13, 2001, for the text of the declaration and background, www.nadir.org/nadir/initiativ/agp/free/imf/bolivia/cochabamba.htm#declaration.

2. Maude Barlow, *Blue Covenant: The Global Water Crisis and the Coming Battle for the Right to Water* (New York: The New Press, 2007), 33.

3. Will Weissert, "Official: 956 Texas Water Systems on Restrictions," *Bloomberg Businessweek*, November 1, 2011; Terrence Henry, "When Wells Run Dry: Spicewood Beach, Texas Is Out of Water," *StateImpact*, January 31, 2012, stateimpact.npr.org/texas/2012/01/31/when-wells-run-dry-spicewood-beach-is-out-of-water; Terrence Henry, "Where Did Spicewood Beach's Water Go?" *StateImpact*, February 2, 2012, stateimpact.npr.org/texas/2012/02/02/where-did-spicewood-beachs-water-go.

4. Henry, "Where Did Spicewood Beach's Water Go?"

5. A.Y. Hoekstra and A.K. Chapagain, "Water Footprints of Nations: Water Use by People as a Function of Their Consumption Pattern," *Water Resource Management* 21 (2007): 35–48. China, India, and the United States together account for more than one-third of the world's total water footprint.

6. Reed Benson, "Alive but Irrelevant: The Prior Appropriation Doctrine in Today's Western Water Law," *University of Colorado Law Review* 83 (2012): 675.

7. Charles Howe, "Policy Issues and Institutional Impediments in the Management of Groundwater: Lessons from Case Studies," *Environment and Development Economics* 7 (2002): 625–41.

8. Daniel Findlay, "Rainwater Collection, Water Law, and Climate Change: A Flood of Problems Waiting to Happen?" *North Carolina Journal of Law & Technology* 10 (2009): 74–95.

9. D. Craig Bell and Norman Johnson, "State Water Laws and Federal Water Uses: The History of Conflict, the Prospects for Accommodation, Part 1," *Environmental Law* 21 (1991): 1–51; Benson, "Alive but Irrelevant"; Findlay, "Rainwater Collection."

10. Howe, "Policy issues."

11. Findlay, "Rainwater Collection."

12. R.N. Palmer, L.K. Sandra, and A.C. Steinemann, "Developing Drought Triggers and Drought Responses: An Application in Georgia," *Journal of Water Resources Planning and Management* 132 (2002): 164–74; J.B. Ruhl, "Water Wars, Eastern Style: Divvying Up the Apalachicola–Chattahoochee–Flint River Basin," *Journal*

of Contemporary Water Research & Education 131 (2005): 47–54; author's observations and interviews of local residents, November 2007.

13. Greg Blustein, "Drought Tightens Grip on Southeast," Associated Press, October 16, 2007.

14. Patrik Jonsson, "South Struggles to Cope with Drought," *Christian Science Monitor*, October 22, 2007.

15. Craig Anthony Arnold, "Water Privatization Trends in the United States: Human Rights, National Security, and Public Stewardship," *William & Mary Environmental Law and Policy Review* 33 (2009): 785–849.

16. Dahan Momi and Nisan Udi, "The Unintended Consequences of IBT Pricing Policy in Urban Water," *Water Resources Research* 43 (2007): W03402, doi:10.1029/2005WR004493; Bhakti Lata Devi, "State of Urban Irrigation Demand Management—A Review," *Cooperative Research Centre for Irrigation Futures Irrigation Matters Series* No. 02/09, 2009, www.irrigationfutures.org.au/imagesDB/news/crcif-im0209-web.pdf. For most of the twentieth century, U.S. water customers were charged either a flat rate or a decreasing block tariff; however, in an effort to eliminate overconsumption, many water utilities have turned to increasing block tariffs (36 percent of them by 2004).

17. John Whitcomb, "Evaluation of Irrigation Restrictions in East-Central Florida," report prepared for St. Johns River Water Management District, Palatka, Florida, June 2006, b2bcontentsolutions.com/documents/B2B_SJRWMDIrrigation RestrictionReport2006.pdf.

18. Douglas Kenney, Roberta Klein, and Martyn Clark, "Use and Effectiveness of Municipal Water Restrictions During Drought in Colorado," *Journal of the American Water Resources Association* 40 (2004): 77–87.

19. Jessica Garrison, " 'Major Blowouts' of L.A. Water Pipes Rise Sharply," *Los Angeles Times*, September 19, 2009; David Zahniser and Phil Willon, "Water Conservation Program Caused L.A.'s String of Water Main Breaks, Report Finds," *Los Angeles Times*, April 13, 2010.

20. Sheila Olmstead and Robert Stavins, "Managing Water Demand: Price vs. Non-Price Conservation Programs," Pioneer Institute White Paper No. 39, Pioneer Institute for Public Policy Research, Boston, July 2007, www.ebcne.org/fileadmin/misc/WaterPrice_01.pdf.

21. Emma Aisbett and Ralf Steinhauser, "Does Anybody Give a Dam? The Importance of Public Awareness for Urban Water Conservation During Drought," Environmental Economics Research Hub Research Report No. 100, Social Science Research Network eLibrary, March 2011, ageconsearch.umn.edu/bitstream/107850/2/EERH_RR100.pdf.

22. UNICEF, *Progress on Sanitation and Drinking-Water: 2010 Update Report* (New York: UNICEF, 2010), 18.

23. The account of water rationing in Kadam Chawl that follows is based on interviews and observations by Priti Gulati Cox and the author in Mumbai, December 2, 2010, and January 15, 2012. Also see Priti Gulati Cox and Stan Cox, "An Inside

Look at the Daily Struggle for Water in One of the World's Largest Cities," *Alternet*, January 7, 2011, www.alternet.org/story/149422.

24. World Health Organization, *Domestic Water Quantity, Service Level and Health* (Geneva: WHO, 2003), 24–25.

25. Food and Agriculture Organization, *The State of the World's Land and Water Resources for Food and Agriculture—Managing Systems at Risk* (Rome: FAO, 2011); P. Döll, "Impact of Climate Change and Variability on Irrigation Requirements: A Global Perspective," *Climatic Change* 54 (2002): 269–93; Günther Fischer, Francesco N. Tubiello, Harrij van Velthuizen, and David A. Wiberg, "Climate Change Impacts on Irrigation Water Requirements: Effects of Mitigation, 1990–2080," *Technological Forecasting and Social Change* 74 (2007): 1083–107.

26. Shamsher Samra, Julia Crowley, and Mary C. Smith Fawzi, "The Right to Water in Rural Punjab: Assessing Equitable Access to Water Through the Punjab Rural Water Supply and Sanitation Project," *Health and Human Rights* 13 (2011): 1–14.

27. UNICEF, *Progress on Sanitation and Drinking-Water*, 28.

28. United Nations, *The Millennium Development Goals Report* (New York: United Nations, 2008), 40, www.un.org/millenniumgoals/pdf/The%20Millennium%20 Development%20Goals%20Report%202008.pdf.

29. Manuel Couret Branco and Pedro Damião Henriques, "The Political Economy of the Human Right to Water," *Review of Radical Political Economics* 42 (2010): 142–55.

30. Sukhada Tatke, "Slumdwellers Rely on Ration Shops for Water," *Times of India*, December 19, 2010.

31. Sandeep Ashar, "Brace for Curtailed Water Supply Hours," *Detailed News and Analysis*, October 26, 2009, www.dnaindia.com/mumbai/report_brace-for -curtailed-water-supply-hours_1303135; see also Cox and Cox, "Inside Look."

32. Joan Kenny, Nancy Barber, Susan Hutson, Kristin Linsey, John Lovelace, and Molly Maupin, "Estimated Use of Water in the United States in 2005," U.S. Geological Survey Circular 1344 (2009), pubs.usgs.gov/circ/1344.

33. Ashar, "Brace for Curtailed Water." Meanwhile, a small, elite slice of Mumbai's population does have ready access to plentiful water. One outrageous specimen is the 550-foot-tall, 400,000-square-foot "green" home on posh Altamont Road constructed for the industrialist Mukesh Ambani and his family. It's equipped with a swimming pool, a waterfall, and hydroponic "hanging gardens." The number of bathrooms hasn't been reported, but the house is known to have an "ice room" featuring artificial snow. See Cox and Cox, "Inside Look."

34. United Nations, *Millennium Development Goals Report*.

35. Barton Thompson Jr., "Water as a Public Commodity," *Marquette Law Review* 95 (2011): 17–52.

36. Sandy Cairncross, Jamie Bartram, Oliver Cumming, and Clarissa Brocklehurst, "Hygiene, Sanitation, and Water: What Needs to Be Done?" *PLoS Medicine* 7, no. 11 (2010): e1000365; "Bottled Water Sales Get Refreshed," *Beverage Industry*, July 12, 2011, www.bevindustry.com/articles/84824-bottled-water-sales-get-refreshed.

37. Samra, Crowley, and Smith Fawzi, "Right to Water in Rural Punjab."

38. Branco and Damião Henriques, "Political Economy."

39. "European Declaration for a New Water Culture," Fundación Nueva Cultura del Agua, 2005, Zaragoza, www.unizar.es/fnca/euwater/index2.php?x=3&idioma=en.

40. A. Trevor Hodge, "*In Vitruvium Pompeianum*: Urban Water Distribution Reappraised," *American Journal of Archaeology* 100 (1996): 261–76.

41. David Rosenberg, Samer Talozi, and Jay Lund, "Intermittent Water Supplies: Challenges and Opportunities for Residential Water Users in Jordan," *Water International* 33 (2008): 488–504.

42. Debra Israel, "Impact of Increased Access and Price on Household Water Use in Urban Bolivia," *Journal of Environment Development* 16 (2007): 58–83.

43. Mark Zeitoun, Clemens Messerschmid, and Shaddad Attili, "Asymmetric Abstraction and Allocation: The Israeli-Palestinian Water Pumping Record," *Groundwater* 47 (2009): 146–60; World Bank, "West Bank and Gaza: Assessment of Restrictions on Palestinian Water Sector Development," Report No. 47657-GZ, April 2009.

44. A.K. Chapagain and A.Y. Hoekstra, "Water Footprints of Nations," UNESCO Value of Water Research Report Series No. 16, Appendix, November 2004, www .waterfootprint.org/?page=files/Publications.

45. Zeitoun, Messerschmid, and Attili, "Asymmetric Abstraction and Allocation."

46. "West Bank Suffers Acute Water Shortages," Voice of America, August 2, 2009, www.voanews.com/english/news/a-13-2009-08-01-voa12-68658112.html.

47. UN Office for the Coordination of Humanitarian Affairs, "Analysis: Looming Water Crisis in Gaza," *IRIN*, September 15, 2009, www.irinnews.org/Report/86151; World Bank, "West Bank and Gaza."

48. Susan Spronk, "Water and Sanitation Utilities in the Global South: Re-Centering the Debate on 'Efficiency,'" *Review of Radical Political Economics* 42 (2010): 156–74.

49. K. Moeti and T. Khalo, "Privatisation and Ensuring Accountability in the Provision of Essential Services: The Case of Water in South Africa," *Journal of Public Administration* 43 (2008): 219–30.

50. That is because the elasticity of water demand in this situation is 0.4. See Momi and Udi, "Unintended Consequences."

51. Rick Casey, "Don't Expect Economy of Scale on Water," *San Antonio Express-News*, January 27, 2012.

52. Momi and Udi, "Unintended Consequences."

53. Bernard Barraqué, ed., "Urban Water Conflicts: An Analysis of the Origins and Nature of Water-Related Unrest and Conflicts in the Urban Setting," UNESCO Working Series SC-2006/WS/19, 2006. For example, "In a city that lies along the banks of the Río de la Plata, an inexhaustible source of freshwater, and also sits on the largest reserve of groundwater in the world, large numbers of the inhabitants of the Buenos Aires metropolitan region do not have access to a supply of quality water" (53).

54. Daniel Moss, "At Last, a Human Right to Water," *Yes!*, July 30, 2010.

55. Arnold, "Water Privatization Trends."

56. UNESCO, *Urban Water Conflicts.*

57. Damon Barrett and Vinodh Jaichand, "Privatized Water, the Right to Water and Access to Justice: Tackling UK Water Companies' Policies in Developing Countries," *South African Journal of Human Rights* 23 (2007): 543–62.

58. Ibid.; Couret Branco and Damião Henriques, "Political Economy."

59. The city of Cochabamba signed a contract, but the popular uprising forced it to abandon the agreement.

60. Degol Hailu, Rafael Osorio, and Raquel Tsukada, "Privatization and Renationalization: What Went Wrong in Bolivia's Water Sector?" International Policy Centre for Inclusive Growth, 2009, www.inesad.edu.bo/bcde2009/A3%20Hailu%20 Osorio%20Tsukada.pdf.

61. Maude Barlow and Tony Clarke, *Blue Gold: The Battle Against Corporate Theft of the World's Water* (New York: The New Press, 2005), 154–56.

62. Jackie Dugard, "Can Human Rights Transcend the Commercialization of Water in South Africa? Soweto's Legal Fight for an Equitable Water Policy," *Review of Radical Political Economics* 42 (2010): 175–94.

63. Public Citizen, "Is This What Efficiency Looks Like? Prepayment Water Meters," 2010, www.citizen.org/cmep/article_redirect.cfm?ID=8210.

64. Patrick Bond and Jackie Dugard, "The Case of Johannesburg Water: What Really Happened at the Pre-Paid 'Parish Pump'?" *Law, Democracy, and Development* 12 (2008): 1–28.

65. Spronk, "Water and Sanitation Utilities"; Couret Branco and Damião Henriques, "Political Economy"; L. Mehta and O. Mirosa Canel, "Financing Water for All: Behind the Border Policy Convergence in Water Management," Institute of Development Studies Working Paper No. 233, 2004, www.watergovernance.org/documents/ WGF/Reports/Water_Governance_trends_and_needs_paper.pdf; Odete Maria Viero and Andre Passos Cordeiro, "Public Interest vs. Profits: The Case of Water Supply and Sewage in Porto Alegre, Brazil," Dynamics of Urban Change, University College London Department for International Development, undated, www.ucl .ac.uk/dpu-projects/drivers_urb_change/urb_infrastructure/pdf_public_private_ services/W_WaterAid-Public_Porto%20Alegre.pdf.

66. Viero and Cordeiro, "Public Interest vs. Profits."

67. Arnold, "Water Privatization Trends."

Chapter 5: Our Monthly Bread

1. Laura Cugusi, "Egypt's Organic Food Seduces the West and Egyptian Farmers," *Al-Masry Al-Youm*, February 5, 2011.

2. Countries are examined chapter by chapter in Per Pinstrup-Andersen, ed., *Food Subsidies in Developing Countries: Costs, Benefits, and Policy Options* (Washington, DC: International Food Policy Research Institute, 1988). See also Amy Bentley, "Rationing," in *Scribner Encyclopedia of Food and Culture*, vol. 3, ed. S.H. Katz and W.W. Weaver (New York: Scribner, 2003), 576.

3. Associated Press, "As Users Rise, Food Stamps Under Scrutiny," *St. Louis Post-Dispatch*, September 26, 2011; Mark Nord, Alisha Coleman-Jensen, Margaret Andrews, and Steven Carlson, "Household Food Security in the United States, 2009," Economic Research Report No. (ERR-108), U.S. Department of Agriculture, Agricultural Research Service, November 2010.

4. See Stan Cox, *Sick Planet: Corporate Food and Medicine* (London: Pluto, 2008), 117–33.

5. Jean Drèze and Amartya Sen, *Hunger and Public Action* (New York: Oxford University Press, 1991), 88.

6. Nitin Sethi, "Sonia-Backed Food Bill Tabled," *Times of India*, December 23, 2011; K.P. Sinha, Food Corporation of India, interview by the author, Ranchi, Jharkhand, India, December 19, 2011.

7. Drèze and Sen, *Hunger and Public Action*, 105, 272.

8. Lance Brennan, "Government Famine Relief in Bengal, 1943," *Journal of Asian Studies* 47 (1988): 541–66. Brennan adds, "Most of the time there was no restriction on who could use the cheap-grain shops—the government relied for rationing devices on the inconvenience of queuing and the limits on the amount that could be bought at any one time. When, as often happened, the cheap-grain shops ran out of stocks and people were forced into the market, those receiving gratuitous relief or those on test relief were at a significant disadvantage." Drèze and Sen note, "The British Indian administration considered government involvement in food trade or distribution as sacrilegious. This position was grounded on a particular understanding of the teachings of classical economists (especially Adam Smith, John Stuart Mill, and Thomas Malthus) which were sometimes referred to as the 'Infallible Laws of the Great Masters of Economic Science.' Suspicion of government interference with private trade extended also to any kind of public *participation* in food distribution." Drèze and Sen, *Hunger and Public Action*, 124 (italics in original). Bengal was partitioned at the time of independence in 1947, and today this region is divided between the Indian state of West Bengal and the nation of Bangladesh.

9. Elizabeth Whitcombe, "Famine Mortality," *Economic and Political Weekly* 28 (1993): 1169–79.

10. Madhura Swaminathan, "Programmes to Protect the Hungry: Lessons from India," United Nations Department of Economic and Social Affairs Working Paper ST/ESA/2008/DWP/70, October 2008.

11. Three rupees was equivalent to about six U.S. cents at the prevailing exchange rate.

12. Sethi, "Sonia-Backed Food Bill"; Ravish Tiwari, "Food Bill: Govt Looking at Flexible Plan, May Exclude 33% Population," *Indian Express*, July 19, 2012; Jean Drèze, "Food Security, Plan Z," *Hindustan Times*, August 22, 2012. In Drèze's opinion, the Ministry's Plan B "does not even deserve a C or a D—it is more like Z, for zero."

13. Jaideep Hardikar, interview by the author, December 26, 2011, Nagpur, Maharashtra, India.

14. Vijay Jawandhia, interview by the author, December 26, 2011, Wardha, Maharashtra, India.

15. Vijaya, interview by the author via translator, Mumbai, India, January 10, 2012.

16. M.S. Kamath, interview by the author, Mumbai, January 5, 2012. "The PDS is a little wonky," adds Kamath, because customers are required to buy their full month's ration at once. Many do not have enough cash on hand to do so, and sometimes the fair-price shop may not have sufficient supplies of a commodity they wish to buy. Now many shops, including those in Mumbai, allow purchases on a two-week basis and say that if, because of short cash or short supply, a person cannot buy her full allowance, the unused portion of the allowance can be carried over and added to the next month's quota.

17. Swaminathan, "Programmes to Protect the Hungry"; Giovanni Andrea Cornia and Frances Stewart, "Two Errors of Targeting," *Journal of International Development* 5 (1993): 459–96; Reetika Khera, "Trends in Diversion of PDS Grain," Centre for Development Economics, Delhi School of Economics, Working Paper No. 198, March 2011; Department of Food and Government Distribution, "Annual Report, 2010–11," Ministry of Consumer Affairs, Food, and Public Distribution, Government of India, 2011.

18. Pushkar Maitra, Anu Rammohan, Ranjan Ray, and Marie-Claire Robitaille, "Food Consumption Patterns and Malnourished Indian Children: Is There a Link?" Monash University Department of Economics Discussion Paper 19/10, ISSN 1441–5429, 2010; Angus Deaton and Jean Drèze, "Food and Nutrition in India: Facts and Interpretations," *Economic and Political Weekly* 64 (2009): 42–65. Deaton and Drèze concluded, based on statistical analysis, that lower calorie consumption in rural areas was also partly a result of decreasing manual workloads. But the women who still today haul large bundles of wood and pots of water on their heads through the countryside and the men who dig irrigation ditches and plow fields do not appear to be settling into a sedentary lifestyle. And most already had a calorie- and protein-deficient diet even before the decline in consumption began to be reported.

19. Cornia and Stewart, "Two Errors of Targeting"; Khera, "Trends in Diversion"; Swaminathan, "Programmes to Protect the Hungry."

20. Jaideep Hardikar and Dadaji Khobragade (with translation by Hardikar), interview by the author, Nanded, Maharashtra, India, December 28, 2011.

21. Khera, "Trends in Diversion"; Sethi, "Sonia-Backed Food Bill."

22. Vikas Bajaj, "As Grain Piles Up, India's Poor Still Go Hungry," *New York Times*, June 7, 2012.

23. Shikha Jha and Bharat Ramaswami, "How Can Food Subsidies Work Better? Answers from India and the Philippines," Asian Development Bank Working Paper No. 221, September 2010; Jim Yardley, "India Asks, Should Food Be a Right for the Poor?" *New York Times*, August 8, 2010; Tamil News Network, "40% of Poor Denied Benefits Under PDS," *Times of India*, April 8, 2008; Sethi, "Sonia-Backed

Food Bill"; T. Nandakumar, "Food Coupons: The Way Forward," *Economic Times*, April 27, 2010.

24. Shoma Chatterji, "Rioters Against Ration Dealers," *India Together*, October 25, 2007.

25. Gladson Dungdung, interview by the author, December 19, 2011, Ranchi, Jharkhand, India; Sunil Minj and Gladson Dungdung, "Police Atrocities on Adivasis of Saranda Forest: A Fact Sheet by JHRM," *Jharkhand Mirror*, October 10, 2011, jharkhandmirror.org/2011/10/10/police-atrocities-on-adivasis-of -saranda-forest-a-fact-sheet-by-jhrm.

26. Ibid.; Tamil News Network, "Jharkhand to Open 300 PDS Shops to Bring Price Relief," *Times of India*, January 18, 2011.

27. Kaushik Basu, "The Economics of Foodgrain Management in India," India Ministry of Finance Working Paper No. 2/1010, 2010.

28. Ibid.; Subhash Narayan, Amiti Sen, and Vinay Pandey, "Need to Better Target Food Subsidies to Eradicate Poverty: Montek," *Economic Times*, May 3, 2010; Nandakumar, "Food Coupons"; "PDS Consumers Can Soon Have Choice to Buy Goods or Get Cash," *Moneylife*, November 3, 2011; Yardley, "India Asks."

29. Ugo Gentilini, *Cash and Food Transfers: A Primer* (Rome: World Food Program, 2007), 1–2, 7, 10. Theory says that unless the benefit going to a family is larger than the total amount that the family would normally spend on food (and it is almost never that large), in-cash and in-kind benefits are equivalent.

30. World Food Program, "Food for Nutrition: Mainstreaming Nutrition in WFP," Executive Board Annual Session, Rome, May 24–26, 2004, Agenda Item 5: Policy Issues, WFP/EB.A/2004/5-A/1.

31. R. Breunig, I. Dasgupta, C. Gundersen, and P. Pattanaik, "Explaining the Food Stamp Cash-Out Puzzle," U.S. Department of Agriculture, Economic Research Service, Food Assistance and Nutrition Research Report No. 12, April 2001; Neil Bruce and Michael Waldman, "Transfers in Kind: Why They Can Be Efficient and Nonpaternalistic," *American Economic Review* 81 (1991): 1345–51; Gentilini, *Cash and Food Transfers*.

32. K.P. Sinha, interview by the author, December 20, 2011, Ranchi, Jharkhand, India.

33. "ID Design Reflects India's Development Potential," *People's Daily*, November 2, 2011. Fingerprints alone would not provide sufficiently certain identification and, according to one official, would be difficult to obtain from many millions of "people who have worked their whole lives, especially those in some remote areas whose fingerprints have been worn off due to a life of hard labor."

34. Tamil News Network, "Rahul Backs UID, Says It Gives Voice to Every Person," *Times of India*, October 20, 2011; Usha Ramanathan, "The Myth of the Technology Fix," *Seminar Web Edition*, January 2011, www.india-seminar.com/2011/617/617_ usha_ramanathan.htm.

35. "Students Confront Nilekani on Aadhaar," *The Hindu*, January 8, 2011.

36. Khera, "Trends in Diversion"; Jean Drèze, "The Task of Making the PDS Work," *The Hindu*, July 8, 2010.

37. Drèze, "Task of Making the PDS Work."

38. Drèze and Sen, *Hunger and Public Action*, 260.

39. "Records of the Strike at Deir el Medina Under Ramses III," in *An Introduction to the History and Culture of Pharaonic Egypt*, www.reshafim.org.il/ad/egypt/texts/turin_strike_papyrus.htm.

40. Gouda Abdel-Khalek, interview by the author, Cairo, February 20, 2012.

41. I.J. Gelb, "The Ancient Mesopotamian Ration System," *Journal of Near Eastern Studies* 24 (1965): 230–43.

42. John Romer, *Ancient Lives: Daily Life in Egypt of the Pharaohs* (New York: Holt, Rhinehart, and Winston, 1984), 116–23.

43. Harold Alderman, "Food Subsidies in Egypt: Benefit Distribution and Nutritional Effects," in Pinstrup-Andersen, ed., *Food Subsidies*, 171.

44. The United States has about an acre of cropland per person; the world average is a little over half an acre.

45. Agence France-Presse, "Shortage Cuts Egyptians' Access to Daily Bread," *Daily Star*, April 8, 2008.

46. Tamar Gutner, "The Political Economy of Food Subsidy Reform: The Case of Egypt," *Food Policy* 27 (2002): 455–76; Karima Korayem, "Food Subsidy and Social Assistance Programme in Egypt; Assessment and Policy Options," Working Paper for the Egyptian Ministry of Social Solidarity and World Food Program, October 14, 2010 (manuscript provided to the author by Dr. Korayem); Karima Korayem, interview by the author, February 19, 2012, Cairo.

47. Jill Carroll, "Bread Graft Taxes Egypt's Poorest," *Christian Science Monitor*, July 30, 2007; David Biello, "Are High Food Prices Fueling Revolution in Egypt?" *Scientific American*, February 1, 2011; Associated Press, "Thousands Clash with Police in Egyptian Bread Riot," *USA Today*, June 8, 2008.

48. Frank Ricciardone, "Mahalla Riots: Isolated Incident or Tip of an Iceberg?" U.S. Embassy Cairo, cable 08CAIRO783, April 16, 2008, released by Wikileaks on August 30, 2011, www.wikileaks.ch/cable/2008/04/08CAIRO783.html; Alexandra Sandels, "22 Convicted for Food Rioting in Egypt's 'Mahalla 49' Case," *Menassat*, December 17, 2008.

49. Nadine El-Hakim, senior program officer for the World Food Program, interview by the author, Cairo, February 19, 2012.

50. Sarah Daoud, "Officials Speak of Subsidies Amid Rising Social Unrest," *Daily News Egypt*, January 28, 2011; "Egypt's Regime Orders Ministers to Avoid Giving Provocative Statements on Subsidizing," *Ikhwan Web*, January 11, 2011. On January 27, with throngs of angry demonstrators in the streets, the director of the Middle East Studies and Research Centre was still insisting that although living standards for low-income people had become worse than they were when the 1977 riots broke out, "the ordinary Egyptian nowadays is unable to stage wide protests because he has become fragile. Egyptians in 1977 were more politicized than now and the regime's security grip was less strong." That turned out to be one of many spectacularly bad predictions. See "Current Protests in Egypt Recall

'Bread Riots' of 1977," *International Business Times*, January 27, 2011. And even as the uprising swelled, a senior FAO economist asserted that because the subsidy system ensures an affordable food supply in Egypt, even a 20 to 30 percent rise in prices on the open market "shouldn't spark a big problem or discontent among that section of society." See Steve Chiotakis, "Egypt's Food Subsidy Program Is a 'Strategic National Security,'" *Marketplace*, February 1, 2011.

51. Carroll, "Bread Graft"; "Egyptian Unable to Get Ration Card Attempts Self-Immolation," *Al Masry Al Youm*, January 24, 2011; Krista Mahr, "Bread Is Life: Food and Protest in Egypt," Ecocentric blog, *Time*, January 31, 2011; Kevin G. Hall, "Egypt's Unrest May Have Roots in Food Prices, US Fed Policy," McClatchy Newspapers, February 1, 2011; Paul Waldie, "How Governments Are Reacting in the Face of Food Riots," *Globe and Mail*, February 1, 2011. A few observers insisted that access to food was not a factor, however; see Caroline Henshaw, "The Politics of Food Prices in Egypt," *Wall Street Journal*, February 1, 2011.

52. Emad Mekay, "More Arabs Protest Rulers with Self-Immolations," Inter-Press Service, January 19, 2011; Michelle Chen, "Bread and Butter Revolution: Egypt's Workers Mobilize for a New Future," *In These Times*, February 11, 2011; Karima Korayem, interview by the author, February 19, 2012, Cairo.

53. Mostafa Abdelrazek, "Egyptian Poor Fail to Feel Benefits of Economic Recovery," *Egyptian Independent*, December 26, 2010; "Arab Spring Undermines Support for Economic Liberalization Policies in the Middle East," Arabic Knowledge@Wharton, July 26, 2011, knowledge.wharton.upenn.edu/arabic/article.cfm?articleid=2695.

54. Nadine El-Hakim, interview by the author, Cairo, February 19, 2012.

55. Akhter Ahmed, Howarth Bouis, Tamar Gutner, and Hans Löfgren, "The Egyptian Food Subsidy System: Structure, Performance, and Options for Reform," International Food Policy Research Institute Research Report 119, October 2001; Monal Abel-Baki, interview by the author, Cairo, February 19, 2012.

56. Korayem, "Food Subsidy."

57. Gouda Abdel-Khalek, Minister of Supply and Internal Trade, Government of Egypt, interview by the author, Cairo, February 20, 2012.

58. Ashraf, a farmworker, interview by the author, Daushur, Egypt, February 21, 2012, trans. Maged Nosshi.

59. Taheya, interview by the author, Harannia, February 18, 2012, trans. Maged Nosshi.

60. Korayem, "Food Subsidy."

61. Ibid.; Gutner, "Political Economy of Food."

62. Maggie Michael, "Corruption Plagues Egypt's Bread," *USA Today*, April 10, 2008.

63. Gutner, "Political Economy of Food."

64. Nadine El-Hakim, interview by the author, Cairo, February 19, 2012.

65. Gouda Abdel-Khalek, interview by the author, Cairo, February 20, 2012.

66. John William Salevurakis and Sahar Mohamed Abdel-Haleim, "Bread Subsidies in Egypt: Choosing Social Stability or Fiscal Responsibility," *Review of Radical Political Economics* 40 (2008): 35–49.

67. Abdel-Khalek, interview by the author.

68. El-Hakim, interview by the author; Korayem, "Food Subsidy."

69. Taheya, interview by the author, Harannia, February 18, 2012, trans. Maged Nosshi.

70. Altef, a farmworker, interview by the author, Daushur, Egypt, February 21, 2012, trans. Maged Nosshi.

71. Mona El-Fiqi, "Row Brewing over Subsidy Reforms," *Al-Ahram Weekly*, December 6–12, 2007.

72. Korayem, "Food Subsidy."

73. Karima Korayem, interview by the author, Cairo, February 19, 2012.

74. Merrit Kennedy, "The Challenge for President Morsi: Unite Egypt," *Weekend Edition Sunday*, NPR, July 1, 2012, www.npr.org/2012/07/01/156043438/the-challenge-for-president-morsi-unite-egypt. The Morsi Meter's URL was morsimeter.com/en.

75. Marian Fadel, interview by the author, Cairo, February 20, 2012.

76. Agence France-Presse, "Iraq Diverts F-16 Budget for Food Rations," *Middle East Online*, February 15, 2011.

77. Jessica Leeder, "Cuba Drops Potato from Ration Books, Signaling Shift," *Globe and Mail* (Canada), November 12, 2009.

78. Neville Edirisinghe, "A Study of the Food Grain Market in Iraq," World Bank and World Food Program Reconstructing Iraq Series, Working Paper No. 3, December 2004; World Bank, "Considering the Future of the Iraqi Public Distribution System," Restricted Distribution Report, June 28, 2005, siteresources.worldbank.org/IRFFI/Resources/ExecutiveSummary-PDSReportJune2805.doc.

79. World Food Program, *Comprehensive Food Security and Vulnerability Analysis in Iraq* (Geneva: World Food Program, 2008), 15.

80. World Bank, "Considering the Future."

81. "Iraq Government Vows to Improve Food Aid System," Reuters, February 21, 2011; World Food Program, *Comprehensive Food Security*.

82. Usama Rekabi, interview by the author via the Internet, January 14, 2012.

83. Ibid.; World Bank, "Considering the Future." And, added the World Bank (perhaps recalling the 2004 disappearance of whole pallets of shrink-wrapped Iraqi currency notes amounting to as much as $18 billion), Iraq remained a dangerous enough place that hauling such large quantities of cash around the country would not be wise; expansion of banking service and electronic funds transfers would seem to be a solution to that problem. See "Missing Iraq Cash 'as High as $18bn,' " *Al Jazeera*, June 19, 2011.

84. World Food Program, *Comprehensive Food Security*; Rekabi, interview by the author.

85. World Bank, "Considering the Future."

86. Reuters, "Iraq Government Vows"; "Protesters Demand Jobs and Basic Services," *Al Arabiya*, February 4, 2011; Nizar Latif, "Iraqis Step Up Protest in Job and Food Crisis," *The National*, February 6, 2011; Agence France-Presse, "Iraq Diverts."

87. Minutes from a December 2011 meeting in Ramadi, Iraq, between members of the Anbar Provincial Council and representatives of the UN World Food Program, obtained from an American aid official in Baghdad.

88. Rekabi, interview by the author.

89. Medea Benjamin and Joseph Collins, "Is Rationing Socialist? Cuba's Food Distribution System," *Food Policy* 10 (1985): 327–36.

90. Ibid.

91. Ibid.

92. Ibid. Even Benjamin and Collins, sympathetic as they were to the goals of the Cuban revolution, had noted that it would be far cheaper for the government to let prices rise and compensate families with cash than to subsidize and ration. "But," they lamented, "in the ration system the Cuban leadership appears to have locked itself into the broadest and certainly most expensive system, one that was developed in an emergency and quite probably has long outlived much of its usefulness."

93. Ralph Huenemann, "Urban Rationing in Communist China," *China Quarterly* 26 (1966): 44–57.

94. Peter Gattrell and Mark Harrison, "The Russian and Soviet Economies in Two World Wars: A Comparative View," *Economic History Review* 46 (1993): 425–52; Oleg Khlevnyuk and R.W. Davies, "The End of Rationing in the Soviet Union, 1934–1935," *Europe-Asia Studies* 51 (1999): 557–609; Aron Katsenelinboigen, "Coloured Markets in the Soviet Union," *Soviet Studies* 29 (1977): 62–85.

95. José Alvarez, "Overview of Cuba's Food Rationing System," Document FE482, Department of Food and Resource Economics and Florida Cooperative Extension Service, University of Florida, 2004.

96. Peter Rosset, Braulio Machín Sosa, Adilén María Roque Jaime, and Dana Rocío Ávila Lozano, "The Campesino-to-Campesino Agroecology Movement of ANAP in Cuba: Social Process Methodology in the Construction of Sustainable Peasant Agriculture and Food Sovereignty," *Journal of Peasant Studies* 38 (2011): 161–91.

97. Collin Laverty, *Cuba's New Resolve: Economic Reform and Its Implications for U.S. Policy* (Washington, DC: Center for Democracy in the Americas, 2011), 17.

98. Claes Brundenius, "Revolutionary Cuba at 50: Growth with Equity Revisited," *Latin American Perspectives* 36 (2009), 31–47; Carmelo Mesa-Lago, *Reassembling Social Security: A Survey of Pensions and Healthcare Reforms in Latin America* (Oxford: Oxford University Press, 2008), 155–66; Albert Noguera, "Estructura social e igualdad en la Cuba actual: La reforma de los noventa y los cambios en la estructura de clases cubana," *European Review of Latin American and Caribbean Studies*, 76 (2004): 45–59.

99. Patrick Symmes, "Thirty Days as a Cuban," *Harper's Magazine*, October 2010. The article by Symmes is an account of his attempt to live and eat for a month on a Cuban journalist's salary in Havana.

100. Oscar Espinosa Chepe, "¿El fin de 'la libreta'?" *Encuentro*, November 16, 2009.

101. Symmes, "Thirty Days as a Cuban"; Kathryn Peters, "Creating a Sustainable Urban Agriculture Revolution," *Journal of Environmental Law and Litigation* 25 (2010): 203–48.

102. Agence France-Presse, "Cubans Hope Economic Reforms Will Save Country from Bankruptcy," *Jamaica Observer*, April 19, 2011.

103. Patricia Grogg, "Cuba Faces Elusive Horn of Plenty," *Havana Times*, November 2, 2011; Agence France-Presse, "Cubans Hope Economic Reforms Will Save Country from Bankruptcy," *Jamaica Observer*, April 19, 2011; Nick Miroff, "Amid Reforms, Cubans Fret Over Food Rations Fate," NPR, October 22, 2010; see also Laverty, *Cuba's New Resolve*.

104. Garry Egger and Boyd Swinburn, *Planet Obesity: How We're Eating Ourselves and the Planet to Death* (Crows Nest, NSW: Allen & Unwin, 2010), 110.

105. Garry Egger, Boyd Swinburn, and Amirul Islam, "Economic Growth and Obesity: An Interesting Relationship with World-Wide Implications," *Economics and Human Biology* 10 (2012): 147–53.

106. See Symmes, "Thirty Days as a Cuban," regarding the effectiveness of the Cuban diet for weight loss.

107. Rachel Davey, "The Obesity Epidemic: Too Much Food for Thought?" *British Journal of Sports Medicine* 38 (2004): 360–63. Davey pleads the case for rationing over voluntary programs: "Possible solutions that have political implications are never popular, but that does not mean that they should not be aired. This is particularly appropriate for major problems such as obesity where the food supply plays a major role. Those who make suggestions favouring regulations are often intimidated by the public furore initiated by those adversely affected. But will anything less than regulations work? We can learn from the example of tobacco. Warning people of the dangers of smoking had little effect on cigarette consumption, but regulations on advertising and legislated restrictions on where people could smoke reduced smoking incidence dramatically."

108. Kristina H. Lewis and Meredith Rosenthal, "Individual Responsibility or a Policy Solution—Cap and Trade for the U.S. Diet?" *New England Journal of Medicine* 365 (2011): 1561–63.

109. Anthony McMichael, John Powles, Colin Butler, and Ricardo Uauy, "Food, Livestock Production, Energy, Climate Change, and Health," *The Lancet* 370 (2007): 1253–63. Others have challenged McMichael et al.'s calculations and questioned their conclusions. See Jan Deckers, "Should the Consumption of Farmed Animal Products be Restricted, and If So, by How Much?" *Food Policy* 35 (2010): 497–503; for mutual reinforcement of climate and obesity problems, see Egger and Swinburn, *Planet Obesity*, 52–64.

110. McMichael, Powles, Butler, and Uauy, "Food, Livestock Production."

Chapter 6: Painful Questions, Elusive Answers

1. Peter Ubel, *Pricing Life: Why It's Time for Health Care Rationing* (Cambridge, MA: MIT Press, 2000), 183.

2. Leonard Nelson III, "Rationing Health Care in Britain and the United States," *Journal of Health & Biomedical Law* 7 (2011): 175–232.

3. Mary Ann Baily, " 'Rationing' and American Health Policy," *Journal of Health Politics, Policy and Law* 9 (1984): 489–501.

4. Ibid.

5. "Historical," Centers for Medicare and Medicaid Services, U.S. Department of Health and Human Services, 2011, www.cms.gov/NationalHealthExpendData/02 _NationalHealthAccountsHistorical.asp.

6. Mary Ann Baily, telephone interview by the author, April 17, 2012.

7. Ibid.

8. Angie Drobnic Holan, Katie Sanders, Aaron Sharockman, "Fact-Checking Rick Scott on the Health Care Law," *PolitiFact Florida*, July 2, 2012.

9. Michael Cannon, "GOP Plan: Huge Opportunity to Improve Health Care," *San Antonio Express-News*, April 7, 2011; Julie Rovner, "Budget Office: GOP Medicare Plan Could Lead to Rationing," NPR, April 6, 2011; Angie Drobnic Holan, "Politi-Fact's Lie of the Year: 'Death Panels,' " *PolitiFact*, December 18, 2009.

10. Alan Maynard, "Rationing Health Care: An Exploration," *Health Policy* 49 (1999): 5–11.

11. Mary Ann Baily, "Futility, Autonomy, and Cost in End-of-Life Care," *Journal of Law, Medicine, and Ethics* 39 (2011): 172–82.

12. These two classifications—absolute scarcity versus relative scarcity and explicit versus implicit rationing—are explained at length in Ubel, *Pricing Life*, 13–30. Ubel discusses an oft-employed third distinction, necessary versus beneficial care, in order to demonstrate that "necessary" is a vague and confusing term that adds nothing useful to the discussion, while "beneficial" is subject to measurement and helps focus the discussion.

13. Uwe E. Reinhardt, " 'Rationing' Health Care: What Does It Mean?" *New York Times*, July 3, 2009.

14. The four differences between health care and other commodities that follow were outlined in Baily, " 'Rationing' and American Health Policy."

15. Henry Aaron, William Schwartz, and Melissa Cox, *Can We Say No? The Challenge of Rationing Health Care* (Washington, DC: Brookings Institution Press, 2005), 131–32.

16. Laura McGough, Steven Reynolds, Thomas Quinn, and Jonathan Zenilman, "Which Patients First? Setting Priorities for Antiretroviral Therapy Where Resources Are Limited," *American Journal of Public Health* 95 (2005): 1173–80.

17. David Adams, *The Greatest Good to the Greatest Number: Penicillin Rationing on the American Home Front, 1940–1945* (New York: Peter Lang, 1991): 67–70.

18. Ibid., 74.

19. Ibid., 9, 18, 78, 87, 89.

20. P. D'Arcy Hart, "A Change in Scientific Approach: From Alternation to Randomised Allocation in Clinical Trials in the 1940s," *British Medical Journal* 319 (1999): 572–73; Alan Yoshioka, "Use of Randomisation in the Medical Research Council's Clinical Trial of Streptomycin in Pulmonary Tuberculosis in the 1940s," *British Medical Journal* 317 (1998): 1220–23; William Silverman and Iain Chalmers, "Casting and Drawing Lots: A Time Honoured Way of Dealing with Uncertainty and Ensuring Fairness," *British Medical Journal* 323 (2001): 22–29.

21. The above quotes and the descriptions of the committee's work that follow are from Shana Alexander, "They Decide Who Lives, Who Dies," *Life*, November 9, 1962. See also Albert Jonsen, "The God Squad and the Origins of Transplantation Ethics and Policy," *Journal of Law, Medicine, and Ethics* 35 (2007): 238–40.

22. David Mechanic, "Dilemmas in Rationing Health Care Services: The Case for Implicit Rationing," *British Medical Journal* 310 (1995): 1655–59.

23. Alexander, "They Decide."

24. McGough, Reynolds, Quinn, and Zenilman, "Which Patients First?"

25. Adams, *Greatest Good*, 4–5; "Foreigners to Be Banned from Having UK Organ Transplants," *Daily Mail*, July 31, 2009; Associated Press, "S. African Hospital Charged in Organ Trafficking," *USA Today*, September 16, 2010; Mark Stein, "The Distribution of Life-Saving Medical Resources: Equality, Life Expectancy, and Choice Behind the Veil," *Social Philosophy and Policy* 19 (2002): 212–45.

26. American Society for Transplantation, "Statement of Ethics," revised October 2002, www.a-s-t.org/about/statement-ethics.

27. Ubel, *Pricing Life*, 62–63.

28. Andrew A. Herring, Steffie Woolhandler, and David U. Himmelstein, "Insurance Status of U.S. Organ Donors and Transplant Recipients: The Uninsured Give, but Rarely Receive," *International Journal of Health Services* 38 (2008): 641–52.

29. Philip M. Rosoff, "Unpredictable Drug Shortages: An Ethical Framework for Short-Term Rationing in Hospitals," *American Journal of Bioethics* 12 (2012): 1–9. The term "tragic choices" has been in common use since the publication of Guido Calabresi and Philip Bobbitt, *Tragic Choices: The Conflicts Society Confronts in the Allocation of Tragically Scarce Resources* (New York: W.W. Norton, 1978). Calabresi and Bobbitt argued that tragic choices include not just the allocation of absolutely scarce lifesaving treatments but also the decisions that must be made when there is a limit on total resources available and all beneficial uses cannot be accommodated.

30. U.S. Department of Health and Human Services, "HHS Pandemic Influenza Plan," November 2005, www.hhs.gov/pandemicflu/plan/pdf/HHSPandemic InfluenzaPlan.pdf.

31. Tia Powell, Kelly Christ, and Guthrie Birkhead, "Allocation of Ventilators in a Public Health Disaster," *Disaster Medicine and Public Health Preparedness* 2 (2008): 20–26. Before outlining criteria, the group stressed that whatever the rationing

system used, it must be the same in all hospitals in the area or state, and the criteria must be made public. They also emphasized that access to ventilators should not be limited to patients suffering from flu and should not go preferentially to essential medical workers; the criteria must include only clinical need. Giving priority to health care workers would not maintain the size of the workforce, because a nurse, for example, who is sick enough to need a ventilator cannot recover sufficiently to return to work before the outbreak has waned. And so many people working in the hospital, from doctors to laundry workers to police, have a high risk of exposure that, if they had priority, there might be no ventilators left for anyone else. With regard to the question "Why doesn't the state just stockpile as many ventilators as would be needed?" the department website explains, "Although New York State continues to purchase and stockpile ventilators, we know that no matter how many ventilators are available overall, in a severe pandemic there will be shortages in individual facilities. This is because so many people will be sick at the same time. The ill will include healthcare workers, so there also will not be enough staff to provide the extra level of care for all patients who need ventilators. Undoubtedly, difficult decisions on ventilator allocation will need to be made. We must recognize this and plan for it." See New York State Department of Health, "Frequently Asked Questions—Proposed Policy on Allocation of Ventilators in an Influenza Pandemic," revised March 2007, www.health.ny.gov/ diseases/communicable/influenza/pandemic/ventilators/faq.htm.

32. Powell, Christ, and Birkhead, "Allocation of Ventilators."
33. On ventilators in Florida, see Sheri Fink, "In Flu Pandemic, Florida's Hospitals May Exclude Certain Patients," *ProPublica*, October16, 2009; on the controversy, see the full series of "Disaster Medicine" articles by *ProPublica* reporters at www .propublica.org/topic/disaster-medicine.
34. Sheri Fink, "Preparing for a Pandemic, State Health Departments Struggle with Rationing Decisions," *ProPublica*, October 24, 2009.
35. E. Cross, S. Goodacre, A. O'Cathain, and J. Arnold, "Rationing in the Emergency Department: The Good, the Bad, and the Unacceptable," *Emergency Medicine Journal* 22 (2005): 171–76.
36. The three questions are paraphrased from Michael Schlander, "The Use of Cost-Effectiveness by the National Institute for Health and Clinical Excellence (NICE): No(t Yet an) Exemplar of a Deliberative Process," *Journal of Medical Ethics* 34 (2008): 534–39; see also D. Mortimer, "The Value of Thinly Spread QALYs," *Pharmacoeconomics* 24 (2006): 845–53.
37. John Harris, "QALYfying the Value of Life," *Journal of Medical Ethics* 13 (1987): 117–23.
38. Stein, "Distribution of Life-Saving Medical Resources." Note that a weighted lottery would involve human judgments and therefore would not be acceptable under Harris's principle.
39. Govind Persad, Alan Wertheimer, and Ezekiel J. Emanuel, "Principles for Allocation of Scarce Medical Interventions," *The Lancet* 373 (2009): 423–31.

40. Stein, "Distribution of Life-Saving Medical Resources."

41. Albert Jonsen, "Bentham in a Box: Technology Assessment and Health Care Allocation," *Law, Medicine, and Health Care*, 14 (1986): 172–74.

42. Singer, "Why We Must Ration." It is not clear why eighty-five-year-olds are used so often as examples.

43. Alan Williams, "Rationing Health Care by Age: The Case For," *British Medical Journal* 314 (1997): 820–22.

44. J. Grimley Evans, "Rationing Health Care by Age: The Case Against," *British Medical Journal* 314 (1997): 822–25; Baily, telephone interview.

45. Persad, Wertheimer, and Emanuel, "Principles for Allocation."

46. Samuel J. Kerstein and Greg Bognar, "Complete Lives in the Balance," *American Journal of Bioethics* 10 (2010): 37–45.

47. See Betsy McCaughey, "Obama's Health Rationer-in-Chief," *Wall Street Journal*, August 27, 2009.

48. Sadath Sayeed, "Assessing the Modified Youngest-First Principle and the Idea of Non-Persons at the Bedside: A Clinical Perspective," *American Journal of Bioethics* 10 (2010): 52–54.

49. Leonard Fleck, telephone interview by author, April 3, 2012; Leonard Fleck, "Just Caring: Health Care Rationing, Terminal Illness, and the Medically Least Well Off," *Journal of Law, Medicine & Ethics* 39 (2011): 156–71.

50. Fleck, "Just Caring."

51. Joanna Coast, "Rationing Within the NHS Should Be Explicit: The Case Against," *British Medical Journal* 314 (1997): 1118–22; see also Samia Hurst and Marion Danis, "A Framework for Rationing by Clinical Judgment," *Kennedy Institute of Ethics Journal* 17 (2007): 247–66.

52. Baily, "Futility, Autonomy"; Len Doyal, "Rationing Within the NHS Should Be Explicit: The Case For," *British Medical Journal* 314 (1997): 1114–18; see also Nelson, "Rationing Health Care."

53. Mechanic, "Dilemmas in Rationing."

54. Ubel, *Pricing Life*, 126–27.

55. Doyal, "Rationing Within the NHS."

56. Philip Ayres, "Rationing Health Care: Views from General Practice," *Social Science and Medicine* 42 (1996): 1021–25. For American doctors' views, see Samia Hurst, Sara Chandros Hull, Gordon DuVal, and Marion Danis, "Physicians' Responses to Resource Constraints," *Archives of Internal Medicine* 165 (2005): 639–44.

57. See, for example, Frank Ackerman and Lisa Heinzerling, *Priceless: On Knowing the Price of Everything and the Value of Nothing* (New York: The New Press, 2004), 98–102.

58. For discussions of QALYs, see P. Dolan, R. Shaw, A. Tsuchiya, and A. Williams, "QALY Maximisation and People's Preferences: A Methodological Review of the Literature," *Health Economics* 14 (2004): 197–208; and M. Rawlins and A. Dillon, "NICE Discrimination," *Journal of Medical Ethics* 31 (2005): 683–84.

59. Ubel, *Pricing Life*, 157–69.

60. Harris, "QALYfying."

61. Ibid. Exclamation point in original.

62. Rawlins and Dillon, "NICE Discrimination."

63. Aaron, Schwartz, and Cox, *Can We Say No?*, 13, 16, 18, 121; Nelson, "Rationing Health Care."

64. Ibid., 21–22. Some analysts say the numbers overstate the problem, however: people on the lists include those who are in a "wait and see" status, when there is question of whether surgery or other treatment is the best course, and sometimes names of people who have decided against treatment or moved away or gotten better or died linger on the lists.

65. Rawlins and Dillon, "NICE Discrimination."

66. Schlander, "Use of Cost-Effectiveness."

67. Claudia Landwehr, "Deciding How to Decide: The Case of Health Care Rationing," *Public Administration* 87 (2009): 586–603; R. Cookson, D. McDaid, and A. Maynard, "Wrong SIGN, NICE Mess: Is National Guidance Distorting Allocation of Resources?" *British Medical Journal* 323 (2001): 743–45.

68. Steven Pearson and Michael Rawlins, "Quality, Innovation, and Value for Money: NICE and the British National Health Service," *Journal of the American Medical Association* 294 (2005): 2618–22.

69. Steve Chaplin, "NICE's Future Without a Veto on the Use of Expensive Drugs," *Prescriber* 22 (2011): 18–25.

70. Pearson and Rawlins, "Quality, Innovation."

71. Laura Clout, "War Hero Refused Treatment by NHS," *The Telegraph*, February 18, 2008; John Coles, "Nearly Blind Man Wins Treatment," *The Sun*, February 28, 2008; Sarah Boseley, "Cancer Drug 'Too Expensive for NHS,'" *The Guardian*, February 1, 2012; Jill Insley and Hilary Osborne, "Abiraterone Prostate Cancer Treatment to Be Covered by Axa PPP," *The Guardian*, February 2, 2012.

72. Chaplin, "NICE's Future"; see also Sarah Thornton, "Return of the Postcode Lottery," *BMJ* 342 (2011): 69.

73. "Doctors: Obese Should Be Refused Treatment," *Daily Mail*, February 3, 2006.

74. Nelson, "Rationing Health Care."

75. Aaron, Schwartz, and Cox, *Can We Say No?*, 40, 42, 44.

76. UPI, "Transplant Policy Was Death Sentence for Boy," *Dubuque Telegraph Herald*, December 3, 1987; Ubel, *Pricing Life*, 3–4.

77. Jonathan Oberlander, Theodore Marmor, and Lawrence Jacobs, "Rationing Medical Care: Rhetoric and Reality in the Oregon Health Plan," *Canadian Medical Association Journal* 164 (2001): 1583–87.

78. David Hadorn, "Setting Health Care Priorities in Oregon: Cost-Effectiveness Meets the Rule of Rescue," *Journal of the American Medical Association* 265 (1991): 2218–25; Oregon Health Services Commission, "Prioritization of Health Services: A Report to the Governor and the 74th Oregon Legislative Assembly," 2007, www.oregon.gov/OHA/OHPR/HSC/docs/R/07HSCBiennialReport.pdf.

79. Landwehr, "Deciding How to Decide."

80. Jeff Goldsmith, "The Road to Meaningful Reform: A Conversation with Oregon's John Kitzhaber," *Health Affairs* 22 (2003): 114–24.

81. Oberlander, Marmor, and Jacobs, "Rationing Medical Care."

82. Jennifer Fisher Wilson, "Oregon Surpasses Struggles of Early Reform and Develops a Road Map for Future Success," *Annals of Internal Medicine* 149 (2008): 149–52.

83. Saul Hubbard, "State Health Reform Bill Passes," *Register-Guard* (Eugene, OR), February 24, 2012; Nick Budnick, "Health Transformation Law's Passage in Salem Leaves Companion Bill in Limbo," *The Oregonian*, February 23, 2012.

84. Rick Attig, "Sensationalizing a Sad Case Cheats the Public of Sound Debate," *The Oregonian*, November 29, 2008.

85. Wilson, "Oregon Surpasses Struggles."

86. Jennifer Bendery, "Single-Payer Health Care Favored by House Progressives if Court Strikes Down Obamacare," *Huffington Post*, June 27, 2012, www.huffingtonpost.com/2012/06/27/house-progressives-single-payer-health-care_n_1630777.html.

87. Nelson, "Rationing Health Care."

88. Rony Caryn Rabin, "Doctor Panels Recommend Fewer Tests for Patients," *New York Times*, April 4, 2012.

89. Baily, telephone interview. On overtesting and overtreatment, see Cox, *Sick Planet*, 1–33; and Shannon Brownlee, *Overtreated: Why Too Much Medicine Is Making Us Sicker and Poorer* (New York: Bloomsbury, 2007).

90. Ubel, *Pricing Life*, 37–40.

91. H. Aaron and W.B. Schwartz, "Rationing Health-Care—The Choice Before Us," *Science* 247 (1990): 418–22.

92. Leonard Fleck, telephone interview by the author, April 3, 2012. The community dialogue project is described in Leonard Fleck, "The Role of Universities in the Construction of Public Reason," *Journal of Public Service and Outreach* 4 (1999): 34–43.

93. Daniel Callahan, "Rationing Medical Progress: The Way to Affordable Health Care," *New England Journal of Medicine* 322 (1990): 1810–13.

94. Callahan, *What Price Better Health?*, 223.

95. Baily, telephone interview. (Baily and Callahan were colleagues at the Hastings Center in New York until Baily's retirement.) Robert Goldberg, "Life-And-Death Matters," *Health Affairs* 23 (2004): 280–81. Goldberg opens his caustic review of *What Price Better Health?* with the sentence "When I grow up, I want to be a bioethicist."

96. Callahan, "Rationing Medical Progress."

97. Aaron, Schwartz, and Cox, *Can We Say No?*, 123.

98. Callahan, *Taming the Beloved Beast*, 207–8.

99. Baily, telephone interview; Michael Maciosek, Ashley Coffield, Nichol Edwards, Thomas Flottemesch, Michael Goodman, and Leif Solberg, "Priorities Among Effective Clinical Preventive Services: Results of a Systematic Review and Analysis," *American Journal of Preventive Medicine* 31 (2006): 52–61.

100. Don Fitz, "Why Does Health Care in Cuba Cost 96% Less Than in the US?" *Links International Journal*, January 5, 2011, links.org.au/node/2082.

101. Jeanette Chung and David Meltzer, "Estimate of the Carbon Footprint of the US Health Care Sector," *Journal of the American Medical Association* 302 (2009): 1970–72.

102. Energy Information Administration, "A Look at Principal Building Activities in the Commercial Buildings Energy Consumption Survey (CBECS)," U.S. Department of Energy, 2000, www.eia.doe.gov/emeu/consumptionbriefs/cbecs/pbawebsite/contents.htm.

103. The ecological consequences can be shocking. In 2008, researchers collected and tested water flowing out of a treatment plant near the city of Patancheru, India. The plant received wastewater from a large cluster of bulk-drug manufacturing plants in and around Patancheru, and the testing of the treated water being released into local streams showed alarming concentrations of the antibiotic ciprofloxacin (commonly known by the trade name Cipro), along with an array of twenty-one other active pharmaceutical ingredients for treating heart disease, liver disease, high blood pressure, depression, sexually transmitted diseases, ulcers, and other ailments—most of them for export. This "floating medicine cabinet" released enough Cipro alone into the environment to treat a city of ninety thousand people. Eleven drugs were present at concentrations higher than any ever before detected in the environment. Martha Mendoza, "World's Highest Drug Levels Entering India Stream," Associated Press, January 26, 2009; Cox, *Sick Planet*, 34–46. Similar levels of pharmaceutical pollution from factories have been observed all over Asia, and in the United States and Europe. See Stan Cox, "The Hidden Costs of Overprescribing Drugs," *Al Jazeera English*, August 24, 2012: National Health Service Eastern Regional Public Health Observatory, "Indicative Carbon Emissions Per Unit of Healthcare Activity," Briefing No. 23, April 9, 2010, www.erpho.org.uk/viewResource.aspx?id=20967.

104. National Health Service Sustainable Development Unit, *Saving Carbon, Improving Health* (London: NHS Sustainable Development Unit; 2009), 36–38.

105. John Agar, "Hemodialysis—Water, Power, and Waste Disposal: Rethinking Our Environmental Responsibilities," *Hemodialysis International* 16 (2010): 6–10; Andrew Connor and Donal O'Donoghue, "Sustainability: The Seventh Dimension of Quality in Health Care," *Hemodialysis International* 16 (2012): 2–5; Cox, *Sick Planet*, 1–20.

106. Friedrich Breyer, "Health Care Rationing and Distributive Justice," in *Perspectives in Moral Science*, ed. M. Baurmann and B. Lahno (Frankfurt am Main: Frankfurt School Verlag, 2009), 395–410.

Chapter 7: Slowing Down with the Joneses

1. Naomi Klein, "Capitalism vs. the Climate," *The Nation*, November 9, 2011.

2. Calabresi and Bobbitt, *Tragic Choices: The Conflicts Society Confronts in the Allocation of Tragically Scarce Resources* (New York: W.W. Norton, 1978), 41.

3. Mark Sagoff, "Should Preferences Count?" *Land Economics* 70 (1994): 127–44.

4. Fairness is so highly prized, in fact, that we all assume we know what we mean when we talk about it; the definition is rarely spelled out. *Merriam-Webster* says that to be fair is to be "marked by impartiality and honesty" and "free from self-interest, prejudice, or favoritism," but a broader definition that includes the notion of equality is often assumed. For example, "justice as fairness" as conceived by the philosopher John Rawls specifies that "each person has an equal right to a fully adequate scheme of equal basic rights and liberties, which scheme is compatible with a similar scheme for all," and that any inequalities that do exist "must be to the greatest benefit of the least advantaged members of society." "Fair," *Merriam-Webster Dictionary* online edition, www.merriam-webster.com/dictionary/fair; John Rawls, "Justice as Fairness: Political Not Metaphysical," *Philosophy and Public Affairs* 14 (1985): 223–51. See a more recent elaboration in John Rawls, *Justice as Fairness: A Restatement* (Cambridge, MA: Harvard University Press, 2001). Amartya Sen asks and answers a deeper question that Rawls raises: "So what *is* fairness? This foundational idea can be given shape in various ways, but central to it must be a demand to avoid bias in our evaluations, taking note of the interests and concerns of others as well, and in particular the need to avoid being influenced by our respective vested interests, or by our personal priorities or eccentricities or prejudices. It can broadly be seen as a demand for impartiality." While stressing the importance of Rawls's approach, Sen notes some deficiencies, including the absolute priority that Rawls gives to liberty, even over access to food and medicine, and his lack of a global viewpoint. Amartya Sen, *The Idea of Justice* (Cambridge, MA: Harvard University Press, 2009), 54, 65–72.

5. Daniel Kahneman, Jack Knetsch, and Richard Thaler, "Fairness and the Assumptions of Economics," *Journal of Business* 59 (1986): S285–S300; Ernst Fehr and Klaus Schmidt, "A Theory of Fairness, Competition, and Cooperation," *Quarterly Journal of Economics* 114 (1999): 817–68; Ernst Fehr and Jean-Robert Tyran, "Institutions and Reciprocal Fairness," *Nordic Journal of Political Economy* 23 (1996): 133–44.

6. David A. Savage and Benno Torgler, "Perceptions of Fairness and Allocation Systems," *Economic Analysis and Policy* 40 (2010): 229–48.

7. Yochai Benkler, "Law, Policy, and Cooperation," in *Government and Markets: Toward a New Theory of Regulation*, ed. Edward Balleisen and David Moss (New York: Cambridge University Press, 2009), 101–12.

8. Ibid.

9. Thorstein Veblen, *The Theory of the Leisure Class* (New York: Modern Library, 1931), 103.

10. Samuel Bowles and Yongjin Park, "Emulation, Inequality, and Work Hours: Was Thorstein Veblen Right?" *Economic Journal* 115 (2005): F397–F412. But there is another question, posed by Bowles and Park: "But why is it the consumption of the leisure class that is emulated rather than their leisure?" Veblen's answer was that because we rarely have personal contact with the people we are emulating, it is chiefly their visible material consumption that works an effect on us. We don't

normally see a tycoon as he's relaxing with a library book in his study, but we can see that he lives in a mansion.

11. Erzo Luttmer, "Neighbors as Negatives: Relative Earnings and Well-Being," *Quarterly Journal of Economics* 120 (2005): 963–1002.

12. James Coleman, "Social Capital in the Creation of Human Capital," *American Journal of Sociology* 94 (1988): S95–S120; John Helliwell and Robert Putnam, "The Social Context of Well-Being," *Philosophical Transactions of the Royal Society of London B* 359 (2004): 1435–46.

13. Anna C. Merritt, Daniel A. Effron, and Benoît Monin, "Moral Self-Licensing: When Being Good Frees Us to Be Bad," *Social and Personality Psychology Compass* 4, no. 5 (2010): 344–57.

14. Nina Mazar and Chen-Bo Zhong, "Do Green Products Make Us Better People?" *Psychological Science* 21 (2010): 494–98.

15. Kendall Eskine, "Wholesome Foods and Wholesome Morals? Organic Foods Reduce Prosocial Behavior and Harshen Moral Judgments," *Social Psychological and Personality Science* (2012): DOI:10.1177/1948550612447114.

16. Sonya Sachdeva, Rumen Iliev, and Douglas Medin, "Sinning Saints and Saintly Sinners: The Paradox of Moral Self-Regulation," *Psychological Science* 20 (2009): 523–28.

17. Uzma Khan and Ravi Dhar, "Licensing Effect in Consumer Choice," *Journal of Marketing Research* 43 (2006): 259–66. Likewise, students who previously had volunteered to spend two hours assisting a foreign classmate with a course assignment donated 30 percent less money when asked if they would like to make a charitable contribution.

18. Benoît Monin, Pamela J. Sawyer, and Matthew J. Marquez, "The Rejection of Moral Rebels: Resenting Those Who Do the Right Thing," *Journal of Personality and Social Psychology* 95, no. 1 (2008): 76–93.

19. Brian Hayden and Rob Gargett, "Big Man, Big Heart? A Mesoamerican View of the Emergence of Complex Society," *Ancient Mesoamerica* 1 (1990): 3–20; Alan Honik, "The Evolution of Fairness," *Pacific Standard*, August 31, 2012; see also Robert Allen, "Agriculture and the Origins of the State in Ancient Egypt," *Explorations in Economic History* 34 (1997): 135–54.

20. Robert Frank, "Positional Externalities Cause Large and Preventable Welfare Losses," *American Economic Review* 95 (2005): 137–41; Bowles and Park, "Emulation, Inequality, and Work Hours"; Richard Wilkinson, *The Impact of Inequality: How to Make Sick Societies Healthier* (New York: The New Press, 2005), 101–43.

21. Richard Easterlin, "Will Raising the Incomes of All Increase the Happiness of All?" *Journal of Economic Behavior and Organization* 27 (1995): 35–47; Richard Easterlin, "Income and Happiness: Towards a Unified Theory," *Economic Journal* 111 (2001): 465–84.

22. Luttmer, "Neighbors as Negatives"; Angus Deaton, "Income, Health, and Well-Being Around the World: Evidence from the Gallup World Poll," *Journal of Economic Perspectives* 22 (2008): 53–72.

23. Hugh Rockoff, e-mail interview by the author, August 12, 2011.

24. Henry Aaron, "The Oregon Experiment," in *Rationing America's Medical Care: The Oregon Plan and Beyond*, ed. Martin Strosberg, Joshua Wiener, Robert Baker, and I. Alan Fein (Washington, DC: Brookings Institution, 1992), 107.

25. The complete argument is in Paul Baran and Paul Sweezy, *Monopoly Capital* (New York: Monthly Review Press, 1966). For a concise summary of the stagnation argument, see Paul Sweezy, "Why Stagnation?" *Monthly Review* 34, no. 2 (1982): 1–11.

26. Zachary Karabell, "Google's Results Reflect Giants' Surge, as Everyone Else Struggles," *Daily Beast*, April 13, 2012; Charles Arthur, "Instagram and Facebook: The Next Tech Bubble?" *The Guardian*, April 10, 2012.

27. John Bellamy Foster, Robert W. McChesney, and R. Jamil Jonna, "Monopoly and Competition in Twenty-First Century Capitalism," *Monthly Review* 62, no. 11 (2011): 1–31.

28. One example must suffice: the conservative blogger Robert Stacy McCain's "No Poor Man Ever Gave Me a Job," *Other McCain*, April 14, 2011, theothermccain.com/2011/04/14/no-poor-man-ever-gave-me-a-job. The much more complex reality is examined in John Bellamy Foster, Robert McChesney, and R. Jamil Jonna, "The Global Reserve Army of Labor and the New Imperialism," *Monthly Review* 63, no. 6 (2011): 1–31.

29. See, for example, this analysis published at the peak of the 2000s boom: Jared Bernstein and Lawrence Mishel, "Economy's Gains Fail to Reach Most Workers' Paychecks," Economic Policy Institute Briefing Paper 195, August 30, 2007, www.epi.org/publication/bp195.

30. François Schneider, Giorgos Kallis, and Joan Martinez-Alier, "Crisis or Opportunity? Economic Degrowth for Social Equity and Ecological Sustainability," *Journal of Cleaner Production* 18 (2010): 511–18.

31. André Gorz, *Ecologica* (London: Seagull, 2010), 152.

32. Juliet Schor, "Sustainable Consumption and Worktime Reduction," *Journal of Industrial Ecology* 9 (2005): 37–50. Other things being equal, the employer gains more when eight employees each work twelve-hour days than when twelve employees each work eight-hour days or twenty-four people work four-hour days. The early labor movement focused on reducing the workday, and decades of hard struggle gradually pushed down annual working hours. Meanwhile, the advance of technology and resulting increases in productivity provided employers an alternative way to boost wealth generation, allowing work hours in industrialized countries to continue edging downward until the 1970s. But work hours have been on the rise again since then. Schor has shown how in recent decades capitalist economies have consistently translated productivity growth into increased levels of output and income rather than reductions in working hours. That employer bias, she argues, has several sources: employers prefer to pay fixed salaries rather than hourly wages because they can often induce salaried employees to work additional hours that are "free to the firm"; full-time or full-time-plus workers are

more dependent on the employer and less likely to leave the firm than are part-timers; the longer the hours worked, the smaller the employer's share of health insurance tends to be when compared with wages and salaries; and, because employers believe in their own ability to skim off the cream of the labor pool when hiring, they resist hiring larger numbers of workers, which would mean going deeper into that pool and taking the risk of hiring workers of lower quality.

33. See Herman Daly, *Steady-State Economics*, 2nd ed. (Washington, DC: Island Press, 1991); Herman Daly and Joshua Farley, *Ecological Economics: Principles and Applications*, 2nd ed. (Washington, DC: Island Press, 2010).

34. Texts of presentations at the 2010 Degrowth Conference in Barcelona, Spain, as well as the "Degrowth Declaration" may be found at www.degrowth.eu. The context of degrowth is explained in Joan Martínez-Alier, Unai Pascual, Franck-Dominique Vivien, and Edwin Zaccai, "Sustainable De-growth: Mapping the Context, Criticisms and Future Prospects of an Emergent Paradigm," *Ecological Economics* 69 (2010): 1741–47.

35. Howard Odum and Elisabeth Odum, "The Prosperous Way Down," *Energy* 31 (2006): 21–32. There are exceptions to this view. See Pascal van Griethuysen, "Why Are We Growth-Addicted? The Hard Way Towards Degrowth in the Involutionary Western Development Path," *Journal of Cleaner Production* 6 (2009): 590–95.

36.   Peter Victor, "Growth, Degrowth and Climate Change: A Scenario Analysis," *Ecological Economics* (2011): doi:10.1016/j.ecolecon.2011.04.013.

37. I have taken these terms from John Bellamy Foster, "Why Ecological Revolution?" *Monthly Review* 61, no. 8 (2010): 1–18; and Fred Magdoff, "Ecological Civilization," *Monthly Review* 62, no. 8 (2011): 1–25. The approach comes under regular examination in the journals *Monthly Review, Synthesis/Regeneration*, and *Capitalism Nature Socialism*, and has recently received a thorough treatment in John Bellamy Foster, Brett Clark, and Richard York, *The Ecological Rift: Capitalism's War on the Earth* (New York: Monthly Review Press, 2010).

38. See, for example, this interview: Max van Lingen, "We Cannot Shop Our Way Out of the Problems," *MRZine*, January 12, 2009.

39. Magdoff, "Ecological Civilization."

40. Fred Magdoff and John Bellamy Foster, "What Every Environmentalist Needs to Know About Capitalism," *Monthly Review* 61, no. 10 (2010).

41. Gorz, *Ecologica*, 58–59, 106, 117 (italics in original).

42. For the trajectory of market failure from Smith to Greenspan, see Cassidy, *How Markets Fail*.

43. Kathleen League, *Adorno, Radical Negativity, and Cultural Critique: Utopia in the Map of the World* (Lanham, MD: Lexington Books, 2011), 48. Italics in original.

INDEX

CELEBRATING INDEPENDENT PUBLISHING

Thank you for reading this book published by The New Press. The New Press is a nonprofit, public interest publisher. New Press books and authors play a crucial role in sparking conversations about the key political and social issues of our day.

We hope you enjoyed this book and that you will stay in touch with The New Press. Here are a few ways to stay up to date with our books, events, and the issues we cover:

- Sign up at www.thenewpress.com/subscribe to receive updates on New Press authors and issues and to be notified about local events
- Like us on Facebook: www.facebook.com/newpressbooks
- Follow us on Twitter: www.twitter.com/thenewpress

Please consider buying New Press books for yourself; for friends and family; or to donate to schools, libraries, community centers, prison libraries, and other organizations involved with the issues our authors write about.

The New Press is a 501(c)(3) nonprofit organization. You can also support our work with a tax-deductible gift by visiting www.thenewpress.com/donate.